Regional Conflict and U.S. Policy:

Angola and Mozambique

ZAIRE

Moshi •

• Mombasa

TANZANIA

Luanda

MALAWI

Kolwezi

Lobito
Benguela

BENGUELA RAILROAD

Lubumbashi

ANGOLA

Ndola

Lilongwe

• Cuito
Cuanavale

ZAMBIA

Lusaka •

• Blantyre

Harare

*CAPRIVI
STRIP*

Bulawayo •

ZIMBABWE

Beira

NAMIBIA

BOTSWANA

MOZAMBIQUE

Walvis Bay •

• Windhoek

*KALAHARI
DESERT*

*INDIAN
OCEAN*

Pretoria •

• Maputo

Johannesburg •

SWAZILAND

*ATLANTIC
OCEAN*

• Durban

SOUTH AFRICA

LESOTHO

Cape Town •

Southern
Africa

REGIONAL CONFLICT AND U.S. POLICY:

Angola and Mozambique

EDITED BY

RICHARD J. BLOOMFIELD

A World Peace Foundation Study

REFERENCE PUBLICATIONS, INC.

Published 1988

Copyright © World Peace Foundation

Printed in the United States of America

Library of Congress Cataloging-in-Publication Data

Regional Conflict and U.S. Policy: Angola and Mozambique / edited by
Richard J. Bloomfield.
    p.   cm. — (A World Peace Foundation study)
    Includes index.
    ISBN 0-917256-45-X : $24.95.   ISBN 0-917256-46-8 (pbk.) : $12.95
    1. Angola—Politics and government—1975- 2.Angola—Foreign
relations—United States. 3. United States—Foreign relations-
-Angola. 4. Mozambique—Politics and government—1975-
5. Mozambique—Foreign relations—United States. 6. United States-
-Foreign relations—Mozambique. I. Bloomfield, Richard J.
II. Title: Regional conflict and US policy. III. Series.
DT611.8.R44 1988
967'.304—dc19   88-23461
                                              CIP

Library of Congress Catalog Card Number: 88-23461
International Standard Book Number: 0-917256-45-X (hardcover)
0-917256-46-8 (paperback)

Reference Publications, Inc.
218 St. Clair River Drive, Box 344
Algonac, Michigan 48001

Contents

Preface

This book is the latest product of more than a decade of work by the World Peace Foundation on southern Africa. The early years of that effort focused on South Africa, the country that is the catalyst for so much that happens in the region. The Foundation's studies examined, in sequence, the prospects and problems for political change in South Africa, how that process affected and was affected by U.S.-South African relations, the future of Namibia, and South Africa's impact on its neighbors.

It was a natural next step for the Foundation to study two countries that have been the targets of South Africa's activist regional politics and that are at the center of efforts by the United States to bring about a regional settlement. Angola and Mozambique have much in common: Portugal as their colonial master until 1975, a long and violent struggle for independence, and for much of the time since then, a fierce guerrilla opposition supported by South Africa. Both countries are at the crossroads where the interests of the United States in regional peace and development intersect with U.S. ideological and strategic concerns. The purpose of the book is to help the public make informed judgments about American policy as it faces these difficult challenges.

I am indebted to a great many people for their help in this project, the more so since I am a neophyte in the region. I especially wish to express my gratitude to Victor de Sa Machado, who, as a director of the Gulbenkian Foundation of Portugal, collaborated with me in organizing a multinational conference on Portuguese-speaking Africa in Lisbon in 1985 that inspired me to produce this book.

I also wish to thank my collaborators in this volume for their patience during the vicissitudes of editing and publication. Finally, my thanks to the trustees of the World Peace Foundation, for their support in this and other endeavors.

—*R.J.B.*

Boston
September 1988

Introduction

ROBERT I. ROTBERG

Angola and Mozambique provide important and unexpected foreign policy opportunities for the new United States administration. Mozambique has already freed itself from the grip of Soviet and East Bloc clientelism. Angola seeks an honorable and safe escape from its government's continued dependence upon Soviet and Cuban military backing. Glasnost, and a profound reconsideration by General Secretary Mikhail Gorbachev of Soviet interests in Africa, makes such radical changes distinctly probable. As a result, United States' policymakers and opinion-formers need to be aware of how significant both Lusophone countries are and will continue to be in the battle for southern Africa. They need to appreciate the political and strategic realities of the region. Angola and Mozambique are moving from a Marxist to a Western embrace; it is critical that the reasons for and the obstacles to the completion of that shift be well understood. The chapters in this book explain it all, and clearly.

Since they were written, too, the collective message of those chapters has become even clearer. In Mozambique, President Joaquim Chissano's regime is locked in a desperate struggle for the territory and for its economic underpinnings with RENAMO (*Resistência Nacional Moçambicana*, the Mozambique Resistance Movement, also known as the MNR). Gillian Gunn's chapter explains how RENAMO began as a Rhodesian-backed counter-insurgency militia and subsequently became a South-African-funded and -equipped force intended to destabilize post-independence Mozambique. By mid-1988, despite South African assertions of innocence and a well-publicized diplomatic renewal of the peace and amity accord of 1984 between Mozambique and South Africa, the war for Mozambique continued brutal and bloody. RENAMO, despite its lack of an articulated political message or any defined ethnic or popular base among the Mozambican people, remained strong militarily. The Mozambican army, in contrast, is intrinsically weak, underpaid, underfed, and undermotivated. Indeed, all of Mozambique is weak and fragile: its infrastructure has deteriorated; its economy is in shambles; its bureaucratic and governmental apparatus, at best hardly robust, is decrepit; the country is much more dependent on South Africa and on Western aid and assistance than it was in 1975. Additionally, Mozambique is a famine zone. Because of the civil war and the government's lack of resources, millions cannot obtain food and are intensely at risk.

The fate of Mozambique is at once a charge upon and a messy challenge to the conscience of the West. In terms of global policy options, Mozambique could be preserved in its newly-discovered Western orientation; it could be preserved both from a return to Soviet client status and from the much more dangerous and more likely possibility that it could slip forever into the bitter embrace of neighboring South Africa.

For very different reasons, Angola is also in danger. South Africa still (in mid-1988) occupies much of southern Angola and shows few signs of being willing to relinquish its strategic hold on a sizable salient of Namibia's northern neighbor. The linkage between South Africa's control over Namibia and its determination to destabilize and influence the future of Angola is discussed in a subsequent chapter. But the intimate and no longer surprising relationship between protection by the Soviet Union and Cuba of the government both helped to install in 1975, Namibia's future, and possible negotiations between white-ruled South Africa and the African National Congress (ANC) and other black opponents of that regime, can hardly be ignored.

Under the Reagan administration, and, in 1988, as a result of United States-Soviet and United States-Angolan-Cuban-South African high level discussions, formulas for the withdrawal of 40,000 Cuban and 20,000 South Africans have been prepared. But what about Jonas Savimbi's UNITA (*União Nacional para a Independência Total de Angola*, or National Union for the Total Independence of Angola), an ethnically-based popular movement which has fought the government of Angola since the mid-1970s, now controls about

40 percent of the country, and probably packs more military punch than the army of Angola alone? The Reagan administration supports UNITA. So does South Africa, massively.

South Africa seeks a UNITA-dominated Angola. The Reagan administration sought to put pressure on Soviet clients, like the Angolans, in order to ease the Soviets out of Afghanistan and to reduce Soviet leverage throughout the Third World. By mid-1988, however, as united as the Soviets, the Americans, the Angolans, and even the Cubans might have become about the importance of leaving Angola to the Angolans, the threatening existence of UNITA and South Africa's relentless determination to maintain hegemony in its region and propel proxies into power in Angola (and Mozambique), made it dangerous for the Cuban buffer between the Angolan army and UNITA to be withdrawn.

Angola, a potentially prosperous (oil, diamonds, and coffee) developing state, promises to pose serious policy questions for a new United States administration. The conferring of diplomatic recognition (advocated throughout this book) is an obvious initiative. So is the withdrawal of military and financial assistance to UNITA (espoused by presidential nominee Michael S. Dukakis and other prominent Democrats). How to persuade Congress to appropriate the level of economic assistance for the reconstruction of Angola and Mozambique is a further executive issue. (The chapters of this book suggest how the economies of both countries deteriorated as a result of Portuguese and post-colonial mismanagement and South African-sponsored hostilities.) Finally, and first in importance, the United States must seek to stop both wars. Doing so means finding ingenious or forceful ways of interdicting South African aid flows and cross-border attacks. That is easier said than accomplished, and its achievement may not (paradoxically) be hastened by the provisions of a draconian anti-South African bill that was making its congressional course to passage in mid-1988.

This book offers no recipe for a resolution of the several conflicts of southern Africa. However, a reading of the chapters on decolonization, on Portugal's evolving role in the modernization of its former colonies, on South Africa's destabilization, on Soviet strategy, on the Cuban aims, on the political experience and internal politics of Mozambique and Angola, and on United States policy, provides the ingredients essential to any well-informed, action-oriented perspective on Mozambique and Angola, and on United States relations with southern Africa.

1: The Legacy of Decolonization

KENNETH MAXWELL

To date almost all the literature on the decolonization of the Portuguese territories in Africa during the mid 1970s has fallen into two categories. It has either been classically "Africanist" in its parameters or, on the other hand, it has been overly concerned with grand strategy—with East-West issues and foreign interventionism. In consequence, one group of scholars tends to see all results as caused by purely African events, while the other group concentrates almost exclusively on actions of the superpowers and their allies. Since the two approaches often represent political or ideological positions, rarely does either side listen to the other, let alone accept that in both positions there is much truth.[1]

Policymakers have also wavered between these two extremes in a manner which has often reflected the salience the problems of Angola and Mozambique assumed on the United States agenda. The inputs of regional specialists have seemingly diminished in direct proportion to the intensity of United States domestic political concern. The intrusion of East-West competition into the independence process in Portugal's southern African colonies made this unavoidable; as also did the involvement of South Africa and Cuba, both highly contentious subjects in the internal American debate over foreign policy. The local, regional and international dimensions are thus inextricably woven into the continuing problems of Angola and Mozambique. The manner in which decolonization occurred made this inevitable, creating constraints on all parties to the conflict which have yet to be superseded. The purpose of this chapter is to describe in general outline how this unfortunate situation occurred.

1. The Regional Context of Portugal's Southern African Colonies

It is important, firstly, to emphasize the regional context of Portugal's former colonies in southern Africa, since multiple interconnections tied both Mozambique and Angola to every aspect of the explosive situation in that area.

In South Africa itself no one doubted that the Portuguese colonies represented a breakwater against the tide of majority rule.

In 1974 Angola had the largest white population in the continent outside of South Africa, and the de facto alliance of South Africa, Rhodesia, and Portugal against insurgency in southern Africa merely confirmed the obvious. Angola bordered on Namibia where South Africa faced increasing diplomatic and military pressure. The burden the Portuguese bore on South Africa's behalf, however, was very considerable indeed: an army of 200,000 in Africa in 1974 and defense expenditures of $425 million in the early 1970s. South Africa, meanwhile, with a gross national product three times that of Portugal, spent about the same amount ($448 million). It is not surprising to note, therefore, that within a year of the Portuguese departure the South African defense budget tripled.[2]

But Angola was no more isolated from its African neighbors to the north and east than it was from the white-ruled territory to the south. Basic sectors of the transportation network of Angola were indispensible links in the infrastructure of all southern Central Africa.

Both Zaire and Zambia depended for essential imports and exports on the ports and railways of Angola. The 896-mile long Benguela Railway connects the mineral-rich heart of the continent—Shaba (formerly Katanga) in Zaire and the copper belt in northern Zambia—to the Angolan Atlantic port of Lobito. In the early 1970s copper—and cobalt, mined as a by-product—accounted for between 94 and 96 percent of Zaire's export earnings. In 1973 Lobito handled 320,000 tons of Zaire manganese ore and 200,000 tons of copper. All alternatives to the Benguela route involved major physical and political difficulties. Both Zaire and Zambia, for obvious reasons, were therefore deeply involved in Angolan politics. President Mobutu of Zaire was the major supporter of Holden Roberto's FNLA (*Frente Nacional de Libertação de Angola* or Front for the National Liberation of Angola), and Roberto, to solidify his Zairian connections, had married Mobutu's sister-in-law. President Kenneth Kaunda of Zambia had supported the MPLA (*Movimento Popular de Libertação de Angola* or Movement for the Popular Liberation of Angola) and had allowed it to use Zambia as a base for guerrilla activities in eastern Angola after 1966. Kaunda also supported Jonas Savimbi in 1966.

Mozambique, was, of course, much more dependent on the South African connection than was Angola. Malyn Newitt, in fact, called southern Mozambique under colonial rule one of the first neighboring areas to have become a "Bantustan." In addition, the last years of the anti-colonial struggle were marked by the inevitable intrusion of problems arising from the parallel conflict in Rhodesia. FRELIMO (*Frente de Libertação de Moçambique*) also enjoyed sanctuaries and the support of Mozambique's northern African neighbor—Tanzania. In sum, the complex inter-relationships in the region and the danger of escalating conflicts were intrinsic to the geographical location of Portugal's African empire. The process of decolonization was thus bound to be an extremely complex, dangerous affair, with racial, economic, and ideological overtones that reached far beyond the boundaries of Portugal and her African territories.

2. Linkages—Formal and Informal

The second important element of linkage is the particular nature of the United States relationship with Portugal and by extension with Portuguese Africa. This had two distinct aspects. First, the relationship which existed as a consequence of both nations' participation in NATO. Secondly, the connection which existed as a result of the bilateral treaty arrangements governing United States use of the airbase facilities in the Azores. Portugal had been a member of NATO since 1949, though Salazar at the time had been careful to state that Portugal's participation in it did not signify acceptance of the liberal and democratic principles stated in NATO's charter. NATO's Iberian-Atlantic Command Headquarters (IBERLANT) is situated outside Lisbon overlooking the narrow entrance to the Tagus estuary. It is in the NATO context that the famous (or infamous) policy review of United States relations with southern Africa, which took place early in the Nixon administration, must be seen. In the summer of 1969 an inter-departmental group established to review United States policy options in the region reported to the National Security Council that "the outlook for the rebellion (in Portuguese Africa) is one of continued stalemate, the rebels cannot oust the Portuguese and the Portuguese can contain but not eliminate the rebels."[3] Nixon had promised Franco Nogueira, the Portuguese foreign minister, soon after taking office, that he intended to rectify the errors of past United States dealings with Portugal.[4] He was true to his word. In 1970 the United States began to move closer to both South Africa and Portugal.

The irony was, of course, that NATO and the United States began to find the notion of "pluricontinental Portugal," the idea that Portugal was an intercontinental country with European and African provinces (the central ideological—or mystical—tenet of the Salazarist African policy), to be a very convenient fiction just at the time when the whole edifice was about to collapse. NATO's charter excluded it from the South Atlantic, but United States and European naval circles, in response to growing Soviet naval power, had been voicing criticism of this stipulation for a number of years. After 1970, in fact, the United States Navy made increasing use of Mozambican and Angolan ports and was especially interested in the port of Nacala in Mozambique which, with the proper technical facilities, could contain the entire United States Seventh Fleet. In mid-1973, the Supreme Allied Command Atlantic at Norfolk, Virginia, on instructions from the NATO Defense Planning Committee (a committee of NATO defense ministers), began contingency planning for air and naval operations in defense of southern Africa, and carried out surveys of the state of communications, airfields, and ports of Portugal's Atlantic islands and African colonies.[5] United States Secretary of State Henry Kissinger, while visiting Lisbon in December 1973, a mere four months before the coup d'état which overwhelmed the Caetano regime, was seeking indirect means to provide sophisticated ground-to-air "red-eye missiles," and other equipment to Portugal for use in Africa, a commitment which contradicted previous United States policy.

3. The Azores: Bait and Trap
Relationships between the United States and Portugal since the end of World War II had always had a special cast to them because of the Azores base. The Salazar regime had been very skillful at using the Azores base agreement to deflect United States efforts to get Portugal to modify its intransigent stance in Africa and to plan for the transfer of power in its colonies.

The strongest United States pressure in favor of African independence had been exerted during the Kennedy administration, leading to the imposition of a boycott on the sales of arms for use in Africa.[6] In Portugal itself, during this particular period, there was considerable opposition to Salazar, especially over colonial policy. The election campaign of General Humberto Delgado in 1958 had led to large-scale popular mobilization, and the regime was shaken by disgruntlement within the military. There were also favorable external conditions for change. The years between 1958 and 1961 represented the grand period of African independence, with former British and French colonies stampeding toward nationhood. The Kennedy administration adopted an activist policy in Africa, going so far as to give help to Holden Roberto in Angola, and to Eduardo Mondlane in Mozambique, as well as maintaining liaison via the CIA with disaffected generals in Portugal itself.

But by 1962-63 the moment when the possibility of change existed had passed. Salazar thwarted the military plot against him, a major motive of which had been the military's reaction to his intransigent position on Africa. The various opposition forces in Portugal faltered, and Salazar played the Azores card by threatening not to renew the base agreement. The chaos in the Congo (now Zaire), the Bay of Pigs episode, and the Cuban missile crisis had all meanwhile hardened people's attitudes.

A combination of internal and external factors between 1968-71 again opened up the possibility of movement. The internal factors were the incapacitation of Salazar and the accession of Marcelo Caetano as head of government. Caetano's arrival awoke a great deal of hope for change, bringing as he did younger and more European oriented people into the administration and the National Assembly. It was thought that they might be able to effect some change both internally and externally. Caetano himself hoped for some liberalization of colonial policies.

The irony is that, at the precise point when in Portugal some external pressure might have produced results, the Nixon administration concluded that (as the National Security memorandum put it) "the Portugese are in Africa to stay." This period ended with the murder of Amílcar Cabral in 1973, which foreclosed any possibility of a negotiated settlement with PAIGC (*Partido Africano da Independência da Guiné e Cabo Verde*, or African Party for the Independence of Guinea and Cape Verde), the liberation movement in Guinea-Bissau and Cape Verde. The "liberals" in Portugal had already resigned from the National Assembly in Lisbon, wiping out the possibility of liberal reform in Portugal and of an orderly disengagement in Africa.

4. The Importance of Linkages

Portugal's long delay in following her European neighbors in coming to terms with African nationalism had another consequence. In the 1940s the

Soviet Union had no possibility of involvement in African affairs; by the 1960s the Soviets were an element, but a marginal one; by the 1970s the Soviet Union's capacity to influence events in Africa was substantial. The role of the United States had also grown with time.

The arrival of the United States and the USSR on the African scene in fact marked a broader shift in international power. Africa had already become a focus of intense rivalry between the two superpowers in the former Belgian Congo in the early 1960s. In the Portuguese territories, however, during the decade between 1963 and 1973, neither great power pushed hard for major changes in the status quo. Soviet aid for the liberation movements in the Portuguese territories was modest in scale—much less than either the Portuguese claimed or the liberation movements wanted; and the same could be said for what Western support the Portuguese managed to squeeze out of their reluctant NATO allies.[7] General Spínola, who was to become provisional president in the wake of the April Revolution, concluded in his book *Portugal and the Future* (Lisbon, 1974), that neither the West nor the East seemed to have any real interest in bringing the conflict to a resolution one way or the other.

It should be noted, however, that for later United States reactions the experience of the early 1960s was to have important ramifications for the process of decolonization in Portuguese Africa. In 1960 the choice made by the Kennedy administration of Holden Roberto as a recipient of covert American aid was a bold measure placing Washington's support behind an armed insurrection against the government of one of its NATO allies. At the time Roberto was supported by the then two most radical independent African governments—those of Kwame Nkrumah in Ghana and of Sekou Toure in Guinea. Despite the later withdrawal of Washington's support and the 1970 Nixon-Kissinger decision to move closer to Lisbon and the white minority regimes in southern Africa, these early connections remained. When in 1974 Portugal's position in Africa disintegrated, the alliances forged in the early Kennedy years were resurrected by Kissinger for largely the same reasons they were formed in the first place; that is, for essentially *negative* reasons: avoiding the Marxist-inspired nationalists (the MPLA in particular) for those assumed to be more "pro-Western."

If the nature of relationships established since the 1940s had locked the West, the United States most especially, into a particular set of geo-strategic and personal connections which made it difficult for them to adapt rapidly to the dramatically changed context which came into being in April 1974, the opposite was true for the liberation movements, especially those movements strongly marked by a Marxist ideological formation.

During the late 1940s Agostinho Neto was a central committee member of the youth section of the United Democratic Movement in Portugal. Within this broad antifascist coalition, an organization known by the unfortunate acronym MUD, the Portuguese Communist party was an important element. Africans were active in MUD, among them Amílcar Cabral (PAIGC) and Marcelino dos Santos (FRELIMO). MUD was also a testing ground for many of those who emerged in civilian leadership roles in Lisbon after April 25, 1974, most notably the Socialist leader, Mário Soares.[8] If those connections in the anti-Salazar underground made Neto suspect to Washington, they were to stand him in good stead in Portugal after the April 25 coup. Unlike Holden Roberto, leader of the Zaire-based FNLA—who had spent less than two years in Angola in his whole life, and almost no time in Portugal, and Jonas Savimbi who had been educated in Switzerland—Agostinho Neto knew the Portuguese Left from the inside. In the chaotic situation in Portugal between 1974 and 1975 this was an important strategic asset for the MPLA.

The MPLA also enjoyed exclusive relations with the major liberation fronts in Portuguese Guinea (Guinea-Bissau) and Mozambique. Neto's personal relations with the leaders of both PAIGC and FRELIMO went back to his student days in Lisbon, and they had been fortified after 1961 by a formal structure of mutual consultation among the three movements. All three movements had long-standing formal relationships with leading members of the nonaligned Afro-Asian and Latin American Solidarity Organization, founded in Havana in 1966. Some of Cabral's most important statements of revolutionary theory were delivered at the Havana conference. Cabral observed then that the Cuban revolution "constitutes a particular lesson for the national liberation movements, especially for those who want their national revolution to be a true revolution." There was never any mystery about these views, and about the fact that ideological affinity had been translated into concrete aid. Moreover, the establishment of diplomatic ties between Zaire and China in late 1973 and the decision of the Chinese to train the FNLA in 1974 had galvanized Soviet concern about Chinese objectives in Africa. The Soviets had consistently supported the national liberation movements: their support for the MPLA went back to 1958; and despite a cooling of the Soviet relationship with Neto during the 1970s, Soviet support

throughout went to one or the other of the MPLA's factions throughout
the period of armed struggle against the Portuguese.

The important general point about this history is to emphasize that the
lines of conflict and alliance in Portugal and Africa were clearer than they
appeared to be on the surface. When, as a result of exhaustion by colonial
wars, the prospect of outright military defeat in Guinea-Bissau, and the
pressure of economic problems at home, the Armed Forces Movement (MFA)
overthrew the decrepit dictatorship in Lisbon, the repercussions of this action was almost bound to be startling. Portugal was a NATO ally,
anachronistic and at times embarrassingly stubborn, but nevertheless an
ally that had no doubt whatsoever on which side it stood in a bipolar world.
The United States, because of the intimacy of its relationships with the dictatorship, was unsettled by change in Portugal and was especially unprepared
for the sometimes bewildering reversals and turmoil that were the immediate
consequences of the coup. And the United States, unlike its geopolitical rivals,
the Soviet Union and Cuba, had next to no relationships with the old
clandestine opposition in either Portugal or with the national liberation
movements in the African territories. These lines of conflict and alliance were
to have critical implications for the internationalization of the decolonization process which is the cause of our present policy dilemmas.

5. The Process of Decolonization

The international context within which the Portuguese coup d'état of 1974
occurred and the background against which it unfolded is therefore essential to any understanding of the path the consequent decolonization took.
First, however, it is essential to point out the critical link between decolonization in Africa and the revolution in Portugal. This was a factor largely ignored by policy makers at the time especially in Washington, which gave
a tactical advantage to the Marxist oriented forces in both Europe and Africa.

In the first months after the April 25, 1974 coup in Lisbon, the young officers of the Armed Forces Movement (MFA) stayed very much in the
background, preferring to remain as anonymous as possible. The MFA's am-
biguous phrases about colonial policy in their political manifesto, which spoke
of the "need for a political not military solution," had been, if anything,
an understatement of their real feelings. The MFA's program and the then
more widely known proposals in General Spínola's book *Portugal and the
Future,* which spoke of a Portuguese style "commonwealth," set out

positions which were in fact diametrically opposed to one another. The nature of the coup, especially its swift, popular, and bloodless success, disguised for a time the seriousness of the divergence which existed. But the conflict staked out at the beginning was at its heart a conflict between immediate decolonization and gradual disengagement in Africa. As one of the members of the MFA put it in late 1974: "We have no desire to construct a neocolonial community, we are interested more in the formation of a Socialist inter-dependence, and that only to the extent that our brothers in Guinea, Mozambique, and Angola accept, desire and demand."

The emergence of such "Third World" notions within the military establishment of their enemy, as well as the growing de facto alliance between the radical wing of the MFA and the communists in Portugal, which was also taking place at this time, were watched by the Marxist movements in Africa with considerable interest. They realized very quickly that it provided them with a wedge to speed up the process of decolonization and a guarantee that, where competing nationalist groups existed, those such as the MPLA, that enjoyed long-time connections with the old Portuguese clandestine opposition, would receive special consideraton.

The combination of eclectic Marxism and nationalism in the MFA's philosophy, provided the basis for convergence between the PAIGC, and FRELIMO on the one hand and the MFA on the other. This unique, if temporary, alliance between the colonialist officer corps and its opponents was made possible both by the timing and the special circumstances of the liberation movement struggles and by the backwardness of Portugal which the MFA officers so resented.

The alliance was bound to be temporary, of course, because, whereas the liberation movements had clear objectives, the MFA did not. The liberation movements were committed by necessity to a permanent condition—national independence—while the MFA's commitment, important as it was, remained a commitment to a process that would end once the colonies were free. Nevertheless, temporary though it might be, the momentum which the convergence of views between former enemies brought to the internal politics of Portugal and to the timetable of decolonization in Portuguese Africa proved to be irresistible. It led to rapid settlements in Guinea-Bissau and Mozambique, and culminated in the Alvor agreement of January 15, 1975 between the Angolan liberation movements and Portugal.

It is important to note therefore that, after the 1974 coup in Lisbon, the liberation movements had long-time supporters in influential places who proved to be highly effective allies. Spínola's views of the Lusitanian (Portuguese) commonwealth were totally inappropriate to the real situation in which Portugal found herself. The armies in Africa were simply unwilling to act in any way which prolonged their stay in the overseas territories. Brazil, a supposed partner in Spínola's concept, has decided to cut its losses and make its own approaches to the new Portuguese-speaking states emerging in Africa. Brazil recognized Guinea-Bissau on July 18, one week before Spínola himself made his declaration of July 27 that Portugal would begin an immediate transfer of power in its African colonies. By then 84 countries had already recognized Guinea-Bissau.

A strenuous secret diplomacy had laid the basis for settlements with both PAIGC and FRELIMO. The diplomacy that arranged them emanated largely from Algiers, and from Lusaka in Zambia. The process of making the settlements helped to bring Spínola down, while also guaranteeing relatively rapid and smooth transitions in both Guinea-Bissau and Mozambique.

The underlying reasons for this African success were that Washington and Western Europe could not distinguish the forces at play in the Portuguese situation, and were initially more concerned with situations in Europe than in Africa. No such misjudgment took place within the liberation movements. They, after all, knew the Portuguese and were aware of their weaknesses. They knew the leaders involved, some of them only too well, and above all they knew that real power in Portugal at this time was held by the MFA leaders, and that a tacit alliance with them could be made against Spínola.

6. The Independence of Mozambique

The speed with which the transfers of power to PAIGC and FRELIMO took place during 1974 therefore owed much to the dynamics of the process over the first eight to nine months after the coup in Lisbon. Henry Kissinger claimed after the event that the United States did not oppose the accession to power by "radical movements" in Guinea-Bissau and Mozambique. This is only partly true: the United States, in fact, was extremely disturbed about the consequences of the independence of the Cape Verde Islands under the auspices of the PAIGC, and there is evidence that the United States did contemplate support for anti-FRELIMO movements in Mozambique. It was not the lack of desire, but lack of capacity, that prevented the United States or anyone else interfering with the decolonization process in either country. The Portuguese Armed Forces Movement recognized the necessity of dealing exclusively with the PAIGC and FRELIMO and worked with them closely. The Portuguese also took firm action to suppress diversionary attempts. As a result, the opportunity for effective interference in the decolonization of Guinea-Bissau, Cape Verde, and Mozambique never arose and the process was very rapid.

Like Guinea-Bissau and Cape Verde, Mozambique also enjoyed the advantage of a united and effectively-led liberation movement. FRELIMO had originated as a coalition of small exile groups based in then Tanganyika in 1962. Its first president was Eduardo Mondlane, who had been educated in the United States. Mondlane had received clandestine support from the United States during the Kennedy administration (as well as overt support from the Ford Foundation). Mondlane was, however, assassinated in 1969. A new leadership under the army commander Samora Machel succeeded in overcoming serious internal factionalism. It also pursued an effective military campaign against the Portuguese, encompassing the northern part of Mozambique and, later, the Tete district along the Zambezi River. FRELIMO was in a strong enough position in 1974 to refuse compromise unless the Portuguese offered to withdraw. Like the PAIGC in Guinea-Bissau, it was able to reach a local ceasefire arrangement with the Portuguese military in Mozambique ante-dating Lisbon's own acceptance of the inevitability of independence.

South Africa's attitude to a FRELIMO government in Mozambique was also consistent from the beginning. "A black government in Mozambique holds no fear for us whatever. We are surrounded by black governments as it is, and we ourselves are in the process of creating some more by leading our own black Homelands to independence" is how Balthazar Johannes Vorster put it. Vorster went on to cite the collapse of Portugal's rule as "proof" that apartheid was a correct policy. ("The root of the trouble in all these territories," Vorster commented, "was that the Portuguese policy was one of assimilation—which was a negation of the nationhood of these peoples.")

Joaquim Chissano, then head of the transitional government, reciprocated by downplaying FRELIMO's desire to expand the revolutionary cause to its neighbor. "The duty of the new government [is] to study the real relations existing between South Africa and Mozambique." FRELIMO did not pretend "to be Messiahs or saviours of South Africa," he added. In fact FRELIMO and Vorster agreed to honor past agreements, concerning the ports of Beira and Lourenço Marques (Maputo), Mozambican labor use in South Africa, and the Cabora Bassa power scheme.

The rapid withdrawal of the Portuguese from Mozambique also coincided with the period during which South Africa was attempting a policy of *détente* with black Africa. In Portugal's East African colony there was very little South Africa could do in the short term to influence the outcome once it became clear, in September of 1974, that the Portuguese military in the colony, under the leadership of Vitor Crespo, would tolerate no interference with the smooth transfer of authority to FRELIMO. An independent Mozambique, even if ruled by a Marxist government, would be extremely vulnerable to South Africa and economically dependent on the goodwill of Pretoria. Mozambique and South Africa were bound together by a mutual dependency. Much of Mozambique's foreign earnings depend on the use of its port and rail facilities by South Africans as well as on the earnings of Mozambique workers in the South African gold mines. South Africa relied on Mozambique for more than 25 percent of its mining labor force. It needed the energy that would come from the Cabora Bassa dam. In addition, South Africa's own ports were over-congested. The South African government also hoped that good relations with FRELIMO would discourage any aid to guerrillas in Zululand and the eastern Transvaal. The South African government even thought, in September of 1974, that a similar policy might work in Angola, although the South Africans noted that *both* MPLA and FNLA were reported to be planning guerrilla operations against South Africa once they gained power. UNITA said it wanted only peace with South Africa and that its policy was "non-interference" with neighboring states. At this time UNITA was wooing white supporters within Angola, anticipating pre-independence elections such as those also planned in Portugal for 1975. Angola, however, was for all parties to be a very different case.

7. Angolan Exceptionalism

The interconnection between the course of events in Portugal and the decolonization process had decisive impact in Angola—recognized by all sides as the most difficult and most important test of Portuguese intentions. Several of the factors that had contributed to the MPLA's weakness as a guerrilla organization proved to be sources of strength in the different circumstances which emerged after the Lisbon coup. The MPLA's urban intellectual and cosmopolitan leaders had always strongly opposed tribalism and racism and had enjoyed long-term relationships with the old anti fascist opposition in Portugal, especially the communists. *Assimilados,* mulattoes, and whites had from the beginning found places in its higher echelons. The MPLA enjoyed wide support from urbanized Africans who tended, whatever their ethnic or linguistic background, to form a distinct group in relation to the rural majority. MPLA had always had difficulty appealing beyond its base, especially in the FNLA-dominated Bakongo backlands of the north. MPLA support was concentrated, however, in the strategically located central zone of the country, along the 263-mile railway from Luanda to Melange, among the 1.3 million Kimbundu-speaking peoples, one of Angola's four main ethnic-linguistic groups. MPLA support was almost monolithic among the African population of Luanda and in its teeming slums (*musseques*). But above all, the MPLA enjoyed exclusive relations with the major liberation fronts in Portuguese Guinea and Mozambique, both of which by the autumn of 1974 had successfully negotiated settlements with the Portuguese.

Angola, however, was always close to the center of the struggle between General Spínola and the Armed Forces Movement during the first turbulent months following the Lisbon coup. Out-maneuvered in July, 1974 in the agreement with PAIGC over Guinea-Bissau, and thwarted in early September over Mozambique, Spínola attempted to retain personal control of the Angola negotiations.

The Spínola plan for Angola depended heavily on the collaboration of President Mobutu of Zaire. On September 14, 1974, Spínola flew to the island of Sal in the Cape Verde archipelago and met secretly with President Mobutu. Spínola's formal proposals for an Angolan settlement, which were made public at this time, envisioned a transitional two-year period during which a provisional government would be formed of representatives from the three nationalist groups (FNLA, MPLA, and UNITA), together with representatives of the major ethnic groups and the white population. Elections would follow for a constituent assembly with the franchise based on universal suffrage. The private understanding reached between Mobutu and Spínola at Sal remained secret, but was based on their common desire to see MPLA neutralized and if possible eliminated. Vice Admiral Rosa Coutinho, Portuguese high commissioner in Angola, who had not been informed of the meeting, described the objectives later as being "to install Holden in first place, with Chipenda and Savimbi at his side, and to eliminate Neto."

Spínola, when insisting that no negotiations take place with MPLA, said of Neto: "He received his orders from Moscow."

Like so many cf Spínola's projects, his plans for Angola were not without shrewdness. In 1974, the Portuguese military was under less pressure in Angola than in either Guinea or Mozambique. At the time Spínola met with Mobutu, there were still 60,000 Portuguese troops in the colony and beyond that an extensive paramilitary network. The secret police (PIDE/DGS) continued to operate in Angola under the authority of the chief of staff, and were renamed the police of military information (PIM). Like the MPLA, Holden Roberto's FNLA had not yet agreed to a ceasefire, and in terms of the military struggle the FNLA was by far the most formidable opponent of the Portuguese army. Mobutu was the obvious person to deal with, since Roberto depended entirely on Zairian support and certainly could not function without it. Jonas Savimbi and UNITA had already agreed to a ceasefire in June and opened negotiations with a variety of white civilian and business groups. UNITA in mid-1974 consisted of less than 1,000 trained guerrillas (probably close to 400) with ancient and inadequate weapons. Savimbi appears to have enjoyed covert "protection" from Portuguese military intelligence and PIDE for some years, the objective being to split nationalist groups along tribal lines in eastern and southern Angola following the early successes of MPLA penetration into these regions after 1966.

On August 8, 1974, moreover, 400 MPLA militants meeting in Lusaka had split three ways: 165 delegates supporting Neto: 165 Daniel Chipenda; and 70 Mário de Andrade. Chipenda's group represented the major fighting force of the MPLA within Angola proper, and Chipenda himself had been elected president of MPLA at a rump session of the conference. Chipenda, despite his temporary role as a Moscow protégé, had also at various times been a protégé of almost all the outsiders who had fingers in the Angolan pie, including apparently the Portuguese secret police. At any rate, both Spínola and Mobutu regarded Chipenda as persuadable, given the right inducements. The scenario laid out between them at Sal was thus not entirely implausible, and shortly after his meeting with Spínola, General Mobutu attempted to persuade both Julius Nyerere of Tanzania and Kenneth Kaunda of Zambia of the merits of the project.

The plan failed, however, and for reasons that lay in Lisbon as much as in Luanda. On September 30, 1974, Spínola resigned from the presidency, having failed in his attempt to bypass the MFA and the communists by a popular appeal for support from the "silent majority." Between October 1974 and January 1975, effective power in Portugal was in the hands of the MFA. The MFA strengthened its hand by forming a more broadly based group to oversee its affairs called the Committee of Twenty and constituting an assembly, the so-called Assembly of Two Hundred. During these five critical months the MFA remained united in its commitment to immediate decolonization, since all the diverse Left elements within the movement agreed on the need for a rapid disengagement from Africa. The ascendency within the movement of its leftist elements also brought the Portuguese authorities closer ideologically to the MPLA, allowing it to recuperate from its mid-1974 nadir. Above all, it allowed Agostinho Neto a breathing space to reestablish leadership over his badly divided movement.

Not least of the elements working in the MPLA's favor in these months was the aid the movement received between July 1974 and January 1975, from the Portuguese High Commissioner in Luanda Vice Admiral Rosa Coutinho, soon dubbed the Red Admiral by the white settlers. Rosa Coutinho had a pathological hatred of the FNLA and made no secret of the fact that he regarded President Mobutu as a black fascist. The most important result of Rosa Coutinho's intervention was to thwart a key element in the Mobutu-Spínola plan—the elimination of Agostinho Neto. Although the Andrade faction was reintegrated into the MPLA during the latter part of 1974 (friction reemerged after the MPLA's victory in early 1976), Chipenda, despite a brief rapprochement, was expelled from the MPLA in November.

The temporary resolution of the MPLA's internal squabbles, however, provided a basis for settlement. Under the patronage of President Boumedienne, Agostinho Neto and Major Melo Antunes met in Algiers between November 19 and 31, 1974, and negotiated a ceasefire agreement. A week later, the FNLA and the Portuguese made a similar agreement in Kinshasa. The Organization of African Unity (OAU), which had at different times recognized both the FNLA and MPLA as the sole legitimate nationalist spokesman for Angola, now extended last-minute recognition to Jonas Savimbi's UNITA. In early January 1975 the three nationalist leaders, Roberto, Neto, and Savimbi, came together under the chairmanship of Jomo Kenyatta in Mombasa. They agreed to mutual recognition and the speedy opening of negotiations on Angolan independence with the Portuguese government.

On January 10 the negotiations were moved to the Algarve in Portugal. The leaders of the three movements and their delegations met with the

Portuguese government at the heavily guarded Penina Hotel, and by January 15 had thrashed out a delicately balanced and highly precarious agreement. Leading the Portuguese were General Costa Gomes, who had replaced General Spínola as provisional president of Portugal the previous September; Mário Soares, the foreign minister; Major Melo Antunes; and the high commissioner, Admiral Rosa Coutinho.

The settlement, which became known as the Alvor agreement, set the date of Angolan independence for November 11, 1975. During the transitional period, the country would be administered by a coalition government composed of the three nationalist groups and the Portuguese. The transitional administration would be headed by a presidential college of three, each "president" representing one of the three movements. Lisbon's high commissioner was to control defense and security and to "arbitrate differences." Each movement and the Portuguese would hold three posts in the cabinet. A national army was to be formed, the movements contributing 8,000 men each, while the Portuguese retained a 24,000-man force in the country until independence. The Portuguese troops would be withdrawn by February, 1976. Elections for a constituent assembly were to be held prior to independence. Meanwhile, the three movements agreed to place a freeze on their January, 1975, military positions.

The settlement was no mean achievement. It had been brought about preeminently by the MFA, then at the height of its power and prestige. Dr. Agostinho Neto, president of the MPLA, paid the Armed Forces Movement a quiet tribute at the end of the Alvor meeting. He called the MFA "the fourth Liberation Movement."

8. Why Did Angola Not Follow the Path of Guinea-Bissau and Mozambique?

Until January 1975 the rapidly moving situation in Africa contributed to the dramatic shift to the left in Portugal, while on the other hand the triumph of the MFA over Spínola and then the growing influence of pro-communist elements within the MFA itself also served to aid the purposes of the Marxist movements in Africa.

After March 1975, however, these circumstances were dramatically reversed. The stumbling block was Angola. One of the keys to the implementation of the Alvor agreement, which had been agreed to by *all* the nationalist movements in Angola (FNLA, UNITA, MPLA), was Portuguese collaboration in controlling the internal security situation in Angola until the transfer of power took place. Given the rivalry between and within the nationalist movements, the intrinsic problems in Angola were formidable enough, but it was also the inability of the Portuguese to fulfill their side of the bargain which helped doom the settlement. By March 1975, it was clear that the old cohesion of the MFA had been replaced by an intense internal power struggle, and in addition the left was split by open confrontation between the socialists and communists. In Angola warfare soon broke out between the nationalist movements. The coincidence of the crisis in Portugal and the crisis in Angola are critical to understanding the failure of Angola to follow the relatively smooth transfers which occurred in Portugal's other colonies.

Agostinho Neto was, as always, especially sensitive to the political situation in Portugal. Unlike Holden Roberto, leader of the FNLA, and Jonas Savimbi, leader of UNITA, who left Portugal quickly once the agreements had been signed in January, Agostinho Neto remained in MFA-ruled Portugal, traveled extensively throughout the country, and had lengthy meetings with political and military leaders. It was a critical time in Portugal. The euphoria that followed the fall of the old regime was passing. January 1975 saw a fundamental change in the atmosphere, a beginning of the long struggle between the communists and the socialists. Moreover, within the military itself conflicts were developing—indeed had already developed—which would later split the MFA into warring factions. As shrewd and well-informed a politician as Neto must have seen the storm warnings. They were not hard to recognize. Thus, while the ink on the Alvor agreement was barely dry, the forces that would undo it were already gathering.

Between November 1974 and January 1975, some 10,000 FNLA troops moved into the northeast of Angola. The Portuguese, their soldiers unwilling to become involved in armed confrontation, had virtually abandoned the frontiers. Behind the FNLA regulars came thousands of refugees, returning to the lands they had abandoned in the aftermath of the bloody rural uprising in 1961. As a result, thousands of Ovimbundu workers on the coffee estates were expelled from the region and fled south to their tribal homelands on the central highlands.

On the crowded Benguela-Bie plateau in southern Angola there were serious social and racial tensions too. The Portuguese army's counterinsurgency measures had uprooted thousands of peasants, concentrated them in "secure" village compounds, and in many cases opened up their lands to white settlers. In Luanda, the tension that had remained after serious racial clashes of the previous summer was aggravated by the arrival in February 1975 of heavily armed contingents from the rival nationalist movements. The uneasy standoff between these factions lasted only until March when, coincident with the unsuccessful attempt by General Spínola to seize power from the radicals in Portugal, widespread fighting broke out between the MPLA and FNLA in the Angolan capital. In Caxito, to the north of the capital, the FNLA rounded up MPLA sympathizers and shot and mutilated them.

It was the old nightmare of massacre and reprisal that had been a constant theme in the long Angolan struggle. To the massive internal ebb and flow of people and refugees was now added a mass exodus abroad. First to leave were Cape Verdians. Then came the exodus of whites. In Lisbon they were called the "dislocated" in official jargon; then, the "returned." But they were refugees and several hundred thousand of them poured into Portugal from Africa throughout the summer. Their arrival was a rude awakening for many of those army officers who a few months before had spoken naively about a socialist commonwealth.

One immediate consequence of these developments was that the process of decolonization—which, as it interacted with the internal situation in Portugal, had done so much to propel the country to the left in the months following the coup—now faltered. By the summer of 1975 it was obvious to all that the Portuguese in Angola could not contain outside intervention or control internal security, both obligations which Portugal had assumed under the Alvor accords, and any pretense at a bipartite transitional government collapsed. There was open fighting in Angola, and in Portugal too the military factions were beginning to eye each other ominously.

9. Internationalization

The rapidly deteriorating situation in Angola, however, was especially dangerous because it opened up opportunities for interference by outsiders which had not existed to the same degree in either the case of Guinea-Bissau or Mozambique. In Angola, three nationalist groups, all battle hardened, each with strong ethnic roots, competed with each other as much as they did with the Portuguese. Partly as a consequence of the factionalism within and among the liberation movements in Angola, the Portuguese had been much more successful there from a military point of view than they had been in either Guinea-Bissau or Mozambique. With the exception of UNITA, which in 1974 was a very poorly armed and small organization, each of the other nationalist movements, the FNLA and MPLA, were as much coalitions of exiles as they were effective insurgency forces. This was, of course, in striking contrast to both PAIGC in Guinea-Bissau or FRELIMO in Mozambique, movements which had formidable offensive capacity, controlled large areas of territory, and had developed rudimentary administrative structures. As was mentioned earlier, Angola had, in 1974, the largest white population in Africa outside South Africa. Whites almost totally dominated Angola's agricultural, transportation, and administrative infra-structures. It was partly as a result of these differences from the other territories that Angola took on the importance it did when Lisbon's inability to control the decolonization process became apparent. In Angola, no single movement had the capacity to act with the effectiveness of either PAIGC or FRELIMO, and by the time Angolan decolonization became the prime order of business, the Portuguese were so divided among themselves that they, too, were unable to provide any consistent or effective opposition to the rapid internationalization of Angola's crisis.

Angola, moreover, with a population of about five and a half million, was different in other important ways from all the other Portuguese territories. It was rich in natural resources (oil, diamonds, iron) and agricultural production (cotton, coffee, sisal, maize, sugar, tobacco). Unlike all the other territories, Angola had a favorable trade balance with the rest of the world and a firm basis for real independence. Yet the whole structure of Angola was so dominated by and dependent upon whites that the rapid deterioration of the security situation, and the burgeoning and at times bloody confrontations between the three nationalist movements, soon created panic among them. After March, 1975, as the Angolan whites began to stream out of Angola, they took with them almost everything that made the system of government and economy work, throwing an already confused situation into chaos.

The importance of stressing this chaos in Angola is to point out the contrast it represents from the situations which had transpired in much of the rest of Africa in the period of decolonization. Almost everywhere, except perhaps the Congo, Algeria and, Guinea-Conakry, the transfer of power occurred with the acquiescence (albeit sometimes reluctant) of the colonial power and, in consequence, disruption in administration and in the economy had been surprisingly small. The experiences of outside powers in their relationship with the new African states were therefore not appropriate to the situation which had developed in Angola. There, new circumstances required new policies, which would have to be formulated within an international environment which had itself changed dramatically since 1962.

The failure of Angola to follow the pattern of Mozambique was also increasingly worrying the South African government. In contrast to Mozambique, where South African power and economic suasion would be overwhelming, in Angola, South Africa could exert very little economic leverage over any nationalist government in Luanda. Moreover, because of Namibia, South Africa was vulnerable where its own position was weakest. The temptation to interfere militarily was thus very great, and on the surface seemed to be relatively risk-free, given the divisions between the nationalist movements.[9]

The South African response to developments in Angola had thus to rely more on military capabilities than economic suasion. The defense posture that South Africa's military strategists had adopted during the 1970s also set important limitations to South African options in Angola. While Vorster, the South African prime minister, had been talking of "détente" with neighboring black nations, he had also been rapidly building up the South African defense forces. South African military strategists meanwhile increasingly evoked the Israeli precedent of swift preemptive action, a doctrine of "hot pursuit" in the South African context. The doctrine in "hot pursuit" was used to justify the first armed South African incursion into Angola, while the "defense" of the Cunene dam complex on Namibia's border was used to justify the first permanent installation of South African regular forces inside Angola in early August 1975.

By mid-1975 in fact, Angola had the misfortune to recreate some of the worst characteristics of two previous African crises, the Congo and the Algerian war, combining nationalist forces, all externally dependent, fighting each other, and creating a situation of total insecurity, causing the flight of almost all the white population and the collapse of a great part of the infrastructure of the country. It was an environment where there was *no* effective impediment to outside intervention.

10. Superpower Intervention

The deteriorating situation within Angola was also of concern to Zaire and Zambia. The closure of the Benguela railway in mid-1975 as a result of hostilities in Angola could not have come at a worse time for both countries. Each was in deep political and economic trouble—mainly, though by no means exclusively, as a result of the dramatic drop in world copper prices. It was the Zaire connection, in particular, which trapped the United States in the Angolan crisis.

The special sensitivity to President Mobutu's desires and his effectiveness in promoting them had several causes. First, through late 1974 and 1975 Zaire was facing a major economic crisis, one result of which was to make the international financial community especially solicitous of Zaire, since no one wished to see a precedent set by the potential default on its foreign debt.[10]

Second, Mobutu possessed some very influential private lines of communication with Washington, going back to the epoch of President Kennedy, and by using them he succeeded in circumventing and neutralizing assessments of the situation being made by many experienced African specialists within the intelligence community and the State Department.[11]

Third, as a result of his negotiations with Spínola in 1974, Mobutu had already preempted the strategy to be followed by the West, providing the FNLA with a privileged access to sources of Western support. This was an inevitable consequence of acting in Angola through Zaire. Over the years, the FNLA had become little more than an extension of Mobutu's own armed forces, and Holden Roberto, the leader of the FNLA, was a man linked to Mobutu by marriage and obligated to him for many past favors.[12]

Finally, Zaire played a key role in the overall structures within which the Nixon administration had sought to organize its international relationships, having been designated (in a way which paralleled the United States relations with Iran in the period) as a "regional influential."

One major result of these circumstances was that, when eventually top United States policymakers in Washington began taking a serious direct interest in what was happening in Central Africa, it was largely as a result of the direct and serious measures the Soviet Union was taking to counteract the all-too-obvious attempts by Zaire to exclude the MPLA and Neto from the fruits of the victory which they, with Soviet encouragement, had fought 20 years to achieve. By then, unfortunately, the United States was already trapped within a framework of alliances, assumptions, and past failures from which it was difficult to escape. The salience given in Washington to the fact of communist support for the MPLA served to cover up the fact that the roots of escalation lay in actions in which the United States had been indirectly involved (and after January 1975, directly, when the CIA reactivated its connection with Holden Roberto) through her Zairian client. The African dimension became almost irrelevant in the process. As Helmut Sonnenfeldt, counselor in the State Department and Kissinger's closest adviser on Soviet affairs, explained later, the United States "had no intrinsic interest in Angola as such." But "once a locale, no matter how remote and unimportant for us, becomes a focal point for Soviet, and in this instance, Soviet-supported Cuban military action, the United States acquires a derivative interest which we simply cannot avoid." [13]

11. The War

Preoccupation with Soviet intentions, therefore, overwhelmed the warnings that were pouring in from, among others, the United States consul in Luanda, an interagency task force, and two assistant secretaries of state on the inside; from such respected African specialists as John Marcum and Gerald Bender on the outside; and from Senator Dick Clark in the Congress—all of whom argued that unless a broad based political strategy aimed at conciliating the factions in Angola was substituted for the attempt to favor some at the expense of others, the United States was doomed to face escalating demands with no certainty of success. In those circumstances the solution of the conflict would come through military means, with the United States unprepared and incapable of acting to aid the very forces it had egged into the conflict. At no time, until too late, did the United States give any serious thought to what a purely military solution to the Angolan crisis would involve, so great was the belief that the old and trusted formula of clandestinity, mercenaries, and cash would still work as they had in the past. By the time it became obvious that this was not enough, the only alternative power with the capacity and desire to intervene was South Africa, which was the last thing the West or the anti-MPLA nationalists should have permitted to become obvious. South African intervention at a stroke undermined the Western groups' credibility in African opinion, overwhelmed the doubts that many African states (Nigeria in particular) had about the MPLA and its friends, and made large-scale Soviet and Cuban assistance to Neto respectable.

Nevertheless, as the date set for Angolan independence approached in late October, 1975, the remnant of the old Spínola-Mobutu plan went into operation. The United States-backed Zairian forces moved from the north, as did a combined operation from the south by Portuguese right-wing extremists, South African regulars, and a motley collection of UNITA, FNLA auxiliaries, and Daniel Chipenda. When these forces attempted to take Luanda before

November 11, 1975, much to their surprise they came up against Cuban regulars flown in during the previous weeks in old Britannia transport planes at Agostinho Neto's urgent request. The West's hodgepodge forces thus failed to prevent the MPLA from declaring the independence of Angola under their exclusive auspices in the Angolan capital on November 11.

The Soviet Union's intervention in aid of Patrice Lumumba in 1960, despite its small size and dubious results, had nevertheless been an important turning point. It had marked the first use of transport aircraft in a crisis situation outside the immediate Soviet bloc countries. The creation of the West African naval patrol in late 1970 in order to protect Conakry, capital of Guinea, and indirectly to protect the headquarters of the PAIGC, was also an important step in the Soviets' increased willingness to support clients militarily and to take risks on their behalf. Large-scale Soviet airlift capacity had been much in evidence during the 1973 Middle East war, when the Soviets had made 934 flights to Arab nations, delivering 15,000 tons of matériel in addition to the much larger tonnage shipped by freighter. The United States airlift by C-5 and C-141 to Israel via the Azores in the same period had comprised 568 flights and delivered 23,000 tons of supplies. The Middle East experience, however, had given the Soviets much greater confidence in their ability to influence events in the Third World.

In 1975, direct Soviet aid to the MPLA began in the form of arms deliveries by sea and air via Brazzaville; in March, Russian cargo planes began delivering military equipment, which was later transshipped to Cabinda or Luanda; in April, some hundred tons of arms were delivered, in chartered Bristol Britannias, from Dar es Salaam to MPLA-controlled airfields in central Angola. Two Yugoslavian freighters unloaded weapons in Angola, followed by two East German vessels and an Algerian one. In April, Paulo Jorge of the MPLA visited Cuba in search of specialists to assist with the sophisticated equipment now arriving from the Soviet Union and Eastern Europe which the MPLA's own forces were not yet trained to handle.[14]

Cuban military men knowledgeable enough to use sophisticated equipment were beginning to take part in combat operations by the late spring of 1975. Cuban "advisers" were involved in the fighting at Caxito at the end of May, an engagement where the first tanks were used by the MPLA. In May and June, some 230 Cuban military advisers established training camps at Benguela, Babinda, Henrique de Carvalho, and Salazaro. All these early Cuban arrivals entered via Congo Brazzaville. By mid-August, UNITA found its forces facing Cubans at Lobito. In July the MPLA approached the Soviets for a troop presence in addition to military training experts. The Soviets balked at the suggestion as being too provocative and advised the MPLA to seek such assistance from Cuba. In early August the MPLA mission visited Havana to urge Castro to supply them with troops. In mid-August Castro authorized the logistical planning necessary to mount the sea-and airlift of troops, equipment, and supplies across the Atlantic to Angola. The operation was a complex one, involving the simultaneous arrival in Angola of troops from Cuba and armaments from the USSR.

Meanwhile on July 18, 1975, the United States decided to step up support to the anti-MPLA forces. The "40 committee" (the high-level interagency policy group that advised the president on covert action and to which the CIA was responsible) authorized $14 million in covert assistance to be paid in two installments to the FNLA and UNITA (a sum increased to $25 million in August and $32 million in November). A week before, on July 14, in Angola, the MPLA had expelled its rivals from Luanda. By taking the offensive, it had within two months seized control of twelve of the sixteen district capitals of Angola. In July, Zaire sent a commando company and armored car squadron across the border to Angola and into combat. Daniel Chipenda had flown to Namibia in June to meet in Windhoek with General Hendrik van den Bergh, chief of the South African Bureau of State Security (BOSS). South Africa's support for the FNLA seems to have begun in July and its support for UNITA in September. In mid-August two Zairian paratroop companies joined the action in support of the FNLA. At the same time, regular South African troops occupied the Ruacana and Calac-que pumping stations and the Cunene Dam complex. In September, Soviet 122-millimeter rockets were used for the first time in fighting north of Luanda. These so-called Stalin organs sent the FNLA and Zairian regulars into a panicky retreat. Three Cuban merchant ships left Cuba for Angola in early September after urgent appeals from the MPLA, which now feared a large scale South African invasion augmented by United States assistance, via Zaire, to the FNLA and UNITA. The Soviets had abandoned the idea of a political coalition in March; they were now portraying the FNLA and UNITA in their propaganda as "splintists," and describing the war in Angola not as a "civil war" but as a "war of intervention." Unfortunately for Angola, the war was both a civil war and a war in which outside intervention occurred on a massive scale. The Chinese, looking on from their vantage point in

Zaire, decided to cut their losses. On October 27, 1975, they withdrew all their military instructors from the FNLA. By November, the Portuguese army in Angola was a helpless bystander. The last official Portuguese representative, Leonel Cardoso, and his staff, scuttled quietly away from Luanda the day before independence.

The twin offensives from Zaire and Namibia had, however, come very close to success. In fact, at the moment independence was declared in Luanda in November, the MPLA as a result of Zairian and South African intervention held little more than the capital and a strip of central Angola inland toward Shaba. South African advisers and South African antitank weapons had helped to stop an MPLA advance on Nova Lisboa (Huambo) in early October. Nova Lisboa was the center of UNITA strength and the site of a declaration of an independent state (the "Social Democratic Republic of Angola") by UNITA and FNLA on November 11. By late October, the South Africans had helped turn the tide in the south against the MPLA. A South African-led combat group (ZULU) with armored cars and mortars had traveled four hundred miles from the Namibia border in two weeks, overwhelming the MPLA and Cubans in Benguela and Lobito, thus seizing control of the terminal of the Benguela railroad. In central Angola, a second South African combat unit ("Foxbat") with a squadron of armored cars had moved five hundred miles north toward Luanda and inflicted a severe defeat on the Cubans at Bridge 14 (north of Santa Combo), killing over two hundred of them as well as two hundred MPLA troops. North of Luanda, the FNLA and Zairian troops had again reached Caxito, within a short drive of the capital.

A big Cuban buildup started on November 7, when 650 combat troops were flown to Angola via Barbados and Guinea-Bissau. On November 27, a Cuban artillery regiment and a battalion of motorized and field troops landed on the Angolan coast after a sea crossing of 20 days. The Soviets had meanwhile deployed a naval force in Angolan waters which provided protection to the ships unloading and transshipping arms from Point Noire (Congo) to Angola. Soviet military transports were airlifting reinforcements and arms from late October. The Russians provided MIG-21s, T-34 and T-54 tanks, armored personnel carriers, antitank and SAM-7 missiles, rocket launchers, and AK-47 automatic rifles, in addition to the 122-millimeter rocket launchers, which proved totally effective against the Zairians in particular. (After October, it was said that Zairian regulars went into battle driving in reverse, the better to drive away again when threatened by the Stalin-organs' awesome power.)

The Soviet and Cuban intervention was decisive. It saved the MPLA and their regime, and it profoundly altered the balance of power in southern Africa.

United States Secretary of State Henry Kissinger, like the South Africans, was shaken by the scale of the Soviet and Cuban response. The CIA's Angolan task force at CIA headquarters at Langley had been so confident of success by the Zairian and South African regulars, that on November 11 the members had celebrated Angolan independence with wine and cheese in their crepe paper decorated offices. The arrival of Soviet and Cuban ships and planes; at Pointe Noire and Brazzaville, was observed by United States intelligence surveillance, but the unloading of troops had taken place at night, and strictly imposed discipline during the sea voyage concealed the presence of troops. Not until November did the CIA realize that 4,000 Cuban combat troops were deployed in Angola, a figure which had grown to 15,000 by January 1976. By February 1976, the combined Soviet-Cuban sea and airlift had transported 38,000 tons of weapons and supplies to Angola. Although South African foreign policy had consistently played up the communist threat to Africa, it had clearly not given serious attention to the consequences of a strong conventional communist military presence in the form of some 20,000 Cuban troops. Although South Africa lost only 43 dead in Angola of its over 2,000 troops deployed there, it had by the end of 1976 concluded that, for military and political reasons, it was not in a position to take on a superpower. Meanwhile as a result of press leaks in the fall, the United States was effectively removed from the Angolan competition on December 19, 1975, when overwhelming majorities of both houses of Congress banned covert aid to the FNLA and UNITA. The OAU, in response to the fact that South African intervention had become public knowledge in November, swung from its former neutraility to support of the MPLA as the legitimate government of Angola. South African intervention was especially decisive in the case of Nigeria, the MPLA going so far as to send captured South African prisoners to the OAU meeting in Lagos to prove that South African regulars were in fact involved in the Angolan fighting.

Conclusion

It is ironic that those who had talked the most of "linkage," that is Henry Kissinger and the South Africans, were in fact the least prepared during the

Kissinger and the South Africans, were in fact the least prepared during the rapidly changing circumstances of the critical months between April 1974 and December 1975 to respond to the crisis brought about by the unexpectedly sudden collapse of Portuguese rule in Africa. When it came to manipulating the forces at play, the United States found itself lacking any clear delineation of the interaction between events and personalities in Portugal and Africa, while their geopolitical rivals found themselves with experienced assets in key locations.

The South Africans had talked endlessly of a "communist threat" in South Africa, but they were totally unprepared for the actual intervention of Cuban combat troops with Soviet weaponry and logistical support. Kissinger never seems to have planned for the consequences of a major escalation of the conflict in Angola. He also disastrously misread congressional behavior, especially the congressional opposition to a botched clandestine interference—assumed to be low cost and low risk despite the clear evidence to the contrary. Even here, Castro proved more discerning when it came to predicting possible congressional reaction. Indeed this had been a key element in his decision to provide assistance to the MPLA.

The West's position was fundamentally flawed by the failure to provide any clear objectives for their actions other than the negative objective of denying the MPLA victory. What sort of Angola, for example, did they think a UNITA/FNLA victory would result from? The South Africans seemed to have been thinking of creating some sort of buffer state in the center south of the country. Zaire seems to have coveted Cabinda. The MPLA, in contrast, stood firm to the concept of a unitary state; they held the capital and their main source of ethnic support lay in a broad belt at the heart of the country. This element continues to be a source of strength.

Several likely allies were also noticably missing from the Western lineup. Brazil, for example, which had been among the first to recognize the Neto regime, and Israel, despite Kissinger's entreaties, had the good sense for once to keep clear of the conflict.

None of the conditions which emerged from the Angolan civil war has substantially changed since the mid-1970s. The unfortunate result of the passage of time is if anything to harden positions. It is unlikely that a recounting of the history of how the present situation occurred will alter anything. But it should at least demonstrate how the current impasse came about, and how complicated its resolution is likely to be. It also helps explain why the cases of Angola and Mozambique are so different and likely to remain so.

Perhaps the most unfortunate result of the Angolan conflict is the role Africa has assumed in the domestic politics of East and West. All of which now makes any separation of Africa from the complex web of East-West relations virtually impossible. Actions, produce reactions in politics as in physics. Mr. Brezhnev, for example, played for high stakes in Africa and in the short-term the gains of the Soviet Union were considerable. The debacle in Angola, moreover, coincided with the military defeat of the United States in Vietnam, and the collapse of its Iranian proxy and the consequent shattering of its strategic position in the Persian Gulf and northern Indian Ocean. The issue here is not whether the United States was wise or unwise in any of these actions, or could have avoided them. The point is that the Soviets appeared decisive and successful, the United States indecisive and weak, and that these perceptions aided those in the Soviet Union who urged expansion and weakened those in the United States who urged restraint. It led directly in fact to the so called "Reagan Doctrine," within the frame work of which Angola and Jonas Savimbi play key notes.

Thus, whatever Mr. Brezhnev's short-term gains in Angola and Ethiopia during the 1970s, he gravely miscalculated the consequences of Soviet actions in Africa on United States opinion. If Soviet analysts of the United States thought they were clever in 1975-76 in reading the mood of Congress better than did the old congressional hand, Mr. Gerald Ford, by accurately predicting congressional rejection of administration pleas for increased aid to anti-Soviet forces in Angola, they overlooked the volatile nature of American politics. Post-Watergate flagellation was bound to end sooner or later. The Soviets should not have expected to preen themselves over the shift of "world historical forces" in their favor, assuming that at the same time their adversaries would not take them at their word.

It is, therefore, not enough for American neo-isolationists to say that Africa is far away and insignificant. Africa is very much what we make of it. Perceptions, even myths and obsessions, can at times be more important than events in provoking action. Yet, neither is it always the case that perceptions of threats and strategic challenges reflect real interests or grow from clearly understood roots. Looking back at the rationalization for great power involvement in Africa in the 1880s, the British historians Ronald Robinson and Jack Gallagher concluded that, far from reflecting the interests the powers purported to defend, their strategies were "even more a register of the hopes, the memories, and the neuroses which informed the strategists' picture of the world." Less has changed than might have been expected. Today much of the debate about Angola in particular, both East and West, and on Left and Right, it is no less phantasmagorical than it was a hundred years ago.

Finally it is also worth remembering that Robinson and Gallagher also criticized the theory of imperialism formulated by the English Liberal J.A. Hobson and the Russian Marxist V.I. Lenin. Hobson and Lenin both emphasized the economic or capitalist origins of the scramble for Africa. According to Robinson and Gallagher's interpretation, it was perceived geopolitical threats, caused by concern over strategic routes between Europe and the Indian Ocean, and a combination of nationalistic Islamic revolt in North Africa and expanding conflict within southern Africa that created the coincidence of external and internal pressures that dragged the great powers into deeper involvement and greater competition than they had either intended or desired. The increasing internationalization of Third World conflicts make these arguments surprisingly familiar. Strategists are in hot debate over Soviet expansionism and, again, talk is of the Cape route and naval balances. Even the chronology is strikingly similar, since most historians agree that the process which led to the intensification of imperial rivalries between the great powers was set in motion during the early 1880s.

The conundrum about the role of the United States and the Soviet Union in Africa during the 1980s is that the methods each has chosen to achieve its objectives there, while sufficient to gain temporary success, are not sufficient to guarantee permanent successes. The West, in the final analysis, especially the United States, seems to place faith in economic factors that would gladden the hearts of Lenin and Hobson. On the other hand, the Soviet Union's faith in military leverage and the belief of many African radicals that "superior force" is the means to resolve their dilemmas, will not work either. The danger for both great powers emerges precisely from the fact that the Soviets attempt military solutions to problems that they lack the economic capacity to resolve, while the West seeks to exercise economic influence while lacking a counterbalancing military force.

The second conundrum today is that each of the crises which have stimulated super power rivalry in Africa are peripheral to the fundamental conflicts within the continent. What will really determine the future of Africa will be what happens in South Africa. Yet peripheral crises can narrow the room for maneuver as they have in Angola; these crises can recur at any moment, and undoubtedly, they will.

If the experience of Angola demonstrates anything it is that outsiders who transform conflicts beyond the sphere of their own direct relationships into struggles for advantage are obliged to work through clients who cannot be successfully manipulated. It also demonstrates that acting on the basis of faulty and biased intelligence will constantly present the temptation to escalate commitments to a degree that threatens their bilateral relations and narrows their options for response. It is a trap into which Moscow fell as easily as the Americans, which is why the situation that has emerged from the Angolan episode is potentially so dangerous.

The irony of all this is that the end of Europe's oldest empire in Africa recreated the type of situation that dragged the great powers into the partition of Africa during the nineteenth century. But if the steeplechase is to begin again, let the participants consider the consequences. Russians would do well to remember why Lenin wrote his pamphlet on imperialism. It was to explain the origins of world war. Geostrategists in the West should ponder the words of that great British practitioner of realpolitik, Lord Salisbury, who wondered towards the end of his life what Britain was doing fighting a war "for people whom we despise, and for territory which will bring us no profit and no power." Africans who invite outsiders in to fight old battles might do well to remember that, when this happened before, Africa lost its freedom for a hundred years.

Notes

1. The problem of dealing with the intra-Luso-African dimension of decolonization compounds this problem. African specialists close to the liberation movements find it hard to deal objectively with the interconnections between Portuguese and African events, just as Portuguese specialists often remain locked with the concepts of "Luso-tropicalism." It was in fact the desire to demolish the idea of "Luso-tropicalism" which inspired some of the best American scholarship on the Portuguese in southern Africa, namely the fine books by Gerald J. Bender, *Angola Under the Portuguese: The Myth and the Reality* (Berkeley and Los Angeles: University of California Press, 1978) and Allen F. Isaacman, *The Tradition of Resistance in Mozambique Anti-Colonial Activity in the Zambesi Valley 1850-1921* (Berkeley and Los Angeles: University of California Press, 1980). An extremely sophisticated analysis of the interaction of African society and Portuguese administration (or maladministration) is encompassed in Leroy Vail and Landeg White, *Capitalism and Colonialism in Mozambique* (Minneapolis: University of Minnesota Press, 1980). Antonio de Figueiredo, however, has pointed out that Salazar's policy as well as Gilberto Freyre's development of the idea of Luso-tropicality must be seen in their proper chronological time frame and national context, in *Portugal: Ten Years After the Revolution,* ed. Kenneth Maxwell (New York: Research Institute on International Change, 1984). The classic protagonists in this old debate are, of course, Charles R. Boxer on one side in his *Race Relations in the Portuguese Colonial Empire 1415-1825* (Oxford: Oxford University Press, 1963) and, on the other, Gilberto Freyre, *O Mundo que o Portugues Crio* (Rio de Janeiro: José Olympio, 1940). The violence of the current debate over the relative strengths of endogenous as opposed to external factors is best seen in Kenneth Adelman and Gerald J. Bender, "Conflict in Southern Africa: A Debate," *International Security,* vol. 3, no. 2 (Fall 1978). For an excellent introduction to the Portuguese colonies in Africa see Malyn Newitt, *Portugal in Africa: the Last Hundred Years* (London: Longman, 1981).

2. *World Military Expenditures and Arms Control 1967-1976,* United States Arms Control and Disarmament Agency, Publication 98

(Washington, D.C.: GPO, July, 1978). Also *The Military Balance 1974* (London: International Institute for Strategic Studies).

3. National Security Council Interdepartmental Group on Africa Study in Response to National Security Study Memorandum 39 South Africa. Secret AF/NSDG 69-8, 15 August 1969, 56.

4. See Franco Nogueira, *Dialogos Interditos: a Politica Externa Portuguesa e a Guerra de Africa,* vol. 11 (Lisbon, 1979).

5. United States Congress, House Committee on Foreign Affairs, Subcommittee on Africa, *Review of State Department Trip through Southern and Central Africa* (hearing), 93rd Cong., 12 December 1974, 153-54.

6. The best account of this period is Richard Mahoney, *Kennedy's Ordeal Over Africa* (New York: Oxford University Press, 1982).

7. Portugal received 280 million dollars worth of arms transfers between 1967 and 1976. Most of it came from France: 121 million dollars worth. 50 million dollars worth came from West Germany and only 30 million dollars worth from the United States. See *World Military Expenditures and Arms Control* (Washington, D.C.: GPO, July, 1978).

8. For sores contacts with Neto, see Mŕio Soares, *Wuelle Révoluton* (Paris, 1975). A good synopsis of the decolonization process from the Portuguese point of view can be found in "Groupo de Pesquisa sobre a descolonizacao Portuguesa," in *A Descolonizacao Portuguesa: Aproximação a um estudo*, 2 vols. (Lisbon: Instituto Democracia e Liberdade, 1979).

9. Robert S. Jaster, *South Africa's Narrowing Security Options,* Adelphi Papers, no. 159 (London: International Institute for Strategic Studies, 1980).

10. Nancy Bellieveau, *International Investor* (March 1977): 23-28, and Crawford Young "Zaire: The Unending Crisis," *Foreign Affairs* (Fall 1978): 169-85.

11. *African Contemporary Record,* ed. Colin Legum (New York: Holmes and Mayer), especially vol. 7 (1974-75), A87-A101, and vol. 8 (1975-76), A118-A128.

12. For a sharp insight into strategic thinking in Zaire about the Angolan situation in this important period see Kenneth Adelman, "Report from Angola," *Foreign Affairs* 53, no. 3 (April 1975): 558-74.

13. Helmut Sonnefeldt, "American-Soviet Relations: Informal Remarks,"

Parameters, Journal of the United States Army War College, vol. 6, no. 1:15-16.

14. The literature on the Angolan Civil War is already vast. One of the most balanced accounts is by Colin Legum, in Stephan S. Kaplan, *Diplomacy of Power: Soviet Armed Forces as a Political Instrument* (Washington, D.C.: Brookings Institution, 1981), 570-637. Also see Franz Wilhelm Heimer, *O Processo de Decolonização em Angola 1974-1976* (Lisbon, 1980), and Cord Meyer, *Facing Reality: From World Federalism to the CIA* (New York: Basic Books, 1981).

   For Brazilian policy I have relied on "Polestra proferida na Escuela Superior de Guerra por Italo Zappa," May 31, 1976. On Angola in this period see: Ernest Harsch and Tony Thomas, *Angola: The Hidden History of Washington's War* (New York: Holmes and Maier, 1976; Jim Dingeman, "Angola: Portugal in Africa," *Strategy and Tactics,* no. 56 (May/June 1976); Colin Legum and Tony Hodges, *After Angola: The War over Southern Africa* (New York: Holmes and Maier, 1976); Gerald J. Bender, "Angola, the Cubans and American Anxieties," *Foreign Policy,* no. 31 (Summer 1978): 3-33; John A. Marcum, "The Lessons of Angola," *Foreign Affairs,* vol. 54, no. 3 (April 1976): 407-25; Kenneth Adelman and Gerald J. Bender, "Conflict in Southern Africa: A Debate," *International Security,* vol. 3, no. 2 (Fall 1978): 67-122; Gerald J. Bender, "Kissinger in Angola: Anatomy of Failure," *American Policy in Southern Africa* (Washington, D.C.: University Press of America, 1978), 65-143; and John Marcum, *The Angolan Revolution* (2 vols. Cambridge: M.I.T. Press, 1969 and 1978); Roger Moss, "Castro's Secret War Exposed," *The Sunday Telegraph,* (London: 30 January 1977; 6 February 1977; 30 February 1977); Gabriel Garcia Marquez, "Operation Carlota: Cuba's Role in Angolan Victory," *Cuba Update,* Center for Cuban Studies, no. 1 (New York, April 1977). This is an excerpted account based on the original in Spanish published in Mexico. Also see "United States Policy on Angola," *Hearing Before the Committee on International Relations, House of Representatives, 94th Congress, 2nd session, January 26, 1976* (Washington, D.C.: GPO, 1976), 13; Security Supporting Assistance for Zaire," *Hearing Before the Subcommittee on African Affairs and the Subcommittee on Foreign Assistance of the Committee on Foreign Relations, U.S. Senate, 94th Congress, 1st session, October 24, 1975* (Washington, D.C.: GPO, 1975), 32.

2: Portugal's Policies Toward Angola and Mozambique Since Independence

BY CARLOS GASPAR

In the decolonization of Africa, the former colonial powers typically shaped the process by which independence was achieved, and influenced the political systems and economic structures adopted by the new states. The more freely independence was granted and prepared by the former metropolitan power, the longer it cast its shadow in the post-independence period. As a general rule, the European powers have had a stabilizing influence, at least for a time, on the internal situations and the foreign alignments of the new states.

The most notable exception has been the last imperial European power, Portugal. As a result of the unique circumstances in which Portugal's five African colonies came to independence, Lisbon's control of the process of handing over power was weak at best, and—in the case of the largest colony, Angola—almost non-existent. This power vacuum sucked outside powers into the Angolan civil war, itself a product of Portugal's inability to keep its grip on the decolonization process. This chapter will examine that process as it unfolded in Lisbon, as well as the efforts of successive Portuguese governments to reassert influence in Angola and Mozambique. An attempt

will be made to explain the failure of Portugal to reestablish itself as a significant player in the two countries, and to assess its future prospects in that regard.

The Myth of Integration

The old regime's stubborn resistance to change in its relationship with its
colonies had an ideological foundation—the myth of integration. Portugal
and its overseas dependencies were supposed to form a single cultural entity
and a single plurinational state. That this dream failed is not to say that the
myth has not continued to have serious consequences in the post-colonial
period. This myth was present in the decolonization policies of the military
who took power after the coup d'état of April 25, 1974, and in the military's
vision of post-colonial relations. Furthermore, it has persisted in the debate
over Africa policy down to the present day.

A major consequence of late decolonization was the demise of the
authoritarian regime itself. After the fall of the *Estado Novo* (the "New
State," proclaimed by the 1933 constitution), the issues of a change of regime
in Lisbon and of decolonization became inseparable. It was this reciprocal
interaction between two profoundly complex political processes that constituted the unique circumstances of decolonization in the Portuguese African
colonies. As Portugal revealed its incapacity to transfer power in Angola,
the succession to power in that country came to be decided by an un-
precedented Soviet bloc intervention, which radically changed the situation
in southern Africa. Following this shift, the successor regimes in Angola and
Mozambique chose to become "Marxist-Leninist," as a part of their own
integration strategies, and turned to the Soviet bloc for aid and protection.
No doubt this dramatic reorientation toward the East was itself a major
obstacle to the attempts of Portugal's post-revolutionary governments to play
a relevant role either in regional politics or in its former colonies. Yet, as
we shall see, the persistence of the myth of integration in post-1974 policies
has also been an important factor in Portugal's failure to play an influential
role in the new states.

A Conceptual Framework

It is difficult to understand Portugal's post-colonial policies in Africa
because there has been a lack of an internal consensus over what those policies
should be, as well as an absence of any institutional framework for defining
differences. Thus, the cleavages over African policy have been shifting,
and have also cut across the boundaries between parties and interest

groups. For this reason, this analysis will resort to abstract, ideal categories to characterize the perceptions of political élites on this issue.

The integrationist concept—dominant, if not absolute, in the former authoritarian regime and a pillar of its nationalist legitimacy—carried over into the decolonization policies of the radical military. The vision was that unity between Portugal and its former colonies could be restored after independence on the basis of mutual affinities that were thought to exist—of which one was their relative state of economic underdevelopment.

After events proved the integrationist concept unviable, its proponents concentrated on salvaging its remnants by stressing the priority of a close alliance with the African states, as opposed to greater integration into Western Europe. The principal argument in support of this view was that close relations with Angola and Mozambique were indispensable to maintaining a distinct international role for Portugal, thereby avoiding the external dependence which could result from accession to the European community. While this second concept had strong links to the traditional nationalism of the deposed regime, it nevertheless moved forward away from the traditional integrationist concept. This new approach had its first hesitant appearance in Portuguese presidential diplomacy toward Angola in 1977-78.

The third concept—the liberal approach—also had its roots in the old regime, namely in the "modernizing" currents of its technocrats and business circles. It was to become the prevailing concept among the foreign policy élites of the democratic political parties after 1976, as they restructured Portugal's international position after the decolonization débacle. In this concept, however, relations with the former African colonies were to be subordinated to the priorities of integration with Europe and the West. There was an important internal aspect to this—the consolidation of the democratic pluralist regime established by the 1976 constitution. The liberal concept did not, however, exclude an African dimension in foreign policy. The search for a more active role in southern Africa was one of the aims of both the conservative-liberal alliance in 1979-80 and the socialist-liberal coalition in 1983-85. That the first such effort came in the wake of the Lancaster House conference (at which agreement was reached on procedures for Rhodesia's transition to internationally-recognized independence), and the second when South Africa was preparing to sign bilateral accords with Angola and Mozambique, is perhaps more than a coincidence.

We will now examine how these conceptual approaches evolved in the post-authoritarian period.

Democratization and Decolonization

The military coup d'état of April 25, 1974 that overthrew the old regime in Portugal was precipitated by discontent within the professional military over institutional issues. Its underlying cause, however, was disillusionment of younger officers with the political paralysis and the regime that was ineffectually prosecuting a colonial war that had dragged on for more than a decade. Many of the officers who had campaigned in the African colonies had come to sympathize with the cause of those whom they were fighting. It was natural, therefore, that the struggle for power that ensued in Portugal in the aftermath of the revolution should be bound up with the issue of decolonization. Within the MFA (*Movimento das Forças Armadas* — or Armed Forces Movement, the group within the military that had organized and carried out the coup)—there were two initial currents. One of these supported General António Spínola and the other formed around Major Ernesto Melo Antunes and Colonel Vasco Gonçalves. These two tendencies had both been strongly influenced by the integrationist concept of the old regime, but they differed on how that ideal would be implemented.

General Spínola, president of the republic, was set on a slow process of decolonization which required the continuation of full military deployment in the colonies. The objective was the transfer of power to internal coalitions that would be dominated by representatives of the resident Portuguese communities, at least in Angola and Mozambique. In the meantime, Spínola would consolidate his internal position on the basis of a presidential regime. If he were elected, as he fully expected to be, he could then proceed with his policies for decolonization with full authority.

General Spínola's plans were, however, flawed by a lack of realism. He at first resisted the recognition of the principle of independence for the colonies, and wanted to avoid direct negotiations with the main African nationalist forces in Guinea and Mozambique. In so doing, he underestimated the determination within the ranks of the military to end the colonial wars, while he overestimated the political capacities of the Portuguese communities overseas.

Three months after coming to power, the president had become increasingly isolated, while the stronger radical current within the Armed Forces Movement had succeeded in having him nominate its candidate, Colonel

Vasco Gonçalves as prime minister. In July, Spínola reversed his former position on independence and direct negotiations, opening the way for the recognition of the independence under the PAIGC *(Partido Africano da Independência da Guiné e Cabo Verde* or African Party for the Independence of Guinea and Cape Verde) of Guinea and Cape Verde as well as for the Lusaka Agreement, which set the date for the independence of Mozambique and for the transfer of power to FRELIMO *(Frente de Libertação de Moçambique* or Mozambique Liberation Front), the sole armed nationalist movement in the colony.

These two decisions were congruent with the urge for decolonization that prevailed in the Socialist Party (for which decolonization was a necessary step toward European integration), as well as (for entirely different reasons) in the radical faction in the MFA, which had the advantage of predominant influence in the military overseas. For the radicals, decolonization had to be completed as fast as possible, while they still held uncontested positions of power; their goal was to have the framework for decolonization in place before the general elections scheduled for the spring of 1975. They had a single guiding rule for the transfer of power: negotiations must be with the armed nationalist movements, as these were the only forces with anticolonialist legitimacy—the only ones that would be able to end the war, and the only ones, in their view, that could preserve the unity of the territories and, in the sases of Angola and Mozambique, resist South African interference. This rule disregarded the fundamental differences that existed in each colony, which the radicals ignored, being driven by their belief in the deep political and ideological affinities between themselves and those nationalist movements.

In an extreme version of the radical vision, the lost unity of the empire could be recovered through the "uniqueness" of the decolonization process, in which there would be an alliance between former adversaries, who would constitute military parties that—at the head of left-wing coalitions—would dominate the post-colonial regimes in both Portugal and its former colonies. To underscore the differences between this model and that of General Spínola, the MFA radicals insisted that Portugal's small size and backwardness, which placed it in an unstable position, with one foot in Europe and one foot in the "Third World," made any attempts at creating a neo-colonialist relationship with its former colonies impossible. In addition, they espoused a neutral course that would bring Portugal closer to the prospective non-alignment of the post-colonial states. Finally, their identification with the African liberation movements led them to define the MFA as "the liberation movement of the Portuguese people."[1]

In Guinea-Bissau and Mozambique the implementation of this policy presented no insurmountable problems, and the transfer of power proceeded as called for by the agreements with the PAIGC and FRELIMO. In Angola, however, the two currents in the Portuguese military once again clashed. Even after retreating in the cases of Guinea and Mozambique in July, General Spínola engaged himself all the more deeply in the decolonization of Angola.[2] He proposed a two-year transition period to independence during which there would be a coalition government, with the Portuguese communities represented on a par with the three African nationalist movements, on the grounds that the Portuguese were the largest ethnic group in the territory and that there was no unified African nationalist movement.[3] Furthermore, by 1974 the Portuguese military had largely pacified the territory and the MFA radical faction was not as strong in Angola as elsewhere. Finally, the main nationalist movement, the MPLA (*Movimento Popular de Libertação de Angola*), was deeply divided so that it seemed possible to co-opt its more moderate elements and leave out the "presidential" faction of Agostinho Neto.[4]

Spínola's plan did not survive a confrontation between the president and the MFA radicals and their allies in the Portuguese Communist Party (PCP). The confrontation was in part centered on the issue of Angola, as preparations for a quadripartite summit to settle the decolonization question — although this was quite incompatible with Spínola's scheme — were already being furthered by the government. On the last day of September, Spínola resigned.

The MFA's troubles in Angola were just beginning, however. The presence of three nationalist movements with a claim to legitimacy based on armed resistance made the prospects for a peaceful transition extremely improbable.[5] Nevertheless, by refusing to hold separate negotiations with each movement, the Portuguese government succeeded in forcing them into multi-party negotiations at the Penina Hotel in Alvor, Portugal, on January 10, 1975. This was no mean achievement. The Alvor agreement, signed five days later, looked brilliant on paper. It was clear, however, to all those involved, that at best it was meant as a truce and that none of the liberation movements was ready to comply with its provisions. This being the case, its implementation rested almost exclusively on the enforcement capability of the Portuguese authorities.[6]

The question was which movement would the Portuguese military side with during the approaching confrontation among the three movements. While the military was supposed to be impartial, it was inevitable that—by acting or failing to act—they would have to take sides. Despite their best intentions, it was almost impossible to remain neutral in the midst of what was soon to become a civil war. Agostinho Neto understood this quite clearly. He also had an advantage over his political rivals because of his close ties with left wing forces in Lisbon, especially with the Portuguese Communist Party, and, more importantly because of his very strong standing within the MFA. Neto competed openly for MFA support at Alvor, when he addressed the MFA as the "fourth liberation movement."[7] Together, Neto reasoned, the MFA and the MPLA could defeat the other two groups.

Violence among the three liberation movements began in February, 1975 and was to continue until July, always closely interacting with the successive political and military crises in Lisbon. At the same time, the trends towards regionalization—and internationalization—of the conflict became more and more visible, as each one of the movements started receiving increasing support from regional and international allies. Portuguese diplomacy was incapable of either neutralizing regional interference or of moderating United States hostility towards the MPLA. It also seems not to have tried to influence Soviet policy, even though it was clear that the USSR was determined to support its Angolan allies, perhaps to the limit.[8]

The internal political crisis in Portugal reached its peak during June and July. The radical military and their communist allies had control of the state—or what remained of it—but were still too weak to impose their domination on Portuguese society. Moreover, the MFA radical movement had split, with its more moderate members siding with the democratic parties in a struggle for political survival. During this period, Portugal's role in decolonization came to an end. Mozambique became an independent state under FRELIMO on June 25, 1975. And the battle for Luanda was about to begin.

In July—coincident with the breaking up of the multiparty coalition in Lisbon—the MPLA began a massive offensive against the FNLA (*Frente Nacional de Libertação de Angola*) to gain sole control of Luanda, and in doing so provoked the massive flight of the remaining Portuguese community. Paralyzed, the Portuguese military stood aside during the urban fighting as the MPLA called upon its superior support in the capital. After being expelled, the FNLA, with support from Zaire, mounted an operation to recover Luanda, launched from its northern stronghold.

In the middle of this battle, the Portuguese authorities made one last attempt to intervene. Their proposals were clear cut. The Alvor agreement—

which had just been massively violated by the MPLA—was to be replaced by a tripartite arrangement between Portugal, the MPLA, and UNITA (*União Nacional Para a Independência Total de Angola*).[9] It would declare the FNLA an "anti-national" movement—as it was engaged in an invasion of Angola involving a foreign power—and the two remaining movements would join forces to restore "national unity." In the meantime, the Portuguese military were ordered to stop the invasion from the north, which they did with remarkable efficiency, fighting side by side with the MPLA.

These proposals made some sense from a strategic point of view. The remaining Portuguese military forces, standing alongside the MPLA, would probably be able to hold northern Angola, while UNITA was virtually alone in the south. Apparently, the threat of an invasion by South Africa was not at issue. Together, the two movements on the one hand could limit the risks of the conflict spreading throughout the whole region and on the other hand, might avoid the disintegration of territorial integrity and perhaps moderate further internal ethnic conflicts.

The problem, however, was a political one: the Portuguese side was less than persuaded that such a late alliance could work, and it was convinced that the final outcome would be a single-party regime under the MPLA. Its aims were, at best, tactical—avoiding further escalation until its own withdrawal. In any case, the Portuguese proposals were rejected by Agostinho Neto. The MPLA seemed confident of victory, as it felt assured of extensive Soviet and Cuban support. It did not have to deal with any Portuguese forces that were not unconditional allies in its drive to achieve total control of Angola.

By the end of July, the failure of successive Portuguese policies was quite evident. Only a communist takeover in Lisbon could have resurrected the integrationist vision that until then had inspired Portugal's decolonization policies. As power slipped from the Communist Party's grasp in Portugal, the possibility of the restoration of the "unique" ties between Portugal and its colonies faded. Solidarity between the MFA and the MPLA was shattered in the battle for Luanda, and destroyed on November 11, 1975, when Portugal withheld recognition of the People's Republic proclaimed by the MPLA.

The events of the months until independence compromised Portugal's postcolonial policies in southern Africa even further. As Portugal retreated, escalation (and with it regionalization and internationalization) of the conflict seemed unavoidable, until Soviet and Cuban intervention finally decided the issue of Angolan decolonization. That intervention radically changed the situation in Africa. The post-war balance that had survived successive decolonizations was upset by the retreat of the last of the European colonial powers.

By early 1976, the external conditions that were to shape Portugal's policies towards Angola and Mozambique were roughly defined.

First, the global East-West struggle had become entrenched in Angola as well as in Mozambique, and thus projected its influence throughout southern Africa. The Soviet Union had established its full status as one of the great powers by demonstrating its ability to decide the issue of a distant regional conflict, in which it involved itself to a surprising extent.[10] As a (minor) result this limited the possibility of Portugal taking an independent position towards its former colonies in southern Africa.

Second, the void created by the collapse of the Portuguese "buffer" enhanced the role of South Africa as the regional power—one that had solid strategic as well as economic dimensions. Thus Angola and Mozambique became part of the regional conflict, dependent on external allies for their security. In Angola, the south became (once again) the more threatened area, while Mozambique became vulnerable to the destabilization strategies of its powerful neighbor. This, too, reduced the role of Portugal, as it lacked the will and the resources to counter regional threats against its former dependencies.

Finally, the Soviet Union and Cuba replaced Portugal in Angola to the extent that they were able to take over its security and political roles. Moreover, the post-colonial regimes defined themselves as "Marxist-Leninist."[11] This willingness to imitate the political model of their protectors was also meant to facilitate their own admittance within the Soviet bloc and to consolidate their position as model Soviet allies.[12] In this context, the radical difference between the regime in Portugal and the regimes of its former colonies further excluded Portugal from playing a relevant regional role.

On the other hand, the circumstances and the results of the decolonization process had destroyed the model for post-colonial relations that it was supposed to anticipate, while also setting some of the main patterns of Portugal's future policies. The Angolan debacle demonstrated the error of the integrationist concept. Its unresponsiveness to specific conditions had cleared the way for the worst possible result and showed that it could never be the source of a realistic post-colonial policy. Ideological naiveté—the vision of an alliance between a neutral European power and non-aligned African countries (a vision which in part had its foundations in the traditional anti-communism and anti-Americanism of Portuguese colonial policy)—led to successive mistakes in the search for allies. It also confirmed a deep resistance against coordinating Portugal's position towards Angola or Mozambique with that of other powers. And the inability to implement its decolonization policies in Angola or to avoid the crisis in relations with Mozambique immediately after independence demonstrated that Portugal lacked both the political will and the resources to develop an autonomous post-colonial policy in the region.

In a sense, the only thing that was settled by decolonization was the issue of democratization. The two problems of decolonization and democratization were both solved when the formation of a democratic pluralist regime in Portugal became the priority of all those opposed to a communist takeover in Lisbon.[13] This in turn deepened the cleavage with the former colonies, achieving exactly the opposite of what decolonization was intended to achieve, which was to strengthen the bonds between Portugal and its former colonies.

Back to the Beginning

In the aftermath of the decolonization process, Portugal was left without an overall model for relations with Angola and Mozambique. There was much bitterness in Portugal over the fate of the Portuguese communities in the two former colonies, and over the outcome in Angola.

At first, the Portuguese authorities refused to recognize the People's Republic of Angola proclaimed by the MPLA in Luanda. However, this position was soon to be reversed. The first move came from Foreign Minister Melo Antunes, who stressed that bilateral relations with the MPLA regime were indispensable to protect Portuguese interests in Angola—including those of the refugees—and that recognition was necessary in order to avoid the hegemony of either the Soviet Union or the United States in the former colony. He also argued that recognition of the People's Republic of Angola—following the example of Brazil and a number of Western European states—did not imply recognition of the MPLA regime.[14] This position met with some opposition, namely from Socialist and Popular Democratic representatives in the provisional government. These representatives pointed out that establishing formal diplomatic ties would be tantamount to indirectly legitimizing Soviet and Cuban intervention in the region, thereby sending the wrong signal at the wrong time, and increasing the possibility of further communist expansion in Africa. But their arguments were offset by widespread international recognition of the People's Republic—a situation that might leave Portugal alone with the United States as the only two countries without diplomatic relations with the new regime in Luanda.[15]

In late February 1976—the date previously set for Portuguese military withdrawal by the Alvor accord—Portugal established official diplomatic relations with the People's Republic. But effective diplomatic relations with both Angola and Mozambique were paralyzed for over a year. Meanwhile, the Portuguese Communist Party (PCP) used its channels to the MPLA and FRELIMO to control relations between Lisbon, Luanda and Lourenço Marques (Maputo). During that year a democratic constitutional regime was established in Portugal, while the Socialists formed a minority government that was to define the main lines of post-colonial foreign policy.

According to those lines, foreign policy priorities were centered on European integration, including accession to the European Community, and the stabilization of Portugal's status as a reliable partner in the Atlantic alliance (NATO). These priorities reflected the retreat to a more strict European dimension, associated with democratic consolidation, and the recognition of the need to exorcise remaining neutralist (and Africanist) tendencies that had become associated with authoritarian or military rule in the previous years. Relations with the post-colonial states were only a subordinate priority and, as far as the government was concerned, one that was best met by a wait-and-see attitude.

This lack of interest was a reflection of internal polarization. The PCP continued to enjoy close ties with the MPLA and FRELIMO and these party-to-party relations were made to work against official policies. On the other hand, the Popular Democratic Party (PPD, later PSD), also in the opposition, had established party-to-party relations with UNITA, although accepting the existence of formal diplomatic relations with Luanda. Overriding opponents in his own party, the PPD leader, Sá Carneiro, stressed that those relations were an indispensable means of exerting pressure against the Soviet presence in Angola.[16]

The result of these countervailing forces was paralysis. Formal ties were all but inoperative and were riddled with permanent tensions: Portuguese citizens were frequently arrested, and Portuguese enterprises were nationalized in Angola and Mozambique. The Angolan and Mozambican authorities in turn blamed Portugal either for trying to protect its nationals and its interests, or else for allowing their opponents to conspire against them in Lisbon.

The first break in this stalemate came about in late May 1977 when a coup attempt in Luanda by Nito Alves, a member of the MPLA political bureau, failed. Once more, internal events in one of the former colonies, rather than Portuguese initiative, were the source of change in bilateral relations. Two or three things seemed clear to Lisbon. First, at this stage the MPLA was divided and vulnerable. Second, its Soviet allies had made a mistake—the first one and one that perhaps would not repeat itself. Facing an uncertain outcome, they tried to be with both the *nitista* and the *netista* sides—represented respectively by Nito Alves and by Agostinho Neto, the president of the People's Republic. As a result, a number of PCP members were caught on the wrong side when Cuban troops moved in, at the last moment, to settle the crisis by putting down the *nitista* faction—a case of outright intervention in the internal affairs of a formally sovereign country.

However, there was no common assessment of the consequences of these events. They were interpreted as a defeat by those who had expected that the *nitista* faction would move towards reconciliation with UNITA, and as an opportunity for improving bilateral relations by those who portrayed the *netista* faction as being less radical and less anti-western than the populist and racist *nitista* faction. The latter position prevailed and the president of the Portuguese republic decided on sending a personal emissary to his Angolan counterpart. It was the first act of the presidential diplomacy that was to dominate Portuguese policies towards Angola and Mozambique until 1980, with internally divisive consequences.

The messenger's brief was of a limited and cautious nature. He was to deliver a personal letter to Agostinho Neto, and his activities in Luanda were restricted to fact-finding and were not to involve negotiations. The main point was to make a proposal for a later presidential summit.[17]

The gesture, however, by itself signaled a potential turning point in the enduring stalemate. Moreover, the Angolan authorities seemed to acknowledge their own willingness to restore official diplomatic channels. They chose this moment to cancel the permanent visas of top PCP officials. But this move was not without ambiguity: the MPLA had its own reasons for removing the Portuguese communists from their previous role as mediators between Luanda and Moscow, and this was probably more important than the PCP's position in relations with Lisbon. In any case, Portuguese expectations that the MPLA would take a more independent position were proven wrong. President Neto lost no time in silencing criticism of the Soviet Union in the MPLA ranks, and moved to consolidate relations with his Soviet allies. At the same time, the MPLA reaffirmed its "Marxist-Leninist" position, and relations with Portugal returned to their previous low status.

The May 1977 presidential mission was followed by only a brief interval of détente, and the only remaining outcome of the mission was the proposal for a summit. It was to take place when the MPLA felt it had consolidated its Soviet alliance and restored internal cohesion. Also, consistent with the consolidation of its regime, the MPLA reversed its previous policy toward Zaire, which had previously provided a sanctuary from which dissident attacks could be launched. The MPLA was now able to stabilize the northern region through bilateral agreements with Kinshasa, thus gradually neutralizing what was left of the FNLA in Angola.

The MPLA regime's consolidation was consistent with both internal dynamics—the first revolutionary wave had subsided after the *nitista* coup— and with a more defensive Soviet strategy in southern Africa. This defensive strategy was logical as both South Africa and Zaire had resisted the effects of Soviet intervention and the emergence of radical regimes on their borders.

Beyond internal and regional politics, the MPLA also aimed at opening up its economy to the West on completion of its nationalization policies. Once again this was consistent with its internal needs and with the limits of the Soviet alliance, which did not provide for financial resources and adequate instruments for economic aid. In addition, the Soviets were reluctant to admit either Angola or Mozambique as full partners into the "socialist community of states." [18]

In a sense, the Soviet Union wanted to retain the dominant political and strategic position, while allowing Western interests to provide economic support to its vulnerable and incompetent African allies. The MPLA regime was not in a position to quarrel with this proposed division of roles, and acted accordingly.

Thus, the presidential summit in Bissau in June 1978 was first of all a part of the Angolan policy of détente. On the Angolan side, the main objectives were to bolster the regime's international standing—signaling its openness to relations with the West through a credible and non-intrusive channel—and to establish a framework for bilateral relations. Within this framework they sought to link economic relations with a Portuguese commitment to act against the MPLA's internal opponents by severing Portuguese ties with UNITA and with exiled dissidents. On the Portuguese side, it was a first attempt at defining a revised model for relations with its former colonies.

To begin with, President Eanes undertook extensive political consultations while also seeking to engage the government formally in his enterprise. He was in a good position to build up an internal consensus over African policy and to implement it: he had had no involvement in decolonization, and was not suspected of ideological affinities with the MPLA, much less with its communist faction. Lastly, his institutional position was an advantage given governmental instability.

The first assumption of this emerging policy was that normalization would be a slow and difficult process, mainly because of a continued Soviet presence in Angola, which was believed to be linked to regional insecurity and regime instability rather than to any permanent strategic interests. Thus, Soviet involvement was seen as temporary and reversible. The second (and bizarre) assumption was that for the time being the United States wanted the Soviet Union to stay in Angola and that the United States would support Portugal's efforts in Luanda. The third assumption was that Portugal's status as a Western country should be stressed in dealing with the Angolans in order to remove remaining illusions (if any) about Portugal's neutralist inclinations and to stake out a claim as a link between the People's Republic of Angola and Western Europe.

This new policy was rather unstable. It tried to deny the more permanent effects of the East-West dimension in Angola and southern Africa while at the same time implying that a Soviet presence in Angola should be a reason to revive a southern Atlantic dimension of the Western alliance.[19] On the other hand, even as it underlined Portugal's Western status, it did so mainly to restore the previous priority of the African aspect of its foreign policy. This was seen both as insurance against the risks associated with accession to the European Community, and to blunt the drive towards centering

Portugal's international position in Europe. And, as usual, it refrained from making any real external alliance in developing relations with its former colonies.

In this context, the Portuguese position was less consistent than the Angolan strategy, and the results of the Bissau summit reflected this imbalance. Neto—who described it as "the first step" in bilateral relations—succeeded on three relevant issues. First, the MPLA regime was able to project an image of openness to the West. Second, its legitimization problems were somewhat lessened by the political impact of the presidential summit. Third, it forced upon Portugal an open linkage between bilateral ties—in the form of a general agreement on trade and cooperation signed during the summit— and the isolation of its opponents. In the event, General Eanes publicly committed himself to take action against UNITA networks operating from Lisbon.[20] The signs of reconciliation and of normalization of economic relations were to Portugal's advantage, but they were offset by the linkage imposed by President Neto, which excluded Portuguese diplomacy from any role in mediating between the MPLA and UNITA in the near future.

This was a sign of things to come. The tendency of Portuguese diplomacy to appease the People's Republic of Angola and to underestimate internal opposition in Angola only made for stronger MPLA protests against UNITA's actions in Lisbon. These in turn were answered by further Portuguese declarations stressing unqualified support for the People's Republic. The formal framework of state relations was made to work for Luanda's interests, and overruled the more relevant political and strategic considerations involved in solving the internal conflict in Angola.

Instead of creating vested interests in economic relations with the West in Angola, this policy created interests in such relations with Angola in Lisbon. The policy led to the formation of an internal lobby in Portugal that in turn would reinforce the tendency for unilateral support of the MPLA regime—and later for FRELIMO. This overall dynamic limited the flexibility of Portugal's policies towards both its former colonies, denying Portugal the option of political intervention in the regional and internal conflicts.

Finally, events confirmed the reactive and isolationist nature of Portugal's policies, both in May 1977 and later at the Bissau summit in June 1978. Portugal was reduced to reacting to events and had no capacity to mold them to its own purposes. Portugal lacked the strength to act and to intervene and this weakness was increased by its refusal to seek allies or alliances for a relevant role in either Angola or Mozambique. In any case, its position was too weak to conclude any solid alliances with respect to this dimension of its foreign policy. Without change, Portugal's role could only become more and more irrelevant in face of the powerful international, regional, and internal forces determining the situation in Angola and Mozambique.

The Conservative-Liberal Policies

In December 1979, a liberal-conservative coalition, including the PSD and the Christian-Democrats (CDS), won the elections in Portugal for the first time. Its government enjoyed a parliamentary majority and was the first to be able to stand up to the president of the republic. The prime minister, Sá Carneiro, was determined to challenge what he viewed as "compromises" made between the socialists and the radical military—compromises that he believed perpetuated post-revolutionary instability in Portugal.

One of the compromises that the dominant coalition challenged was the policy towards Angola and Mozambique. The PSD had reservations about the president's previous initiatives on this matter, even suspecting him of trying to involve Portugal in some sort of trilateral cooperation program including Eastern bloc countries and the two former colonies. On the other hand, Sá Carneiro was equally opposed to a close relationship with the United States on African policies and, while insisting on a Western European priority for Portugal's foreign policy, his coalition was not without a pragmatic approach towards Angola and Mozambique.

The main innovation the coalition introduced was to base its African policy on the regional context. A distinction was made between the western and eastern sub-regions in southern Africa—one that matched traditional Portuguese perceptions and regional conditions. In the western sub-region, the Soviet military presence and South Africa's control of Angola's southern border locked both the Soviets and South Africa into rigid positions. The probable outcome of this entrenchment was the persistence of a hot conflict. Portugal could not act autonomously in this context. Lacking the military means to intervene, it could only rely on a normal framework of bilateral relations with the People's Republic (and with South Africa), while at the same time avoiding isolating itself from UNITA, in order not to lose whatever political leverage it could retain.[21] Less parochial than the previous policy, it did not have excessive illusions about the nature of Soviet strategic claims in the region, and it did not attempt to influence external factors that were beyond its reach.

In the eastern sub-region, the situation was rather different. After the Lancaster House conference, Rhodesia was about to attain independence, and the dominant nationalist party was not an ally of the Soviet Union. It was, however, an ally of FRELIMO. Mozambique's president, Samora Machel, had played a moderating role in the negotiations preceding independence, because of his stake in establishing regional stability after years of fighting against Rhodesian-backed insurgents. Mozambique had strong ties with the Soviet bloc and was a self-proclaimed "Marxist-Leninist" regime, but there were no Cuban forces stationed in its territory and its leadership was less dependent on the Soviet Union than the MPLA. This was a result of both ideology and the circumstances of the transfer of power.[22] Also, the internal insurgency against the FRELIMO regime came from a politically unstable entity that could not claim any comparable legitimacy to that of UNITA in Angola.[23]

Furthermore, the Mozambican leadership was in the process of revising its own regional policies. It could expect a solid alliance with Zimbabwe and was engaged in moderating its position towards South Africa. It expected that the internal insurgency would fade away and that regional and internal stability would make available the time and resources needed to restore the economy. Meanwhile, initial illusions over economic cooperation with the "socialist community" had given way to more sober assessments, involving the need to gain access to Western and international economic aid.

Thus, internal changes in Portugal and in Mozambique converged to create the conditions for an ending of the stalemate in bilateral relations. Sá Carneiro took the first step—a polemical one. He solved the problem of negotiations over matters in dispute between Portugal and Mozambique, which concerned the transfer of financial resources, nationalized enterprises, and property, by declaring them to be solved, with each side keeping what it had taken, except for the Cabora Bassa hydroelectric project. In this case Portugal continued to service the debt of the project. Naturally, as the terms were most favorable, Samora Machel did not waste any time in accepting this decision. It was a political decision with the necessary psychological impact to open the way for a better climate in relations between the two countries. The difficult problem that remained was how to transform this opportunity into a solid relationship.

In fact, neither the Portuguese nor the Mozambican authorities were able to secure the necessary conditions for regional (or sub-regional) stability. Both underestimated South Africa's capacity to conduct a destabilization strategy simultaneously on several fronts.[24] The restoration of internal order in Mozambique was dependent on South Africa declining to replace Rhodesia as the main external support of RENAMO (*Resistência Nacional Moçambicana),* and refraining from using Mozambique's economic dependence on South Africa as a weapon. The alternative—always a poor one—was to develop Mozambique's economic role as a gateway to the sea for the land-locked states of Zimbabwe and Zambia. This in turn was dependent on the FRELIMO regime's ability to protect the transportation networks in the Beira and Limpopo corridors against the insurgents. In any case, a shift to this alternative would take several years.

Between 1979 and 1980, the liberal-conservative approach to Portugal's policies toward Angola and Mozambique emerged as an alternative course. Even as it failed to achieve any significant results, it left a strong legacy by demonstrating, first, that it was possible to overcome the traumatic effects of decolonization and, second, that a center-right coalition was more effective than the left-wing in developing relations with the radical post-colonial regimes. Also its emphasis on a regional approach toward the former colonies in southern Africa was to become a lasting feature of Portuguese policy. This also applied to the role of the large Portuguese community in South Africa. Implicit in the emphasis on regional subdivisions was a deliberate decoupling of Mozambique from Angola. This also was in conformity with the bilateral character of post-colonial relations with the former colonies. Up to then, a dualist model—which linked Portugal and all of its former colonies, and that was close to the integrationist tradition—continued to obstruct a realistic policy. Finally, this strategy relied on President Machel's willingness to compete with the MPLA in playing the primary role among the former colonies, thereby making the point that the relative isolation of the People's Republic of Angola was a result of its close Soviet alliance.

The MPLA's response to this pressure came in the form of a lower profile in its relations with Lisbon, but it also refrained from the customary accusation that Portugal was protecting UNITA. Yet this change came precisely at a time when such charges had some substance because of relations between the PSD—Prime Minister Sá Carneiro's party—and the Angolan opposition.[25]

It is difficult to conduct a definitive evaluation of this policy, as it was interrupted by Sá Carneiro's death in December 1980. His successors did not pursue his policy toward Angola[26] and were constantly immersed in internal conflicts until the final collapse of the coalition in early 1983. In any case, it is doubtful that the most important part of the 1979-80 policy—trying to restore some measure of political influence in Mozambique and Angola—could have survived the massive South African destabilization strategy that was to dominate the region over the next three years.

"Hot" regional conflict increased Angolan (and Mozambican) dependence on the Soviet alliance and led to a consolidation of the Soviet and Cuban military presence. At the same time it weakened Angola and Mozambique, pushing their resistance to the limit and fostering internal radicalization and mobilization that in turn served to entrench their political regimes. These factors naturally operated to render Portugal's role a minimal one.

This "minimalism" became, from 1981 to 1983, a sort of mainstream postcolonial policy. No one wanted to go back to the post-decolonization stalemate or to jeopardize a certain degree of normalization that had come about since 1980, even if the prevailing situation lacked solid foundations and even if this meant neglecting more important political and strategic Portuguese interests in southern Africa.

The minimalist line stressed the importance of slowly building up Portugal's role in the region, and of developing marginal economic benefits. It also stressed the need to restore conditions favorable for a massive Portuguese emigration to Angola and Mozambique. The prospects were not, however, encouraging.[27] It was also bent on making relations with the former colonies proof against internal political change, and thus upheld a formal rhetorical consensus about the importance of post-colonial relations both for foreign policy and for economic development. It managed to generate enough political support—on both the right and the left—to survive without having to prove its worth.

Conceptually, the minimalist line was a hybrid. It was typical of internal political conditions during its formative years, after the reelection of President Eanes in 1980 and the beginning of the slow disintegration of the center-right coalition. It shared with the nationalist approach a commitment to an "African calling" and to the need for a strong post-colonial African dimension in foreign policy. This was either for the purpose of safeguarding Portugal's bargaining power in the context of European politics or, in an extreme version, in order to retain its national identity against Europeanization. It had in common with a liberal approach some strong illusions about the effects of the (potential) development of economic relations between the post-colonial radical regimes and the West, and apparently had unrealistic expectations about Portugal's role in the development of Angola and Mozambique. What the two approaches had in common, and what linked them to past expectations, was the permanent objective of reestablishing large Portuguese communities in those two countries. This would compensate for the lack of financial resources with administrative and technical skills. The flow of large contingents of emigrants back to Africa would, it was felt, once again demonstrate the "uniqueness" of the Portuguese "African calling."[28]

Whatever the respective parts of myth and rationality in the formation of this minimalist policy, it is clear that it was more of a fall-back position than a policy. The consensus around it concealed the fact that there was no stable agreement about post-colonial policies and that Portugal did not have the instruments or the resources to act decisively in Angola or Mozambique whether it was a question of political evolution, strategic stability, or economic development.

Once again, only the coincidence of internal and regional change would bring about an opportunity for development in Portugal's policy toward Africa.

The Apprentice Mediator

By 1983, South Africa's destabilization strategies against Angola and Mozambique had changed the regional balance. Both the MPLA and FRELIMO—albeit to different degrees—were ready to come to terms with the far stronger regional power they had to live with.

Increasing expansion of the southern African conflict deterred or limited external intervention. The United States was still determined to try to de-escalate and contain regional conflicts so that the multiple conflict centers could be dealt with separately.[29] The Soviet Union, for its part, remained entrenched in Angola, where it sought to rescue the survival of the Luanda regime rather than to confront the South African threat on the southern border. It remained determined neither to advance nor to retreat, if only to deny its Western adversaries the positions it held.[30] Regional escalation had frozen, rather than removed, the East-West dimension of the conflict.

The combination of these factors, which were beyond the control of lesser powers, created uncertainties as to the stability of external alliances and, along with the illusions of independence, generated instability within the ranks of the surviving regimes. This made their evolution unpredictable, even to the Soviet Union, where official theory qualified their "socialist orientation" as "reversible." [31] In a sense, even if it were slow in coming about, some sort of adjustment to the changed situation was becoming more probable, as Mozambique became stretched to the limit while Angola sought to avoid reaching the same point.

On the other hand, if South Africa did not want to replace the FRELIMO regime in Mozambique, it would have to know when to stop; and in Angola, as it was not ready for direct confrontation with Soviet and Cuban forces, it was unable to overthrow the MPLA regime. Thus in seeking to promote its own security, it had to adjust to more limited objectives—such as the roll-back of SWAPO (South West Africa People's Organization) in southern Angola, and of the ANC (African National Congress) in Mozambique. Otherwise it might risk bringing about a change in America's "constructive engagement" policy that would make its international position even more difficult.

In the meantime after the general elections of 1983 in Portugal, a coalition between the socialist and social-democratic parties was formed under Prime Minister Mário Soares. The socialists were in control of foreign policy in the coalition government and they were set on reviving it after three years of paralysis. Their priority was accession to the EEC[32] and, as in the past, the African dimension was again subordinated to Western and European priorities in foreign affairs.

However, both the 1980 breakthrough and the evolving European framework contributed to making possible a less casual approach to African policy, which had also acquired some relevance in Portugal's relations with the United States. This, along with the increased international importance of the southern African conflicts, resulted in reassessment of the existing policy. Not surprisingly, this meant going back to the liberal concept, entailing, as in 1979-80, the same sort of conflicts between the president of the republic and the government, as General Eanes had not changed his mind over what he considered the elective domain of presidential diplomacy.

If anything, the socialist reformulation of the former liberal-conservative policy was even sharper in opposing a Soviet presence in Angola, more willing to apply East-West "rules of engagement" to the regional conflict, and almost equally determined not to unilaterally support the MPLA regime—even if the new policy did not go so far as to establish party-to-party relations with UNITA.[33] At the same time, it tried to introduce a discreet mediating role, starting with the upgrading of Portuguese intelligence and diplomatic networks in the region.[34] The policy also maintained the differentiation strategy, separating Angola from Mozambique, while developing relations with South Africa, and trying to form triangular relations which would link Pretoria to Maputo (and also Luanda) through Lisbon.

From the start, this attempt at mediation was uneven. It was relevant to the evolution of relations between South Africa and Mozambique. It also to some extent, took into account the change in United States perceptions of the FRELIMO regime which had resulted in the upgrading of bilateral relations in the aftermath of the Nkomati accord which proclaimed a state of "nonaggression and good neighborliness" between the two countries. But Portugal's role regarding Angola was a tangential one. This was because bilateral contacts between Luanda and the United States had become more regular and intense as the United States tried to entrench its own position as a mediator between Pretoria and Luanda, while leaving out the Soviet Union.

However, it must be noted that regular contacts between the American negotiators and Portuguese authorities at the highest level[35] gave the Portuguese an advisory role that was not without relevance. This was evident, for example, when American diplomacy came close to changing its position towards UNITA, giving in to MPLA pressure. The isolation of UNITA would have significantly reduced American leverage over Luanda, and could have blocked the Lusaka process.[36] Nonetheless, Portuguese influence at that time should not be exaggerated. The United States did not want any outside interference in its dealings with Angola. Portugal, moreover, was unable to overcome its own strained relations with the MPLA, and was not able to attain a high-profile role.

In the case of Mozambique, Portugal was to go beyond an advisory role, taking advantage of its better relations with Maputo and of prevailing conditions. In Mozambique, territorial contiguity, the overwhelming salience of South African power, and a much more limited Soviet presence, made it possible for a smaller power to have a better chance in its attempt to act as an intermediary.

On the Mozambican side, conditions were ripe. Survival was the issue for the FRELIMO regime, which had made clear its wish for a regional détente by revising its position on South Africa's internal conflicts. These were now considered to be a "civil rights struggle" rather than a "national liberation struggle." Maputo even expressed the hope that South African élites would be prepared gradually to reform the apartheid regime, and was more than ready to listen to the arguments of Portugal in favor of normalization of its own relations with its neighbor. At one time, even East and West German relations were raised as an example: if those two states, cut across by the dividing East-West line and belonging to adversary coalitions, were able to live together, why could not South Africa and Mozambique? [37]

In South Africa, Portugal tried to influence political and military élites as well as reform-minded business circles. It stressed the positive results for internal security stemming from the removal of the ANC from southern Mozambique and from the external impact of normalization.[38] On the other hand, the fact that Portugal had interests in both South Africa and Mozambique and had some stake in regional (or sub-regional) stability, lent some credence to its mediation effort. Furthermore, it also had a part to play in the RENAMO issue, as one of the RENAMO factions had close links with Portuguese economic interests.

The formulae for a bilateral agreement between Mozambique and South Africa involved a trade-off. On the one hand each side would eliminate support for expendable agents such as the ANC and RENAMO. On the other, South Africa's image abroad would be improved, while Mozambique would be assured of greater potential access to economic aid from Western countries, including the United States.

Of course, while the two main protagonists in the resulting Nkomati agreement were South Africa and Mozambique, for the first time since 1975, Portuguese diplomacy had played an active role in regional politics.

The effects of the Nkomati agreement were by and large disappointing for Mozambique. First, even if the Soviet response was not without bitterness,[39] its calculation that South Africa would not fulfill its side of the bargain proved more to the point. It was thus able to make up for some of its losses as Mozambique remained dependent on external assistance for minimum security in face of a persistent threat. Then, as internal insurgency continued in spite of the agreements, Mozambique was again left facing complete disruption. It therefore had to lean ever more on Zimbabwe's support. This, the alliance between FRELIMO and ZANU (Zimbabwe African National Union) notwithstanding, raised the specter of secession. And finally, the dominant perceptions inside FRELIMO began to change. After the 1984 urban demonstrations in South Africa, it appeared that the apartheid regime was incapable of controlling change, and hence its motivation for regional détente was lessened. All in all, the agreement came closer to unilateral surrender than anything else, and this seemed to be the real objective of South Africa as it continued to resort to the use of raw power against its neighbors.

Failure of the agreement also had an impact on Portugal, as FRELIMO came to accuse the former colonial power of supporting RENAMO. FRELIMO then joined with Angola in late 1984 in a massive campaign against Portuguese diplomacy that signaled an end to Portugal's apprenticeship as a regional mediator.

Portugal failed mainly for two reasons. To begin with, it had no real capacity to attract external support and it could never have successfully engaged in a mediating role without such support, which would have involved making security, political, and economic commitments in order to underwrite the regional agreement. But it also failed on its own, as the political and security aspects of its relations with Mozambique were either unstable or, in the case of a military role, simply non-existent. None of the objectives of Portugal's mediation were attained. Its credibility as a mediator was damaged, its bilateral relations with Mozambique (and with South Africa) were once again paralyzed, and in the end even the MPLA and FRELIMO found common ground in criticizing Portugal, thereby neutralizing previous Portuguese efforts to keep them apart.

During the same period, the MPLA regime developed a parallel, but more effective, defensive strategy towards South Africa. It retreated, in the face of South African control of its southern border, to consolidate its rear. Neto's successor as president of the MPLA, Eduardo dos Santos, signaled his willingness to engage in regional security talks with South Africa, after having previously coordinated his position with his Soviet and Cuban allies in Moscow[40] and while accepting an American mediation in the talks. Angola began its counterproposals by linking the gradual accession of Namibia to independence to an equally gradual redeployment and partial retreat of Cuban army units within Angola.[41] This "counter-linkage"—an answer to the American linkage between Cuban withdrawal and regional security—was mainly directed at the United States and constituted an attempt to soften American policy towards the MPLA.

As a result, at a tripartite conference in Lusaka, South Africa and the People's Republic of Angola reached a partial disengagement agreement. It did not go as far as the Nkomati agreement but it moved beyond the previous resistance to hold public talks. It included a United States guarantee of full withdrawal of South African Defense Forces from southern Angola, a corresponding retreat of SWAPO forces, and a joint monitoring of the area to verify compliance.[42]

The results of the Lusaka accord lacked the significance and the impact of the Nkomati agreement. South African forces remained within reach of their UNITA allies from their positions adjacent to Angola's southern border. The SWAPO retreat was an irrelevant move for the MPLA. On the other hand, the United States engagement consolidated the regional East-West understanding on which the survival of the MPLA rested. It also entrenched the Soviet presence on which the regime was dependent for its internal and external security. In effect, it accentuated existing trends rather than changed them. Finally, none of the relevant issues—the continued South African threat, the Cuban military presence, or internal reconciliation between the MPLA and UNITA—were involved in the accord.

Portugal's position was not a relevant one in the Lusaka process. The dominant perception in Lisbon was that Soviet presence was no more than a passing phase, as the Soviet Union was seen to have no permanent strategic interests in the region. In the same way the United States was represented as being solely motivated by the need to counter the Soviet and Cuban presence. In a sense, the prevailing view was that a return to the previous status quo ante—before the decolonization of Angola had gotten out of hand—was not only possible but merely a matter of time.[43]

This apparent inability to adjust to prevailing conditions had two important consequences for Portugal's policy towards Angola. It justified a wait-and-see attitude as far as political intervention was concerned. No initiatives were taken and there was no interest in searching for political opportunities. As a result the economic factor remained at the core of bilateral relations. Furthermore, the MPLA regime had acquired another instrument to exert political pressure upon Portugal. It was now able to manipulate its extreme sensitivity to competition from other Western powers—such as France or even Spain—in its former colonies. Thus, on the one hand, a more skilled Angolan policy toward Portugal was able to keep political initiative on its side—playing with internal divisions and the fear of competition—while on the other hand Portugal's policy became increasingly focused on economic competition with other Western countries. Portugal thus began to compromise its capacity for a sober assessment of internal conditions in Angola and of its own potential political role.

The second consequence, which was contradictory to the first one, was that the illusions about the restoration of the previous status quo brought Portuguese policy back to the issue of Angola's internal conflict and enhanced Portugal's role as the former colonial power—offering it a chance to make amends and contribute to national unity in Angola.

The old issue of whether to support the MPLA or to force a coalition between the remaining rival movements remained at the center of internal debate over Portugal's policy towards Angola. Several issues were involved: whether single party systems were all but unavoidable in African post-colonial states; whether the MPLA regime was a nationalist or a communist regime;[44] whether the nature of a regime was of any consequence to bilateral relations; whether the MPLA—in spite of deep internal changes—was still the real national movement; whether a coalition with UNITA was at all feasible; and whether Soviet support for the MPLA was a negative or a positive factor from the point of view of Portuguese interests in Angola.[45]

As most of the issues were biased in their formulation, internal debates were inconclusive and deeply divisive. Until 1985—when internal crisis again caused a reassessment of Portuguese policies toward Angola and Mozambique following the emergence of a minority Popular Democratic Party government—those cleavages aggravated enduring tensions between President Eanes and Prime Minister Mário Soares. This caused instability and left policies vulnerable to manipulation from external quarters, not the least of which was the People's Republic of Angola.

This second attempt at consolidating a liberal policy toward the former colonies was a comparative failure. It lasted only until a possible breakthrough—Nkomati—fell apart for the usual reasons: regional conditions beyond control, lack of resources, and internal Portuguese divisions that made continuity in policy impossible. The liberal policy also demonstrated its own lack of consistency towards the Luanda regime, as it went from an initially hostile and firm position to one which retreated in the face of the MPLA's linkage of political and economic aspects of relations between the two countries.[46] In the end, the socialist initiative became imprisoned within the dominant patterns of Portugal's policies toward Angola and Mozambique.

Ten Years After

Ten years after decolonization, the close interaction between the political evolution of Lisbon and of its still embattled former colonies in southern Africa still went beyond the formal ceremonies of state relations. As in the past, this interaction was more intense between Portugal and Angola than anywhere else.

The stability of relations with the smaller post-colonial states in Cape Verde, Guinea-Bissau, and São Tomé e Principe contrasted with the unending sequence of crisis and conflict with Angola and with the sharp oscillations in relations with Mozambique. This contrast refuted the old concept of an homogeneous colonial empire and of the dualist model for post-colonial relations. It also made nonsense of the analysis that blamed decolonization as a whole for the decadence of Portugal's African position. In time, at least two distinct categories emerged in Portugal's post-colonial world: one category included Guinea-Bissau and the chain of Atlantic archipelagos; and the other included Angola and Mozambique.

On the other hand, these categories underlined the importance, in Portugal's policies towards Angola and Mozambique, of the specific circumstances of decolonization, of international and regional dimensions, of regime instability, and of resources.

Mozambique's decolonization had been controlled and comparatively peaceful. In Angola, Portugal failed utterly, thereby opening the way for other external forces that could then determine the extent of Portuguese access to its former colony. Decolonization did not ensure minimum conditions for national unity in either Mozambique or Angola. This led to internal insurgencies that remain unabated. In Mozambique these insurgencies are a result of internal dissent as well as of regional support for FRELIMO's adversaries. In Angola, they represent a continuation of the civil war that began almost immediately after the signing of the Alvor accords in January 1975.

The failure of decolonization must also be linked to the predominance of international and of regional aspects. In Angola, the vacuum left by the Portuguese retreat since July 1975, and the opportunities offered by a civil war between weak movements, made for an escalation of regional and international intervention that continues to this day. In Mozambique, the transfer of power to FRELIMO predictably increased the regional vulnerabilities of the territory.

Moreover, Portugal's withdrawal in 1975 made for a radical change in overall regional conditions. South Africa was left without its "buffer states." Two of these former "buffer states" had become dependent on the Soviet bloc for their security and survival. At the same time South Africa became more exposed to internal conflicts as the wave of decolonization drew closer and came to seem more irresistible.

The increasing complexity of the regional conflict made the southern African situation even less open to crisis management. The risks of further external intervention—even in limited forms—were increased as regional dynamics gradually became dominant.

In this context, there was no place for an autonomous role for Portugal. Its decolonization policies were in part responsible for this radically changed situation and it lacked the resources—including political will—needed for regional intervention. In fact, its autonomy could only result from its ability to insert its own strategies into a larger framework of alliances with other powers that, in turn, also pursued unstable strategies toward the regional conflict. But Portugal was too insecure and too weak to adjust to this larger framework and remained too isolated to be of any regional relevance.

Regime instability was the most important factor in the persistent interaction between the political processes in Portugal and those in its former colonies. The FRELIMO regime, less unstable at first, was more flexible in its relations with Portugal after 1980. While its expectations over Portugal's role tended to fluctuate widely, it avoided extreme positions that could risk bilateral rupture. The MPLA regime, meanwhile, was more unstable internally and from the beginning had stronger links with political forces in Portugal. These made for a tendency to interfere in Portuguese politics. On the other hand, Portugal also remained the distributor of legitimacy in the conflict between the MPLA and UNITA—a position that was constantly at stake in bilateral relations.

Portugal's regime was also an unstable one, being built first of all upon the successive failures of liberalization of the authoritarian regime, and of revolution after its demise.

Even allowing for the necessary distinctions, this convergence of weak and unstable regimes enhanced the impact of internal political factors in post-colonial relations. The continuity of intense, emotional and often irrational interactions between the respective political processes prevailed over the need for a continuity in bilateral relations between independent states. It also meant that it was impossible to stabilize Portugal's policies toward its former colonies. Claims to a broad "national consensus" on post-colonial policies lacked credibility in the face of the deep internal cleavages that still persisted.

Finally, resources represented the oldest of problems. It was, moreover, a problem bedeviled by misconceptions which inhibited sober and pragmatic assessments. Portugal had tried to compensate for this handicap by political and administrative control and through the settlement of large Portuguese communities in Angola and Mozambique and, during the last colonial war, both territories achieved a remarkable level of development. Having lost these instruments, in part because of its own decolonization policies, it went on trying to restore them with remarkable obstinacy and predictably poor results. It still seems difficult to admit Portugal has a limited capacity to play a decisive role in the development of Angola and Mozambique. Portugal has been unable to overcome the constraints caused by its own political instability and limited resources to respond to the challenge of rebuilding destroyed economies and disintegrated societies.

On their own, each one of these aspects should be sufficient to force change upon Portugal's policies and its view of its own post-colonial position. That each obstacle only made old conceptions more entrenched, and policy implementation less effective and less credible, is the enduring predicament of Portugal's policies toward Angola and Mozambique. Incapable of shaping the course of its former colonies, it remains equally unable to sever the historical ties which bind it to them.

NOTES

1. This definition was first presented in the *Plano de Acção Politica,* a manifesto approved by the Revolutionary Council on June 21, 1975.
2. Interview, 1986. Cf. António de Spinola, *Portugal e o futuro* (Lisbon: Arcádia, 1974.)
3. John Marcum. *The Angolan Revolution, Exile Politics and Guerrilla Warfare,* Vol. II (Cambridge, Mass.: The MIT Press, 1978).
4. Kenneth Maxwell, "Portugal and Africa: the Last Empire," *The Transfer of Power in Africa. Decolonization 1940-1960,* ed. Prosser Gifford and W. Roger Louis (New Haven: Yale University Press, 1982), pp.364-66. Cf. António de Spinola. *Páis sem rumo* (Lisbon: Scire. 1978).
5. John Marcum op. cit.
6. The Alvor agreement called for the early formation of an Angolan national army, integrating the armed forces of the three rival movements. The national army would then gradually take over the positions of the Portuguese military. But no one seemed to take these provisions seriously.
7. Neto's baptism was immediately emphasized by the MFA official bulletin. "Angola nos caminhos da liberdade." *Movimento-Boletim do MFA,* No. 9, January 28, 1975.
8. Interview, 1986. Cf. Ernesto Melo Antunes, "Vector africano da política externa portuguesa." (Paper presented at the World Peace Foundation-Calouste Gulbenkian Foundation conference on "Portugal, os Estados africanos de língua portuguesa e os Estados Unidos da América," Lisbon, May 1985).
9. The proposals were presented by the Portuguese Foreign Minister, Melo Antunes, during his last trip to Luanda before independence, in late July 1975. Interview, 1986.

10. Cf., inter alia, Peter Vanemann and Martin James, "The Soviet Intervention in Angola: Intention and Implications," *Strategic Review,* 4-3 (Summer 1976):92-103. Coral Bell, *The Diplomacy of Détente* (London: Martin Robertson. 1976). Bruce Porter, *The USSR in Third World Conflicts 1945-1980* (Cambridge, Mass.: Cambridge University Press, 1984). And, of course, Henry Kissinger, "On World Affairs," *Encounter*, LI, no. 5, (November 1978).

11. A "socialist" or "scientific socialist" orientation was anticipated in official documents since 1974 and 1976, before the official definition in 1977. Whether one is supposed to take this definition as describing the political nature of those regimes has been a polemical issue ever since. Cf. Kenneth Jowitt. "Scientific Socialist Regimes in Africa. Political Differentiation, Avoidance and Awareness." *Socialism in Sub-Saharan African: a New Assessment* in Carl Rosberg, Thomas Callaghy eds., 133-73 (Berkeley University of California Institute of International Studies, 1949). Peter Wiles, ed., *The New Communist Third World* (London: Croom Helm, 1982). Juan Linz, on the other hand, recalls the problem of classifying the European authoritarian regimes of the twenties and the thirties that were set on imitating Italian fascism. Cf. his *Fascism, the Breakdown of Democracy, Authoritarian and Totalitarian Regimes: Coincidence and Distinctions, MS* (1985).

12. The Soviet Union had more than academic doubts about its own African clients being "model allies." Cf. Zaki Laidi. "L'URSS et l'Afrique: Vers une extension du système socialiste mondial?" *Politique Etrangère*, No. 3 (1983):679-99.

13. Including a fraction of the radical military, since the publication of their opposition manifesto, *Documento dos Nove*, which followed the departure of the Socialist and popular-democratic ministers in July 1975.

14. Private documents. These points were stressed by the Foreign Minister Col. Melo Antunes during a conference at the Centro de Sociologia Militar in February 1976.

15. Especially after Brazil and France—two obvious competitors—hastened to recognize the People's Republic of Angola, and to establish full diplomatic relations.

16. Interview, 1986.
17. Apparently this proposal originated in the Foreign Ministry. The Foreign Minister, Medeiros Ferreira, supported the president's initiative over the reservations of Prime Minister Mário Soares. Interviews, 1986.
18. Cf. Zaki Laidi, op. cit. Christopher Cocker, "Adventurism and Pragmatism: The Soviet Union, COMECON and Relations with African States," *International Affairs,* vol. 57, no. 4 (Autumn 1981). Colin Lawson, "The Soviet Union and Eastern Europe in Southern Africa: Is There a Conflict of Interest?" *International Affairs*, vol. 59, no. 2 (Spring 1983).
19. The southern Atlantic dimension of the Atlantic alliance, or the formation of a southern Atlantic alliance, are recurrent issues both in Portuguese and in alliance politics. Cf. Christopher Cocker, *NATO, The Warsaw Pact and Africa* (London: RUSI Defense Studies, Macmillan, 1985). Hervé Coutau-Bégarie, *Géostratégie de l'Atlantique Sud* (Paris: PUF, 1985).
20. Cf. *A Capital,* June 27, 1977.
21. Interview, 1987.
22. Also President Machel held an undisputed preeminence over FRELIMO and the regime. The ideological factor is interesting in itself, as it seems clear that, for some of the FRELIMO leaders, Soviet insistence that theirs was not as yet a proper communist regime was resented as an irritating interference in Mozambique's internal affairs. Even more irritating were Soviet suggestions that the Central Asian Soviet republics were appropriate models for Mozambique's development.
23. In fact, from the outset, RENAMO has been unable to form a stable and unified leadership.
24. Gerard Challiand, *L'enjeu africain: géostratégie des puissances* (Paris: Seuil, 1980). Christopher Cocker, "L'Afrique de Sud, l'Afrique australe et la sécurité régionale," *Politique Entrangère,* no. 2, (1984):287-300.
25. The MPLA apparently protested against ties with UNITA at a secret meeting with the PSD, held at their request in 1980. Interview, 1986.
26. Ties with UNITA were interrupted in early 1981. Interview, 1986.
27. Restoring conditions for a new wave of emigration, especially to Angola, has been a constant concern of Portuguese policymakers. At

first, this means the return of the 1975 refugees, but since 1980 it has referred to new emigrants, and to more skilled emigrants. Cf., inter alia, former foreign minister Sá Machado, quoted in António de Figueiredo, "Portugal and Africa," in Kenneth Maxwell, ed. *Portugal in the 1980s: Dilemmas of Democratic Consolidation* (New York: Greenwood Press, 1986), 98-99.

28.   Ibid., 98.

29.   Michael Samuels et al., *Implications of Soviet and Cuban Activities in Africa for U.S. Policy*, Significant Issues Series, vol. 1. No. 5 (Washington: Georgetown University, Center for Strategic and International Studies, 1979).

30.   On Soviet strategy, Cf. Kurt Campbell's chapter. Cf. also Bruce Porter, op. cit. S.N. MacFarlane, "Intervention and Security in Africa," *International Affairs*, vol. 60, no. 1 (Winter 1983-1984):53-74.

31.   Cf. Zaki Laidi, op. cit. Terry Hough. *The Struggle for the Third World.* Washington, D.C. The Brookings Institution, 1986.(Cl. l)

32.   The accession treaty was finally signed in 1985, before the demise of the Socialist-Social-democratic coalition government formed in 1983.

33.   According to some sources, there were high level contacts between officials of the Socialist party and UNITA, despite the absence of formal relations. Interview. 1986.

34.   After 1983, most of the Portuguese ambassadors in southern African countries were replaced, and relations with intelligence departments were emphasized. Diplomatic contacts also included those with regional insurgent forces, such as UNITA, the ANC, or RENAMO. Interview. 1986.

35.   Contacts between the Assistant Secretary for African Affairs, Chester Crocker, and Frank Wisner, on the one hand, and the Portuguese government on the other, took place at an exceptionally high level, including the Prime Minister and the Foreign Minister. Their contacts with the presidency of the republic were more irregular, and at a much lower level. Interviews. 1986.

36.   Interview. 1986.

37.   Interview. 1986. Also interesting was the internal argument of

FRELIMO, meant to justify Nkomati, which invoked the Soviet-German treaty of 1939 as a precedent, at least as far as ideology was concerned.

38. President Botha was to be an official guest of the Portuguese government after Nkomati, beginning his 1984 European tour in Lisbon.

39. Peter Clement, "Moscow and Southern Africa," *Problems of Communism*, vol. 34, no. 2 (1985):35-44.

40. From 1983 onwards, the tripartite Moscow meetings between the USSR, Cuba, and Angola were publicized, cautiously at first. This Moscow group was convened in January 1984, before the Lusaka accords. The need for some publicity apparently came from the prominence of extensive negotiations between Luanda and the United States—and also with South Africa—before the Lusaka accords. The publicity was meant to indirectly associate the USSR and Cuba with the regional bargaining process.

41. Successive proposals for redeployment were made from 1982 onwards. They were first presented in the final communiqués of bilateral meetings between Cuba and Angola in 1982 and 1984. In November 1984, President Eduardo dos Santos took a more extensive proposal to the UN secretary-general. The proposal was restated in March 1986.

42. The exchange of notes between the People's Republic of Angola and South Africa took place at Lusaka on February 16, 1984.

43. In fact, at the time, the USSR seemed not to be too harsh in its pronouncements against UNITA, and concentrated on denouncing its leader, Jonas Savimbi. Cf. for instance, Anatoli Gromyko, *L'Afrique: "arène de confrontation" ou de coopération?* (Conference at the IFRI, Paris, May 1984).

44. The political nature of the African post-colonial regimes is a silent issue in Portuguese politics, at least as far as public debates are concerned. An exception was the address by President Eanes to the May 1985 World Peace Foundation-Calouste Gulbenkian Foundation conference.

45. The argument on the positive side of Soviet presence in Angola is that since it is precarious by nature, it becomes an interesting counterweight to other possible hegemonies. Cf. José Medeiros Ferreira, *Portugal em transe* (Lisbon: Pandora, 1986), 85-101.

46.   In the aftermath of the MPLA campaign against the Portuguese govern-
      ment in late 1984, Portugal once more gave ground on some issues.
      It even cancelled the transmission of a television program on UNITA,
      giving in to Luanda's pressure.

3: South Africa's Regional Hegemony

By Robert I. Rotberg

South Africa dominates every discussion of Angola and Mozambique. Once it may have been convenient to think of the two nations primarily in the context of lusophonia—as key segments of a post-revolutionary empire linked culturally and linguistically to Portugal. More recently, and to some extent still, both states can be viewed as parts of the Marxist imperium. They have southern Africa's tightest ties to the Soviet Union. Angola and Mozambique are key members of the Southern African Development Coordination Cnference (SADCC), as well as states in the "Front Line" of the free world against South Africa. Both are developing nations. They are impoverished, nondemocratic, socialist, and many other things. But whatever they are, and however they can best be categorized, no contemplation of their future can begin without focusing on the South African factor.

The trade and transportation networks of the southern African region flow through South Africa, and the economies of the members of SADCC are dependent significantly upon that white-run republic.[1] South Africa supplies manufactured goods, capital, services, and sometimes food to large parts of the region. It employs labor from the countries in the region. It has a gross national product and a standard of living which dwarfs its neighbors. But, despite its potential to do so, it is not primarily through economic might, trade flows, and logistical means that South Africa overshadows Angola and Mozambique. Indeed, as much as South Africa is Mozambique's economic patron, drawing labor from Mozambique (and returning remittances equivalent to 40 percent of governmental revenues) and controlling such items as the supply of electricity to its capital, South Africa has little economic relationship with Angola. Angola is not within South Africa's direct economic orbit. Neither in terms of energy, transportation logistics, or normal trade do Angola and South Africa have much to do with one another.

South Africa dominates any analysis of Angola and Mozambique as nations because of its military strength, its regional strategic ambitions, and its determination to remain the hegemonic power of the southern third of the continent. Beginning in the late 1970s, but more intensively in the early 1980s, South Africa achieved a position of regional preeminence. It has employed that preeminence successfully to destabilize Angola and Mozambique—to make it impossible for the governments of either country to organize themselves without giving intimate consideration to the interests and concerns of South Africa.

Ostensibly, neither Angola nor Mozambique wield sufficient potential power of any kind to pose a serious threat to the hegemony of South Africa. However, Mozambique until 1984 welcomed, and Angola still provides, sanctuaries for the African National Congress (ANC), the primary black exile antagonist of white South Africa. In Angola there are a number of ANC training camps. Angola gives assistance to the South West Africa People's Organization (SWAPO), which since 1966 has been attempting to liberate neighboring Namibia (formerly South West Africa) from South African control. Furthermore, both lusophone countries have Marxist ties, and the Angolan government is closely supported by Soviet military advisors and defended by 45,000 Cuban troops.

All of these facts are well known. Since Cuban forces helped the army of the MPLA (*Movimento Popular de Libertação de Angola*, or Movement for the Popular Liberation of Angola) repulse a South African military thrust in 1975, the MPLA, which assumed control of the government of Angola in that year, and South Africa have been antagonists. In the late 1980s those old wounds naturally remain, as does Angola's cooperation with and succor for the ANC and SWAPO. Naturally, Angola is hostile to South Africa. Moreover, although outsiders assert that Angola is too weak seriously to threaten South Africa's hegemonic position, the military strategists of the white regime have since 1978 organized themselves against a "total onslaught" by the Soviet Union and its allies. Whether or not South Africa's military men ever really feared an attack from Angola or Mozambique, or by the Soviets, they talked as if they did.[2] Officially, Soviet supported states have been South Africa's prime enemies.

For all their lingusitic and ideological affinities, Angola and Mozambique are hardly comparable geopolitically, either in any objective sense or in terms of their potential threat capability as far as South Africa is concerned. Angola harbors ANC and SWAPO guerrillas and massive Cuban firepower. It has been solidly and regularly backed by the Soviets, who have supplied high quality aircraft, radar, and advanced tanks, and anti-personnel and anti-tank missiles. The Soviet Union has demonstrated a dedicated attachment to the MPLA, and to the perpetuation of its hold on the government of Angola. But SWAPO is a weakened movement of insurgency, often capable of infiltration, but incapable of upsetting the balance of power in Namibia.[3] The ANC cannot strike directly from Angola against South Africa. Geographically Namibia and Botswana separate the two countries, and the ANC camps north of Luanda lie 1,000 miles from Pretoria.

In contrast, Mozambique no longer gives shelter to the ANC, having in 1984 closed camps within its borders and attempted to deny guerrillas uncontested passage through its terrain toward South Africa. South Africa had threatened Mozambique sufficiently to compel its government to renounce assistance to the ANC. For example, Joaquim Chissano, the new president of Mozambique, in late 1986 said that despite his government's firm support of the ANC, it would not be allowed to use Mozambique as a base for insurgency against South Africa.[4] The treaty of Nkomati recognized South Africa's might, as a neighbor, and also accepted South Africa's already demonstrated ability to harass Mozambique militarily as well as economically. By the Nkomati agreement Mozambique sued for peace.

Angola is distant, but contains lethal Soviet firepower and well-trained alien troops. It also provides a space for sworn antagonists of South Africa. Mozambique, fearful and cowed, does none of the above, at least not wittingly. Moreover, it abuts South Africa. Angola could become an African economic power. Mozambique, with high levels of illiteracy, a rudimentary infrastructure, and few natural resources, seems destined to remain a country in severe need.

Despite such distinctions, South Africa has behaved with equal aggression toward both. In Mozambique, it has done so in defiance of the accord signed at Nkomati. The accord committed South Africa to cease overt and covert support for a movement of internal insurgency known as the RENAMO (*Resistência Nacional Mocambicana* , or Mozambique National Resistance, also known as MNR). Originally invented by Rhodesia to oppose the guerrillas of the Zimbabwe African National Union (ZANU), now the government of independent Zimbabwe, the RENAMO attracted significant South African backing from about 1981 onward. By 1982 South Africa had fashioned and provided the material for a strike force composed largely of Portuguese-speaking whites, mulattoes, and Africans capable of undermining and sabotaging the government of Mozambique's control of its own countryside. Although the RENAMO articulated no detailed political program, it seemed to be fighting to overthrow the Marxist or socialist government of Mozambique, and thus to be acting entirely as a proxy for South Africa. For some time, too, its headquarters was situated within the Transvaal province of the Republic. In late 1986 Assistant Secretary of State Chester Crocker dismissed the RENAMO "as a military organization and not a national liberation movement." "We don't know what its political base is," he said.[5]

Although UNITA (*União Nacional Para a Independência Total de Angola*, or the National Union for the Total Independence of Angola) was created by Jonas Savimbi well before the Portuguese revolution of 1974, it was the least known and least successful of the Angolan nationalist movements before the struggle for independence in 1975. South Africa's incursion was intended to maximize UNITA's chances of overcoming MPLA resistance. Since 1978 UNITA has enjoyed determined South African support: steady supplies of petrol and arms, radar and air cover, intelligence assistance, and the cooperation of actual South African battalions. UNITA, in the late 1980s a formidable fighting unit of about 15,000 men, became prominent well before the RENAMO and always had the ethnic and political legitimacy which the RENAMO has always lacked. Yet neither could have become convincing actors on their local turfs without persuasive South African involvement. UNITA, too, is an instrument of South African regional hegemonic policy.

From 1974, when Mozambique gained independence, South Africa naturally regarded its neighbor as dangerous. Its capital is only 300 miles from Pretoria and Johannesburg, South Africa's Ruhr. Mozambique borders on a volatile area of northern Zululand. Moreover, some of South Africa's gold and coal transits Mozambique on its way to export markets. (In a similar way, Angola's independence posed a threat to Namibia, if not at first directly to South Africa.)

By the mid-1980s, however, the hostility of Mozambique, the near neighbor, had been contained by a series of preemptive strikes and the ingenious insertion of the RENAMO into the already weakened nation, soon also to become drought-stricken and hurricane-bashed. The Nkomati accord signified Mozambique's capitulation. But before too long it was clear to the government of Mozambique, South African denials to the contrary, that the proxy war was still continuing, and would continue so long as Mozambique retained a semblance of its socialist-minded independence.

By the mid-1980s South Africa had also succeeded in harassing the MPLA, thereby greatly mortgaging its efforts to maintain the momentum of independence and development. UNITA had become a formidable force capable of being reckoned an essential part of any process of national reconciliation. Like a much more supine Mozambique, Angola—despite its distance from Pretoria—was tightly enmeshed in the snare of South Africa. Without its acquiescence, neither nation could begin to achieve the kind of stability capable of transforming either country economically and, indeed, even politically.

Angola and Mozambique are not alone in being the object of unwanted South African attention. Lesotho, the smallest, poorest, and most vulnerable of the SADCC and southern African states, has received more than its share. From the mid-1970s, South African opposition to the policies of Chief Leabua Jonathan's government was demonstrated militarily and economically. South Africa objected to the shelter Lesotho gave to ANC cadres. It wanted Lesotho to cease letting ANC guerrillas transit its mountainous domain en route to South Africa's cities. It asked Lesotho to end its rhetorical antagonism to apartheid. In order to give weight to these demands, South Africa exerted rather pointed economic pressure on Lesotho, which it completely surrounds.

Periodically it closed the main border crossing points; it threatened to—and occasionally did—ban the import of mine labor, the impoverished enclave's major source of foreign exchange.

In order to strengthen its already overweening position, South Africa also backed the anti-Jonathan Lesotho Liberation Army (LLA), long led by Ntsu Mokhehle, an old-line nationalist of Marxist persuasion. Periodically unleashed, the LLA attacked Lesotho from camps in South Africa (and the Transkei). By 1985 Lesotho had become reasonably obedient and comparatively cleansed of the ANC. Direct retaliatory strikes (raids on Maseru); conscious destabilization (funding the LLA, and its own attacks); and the employment of economic leverage on the border had proven effective instruments of South African regional policy. Even so, when South Africa sensed that the moment had come to rid Lesotho of Chief Jonathan and any lingering flirtation with the Soviet bloc, it used economic, military, and diplomatic means to encourage, and perhaps fund, a coup by Lesotho's little military brigade. From its inception the new army-led monarchy has behaved in a manner South Africa calls model. In late 1986 Lesotho agreed to permit South Africa to develop the water resources of the smaller nation in order to relieve pressure on the republic's own scarce supplies. They signed an impressive water sharing agreement and a treaty as well.

Swaziland is as small as Lesotho, but much wealthier, and is not completely surrounded by its bigger neighbor. Before and into the 1980s, during the long reign of King Sobhuza II, Swaziland allied itself with South Africa but gave quiet refuge to the ANC, interfering little with the passage of guerrillas from Mozambique into the Transvaal. (Mbabane, Swaziland's tiny capital, is 250 miles from Johannesburg.) However, after Sobhuza died in 1982, aged 83, South Africa employed its financial muscle to gain an even greater influence with the several parties that merged to become his effective political and economic successor. With South Africa's support, a group of chiefs and ambitious commoners within the Liqoqo (the paramount chief's executive council) gained day-to-day control of the monarchy, then nominally under a regent. At its behest, Swaziland in 1983 secretly signed a nonaggression pact with South Africa and began moving vigorously against the ANC. That approach was intensified during 1984, as the secret agreement became known.

Despite opposition within the kingdom to the cabal that ruled the country and controlled the regency, and despite outspoken opposition to the state's pro-South African policy, Swaziland did South Africa's bidding as far as hostility to the ANC and the Soviet bloc was concerned. In 1985, however, power in the Liqoqo shifted and, in 1986, with the coronation of young King Mswati II, Swaziland began to manifest a mildly more independent position. Several of King Mswati's appointments were made from among the ranks of the least pro-South African officials and ex-officials. So much was Swaziland drifting away from its neighbor's firm embrace that, in late 1986, South African security officials entered the kingdom stealthily to snatch Swiss and local nationals supposedly allied to the ANC.

Botswana, strong economically and united politically, but as vulnerable to South African attack and retaliation as Swaziland, before the 1980s had denied the ANC free passage across its terrain. The threat of a South African preemptive strike was always there. On several occasions, including two in 1986, innocent Tswana lost their lives as a result of cross border raids by the larger republic's security forces. In 1984 South Africa pushed Botswana to accept a formal nonaggression pact similar to the ones it had arranged with Swaziland and Mozambique. But Botswana has refused to become a South African satellite. It has preferred the realism of quiet opposition without giving offense. Accepting South Africa's power and the unconstrained manner in which South Africa has pursued its policies of destabilization, Botswana discourages ANC activity within its borders, accepts no official camps, or staging bases, and has behaved toward South Africa with circumspection. South Africa has neither sought to embarrass Botswana economically (its diamonds are exported by air and many white South Africans made a good living from cross-border trade with Botswana) nor has South Africa fostered internal antagonism by proxy. Beyond the raids, there has been no all-out campaign of destabilization.

Malawi has been considered a South African ally since the early 1970s. It accepted economic assistance from South Africa and the two countries have long exchanged ambassadors. With regard to its South African policy, its backing of the MNR, and elderly President H. Kamuzu Banda's disdain for the leadership of his socialist-minded neighbors, Malawi has long been out of step with black Africa and the countries of SADCC, in general, and with fellow President Kenneth D. Kaunda of Zambia and President Robert Mugabe of Zimbabwe in particular. There has been no question of

South Africa needing to destabilize Malawi, although South Africa may attempt to play a role in the post-Banda succession struggle). Malawi is firmly within South Africa's regional orbit.

Not so Zambia and Zimbabwe. Raids into both countries from South Africa in 1986 were meant to remind them, as habitual critics and antagonists of white South Africa, that South Africa still had a long and potent reach. It had earlier employed its geographical dominance of Zambia and Zimbabwe's main rail links and port outlets to demonstrate undoubted economic muscle. By curtailing the free exchange of locomotives and wagons, and by imposing elaborate "customs" checks at the Zimbabwe border, South Africa impeded the expeditious export of copper and other raw materials, and the import of consumer goods. South Africa is also suspected of backing the Ndebele rebels who pillaged, murdered, and created disorder in southwestern Zimbabwe from 1981 to 1984. Zimbabwe has further accused South Africa of other attempts to subvert the new nation, by such acts as the destruction of combat aircraft, the sabotage of local military installations, and the assassination of ANC leaders living in the country.

Despite the fact that Zambia has, since its independence in 1964, welcomed the ANC and SWAPO, and that the ANC's headquarters is in a section of Lusaka, the capital of Zambia, South Africa has never succeeded in fomenting internal insurrection against the Kaunda government. It has raided with impunity, but since SWAPO moved its camps into Angola, preemptive strikes have become episodic. Zambia is, after all, distant from South Africa, and the ANC headquarters in Lusaka is a political and not a military encampment. The ANC no longer trains its operatives in Zambia, either.

By 1987, as a result of the adroit deployment of a varied catalogue of destabilizing devices, but primarily by the enhancement of formidable insurgency movements in Angola and Mozambique, South Africa had achieved a position of virtually unchallenged geostrategic preeminence in all of Africa south of Zaire and Tanzania. It has had no local or even global rivals for a position of hegemonic primacy which it only began to assert about 1980. Despite South Africa's own unstable core, this South African victory exceeded the expectations of even the country's most optimistic planners. Mozambique, Swaziland, and Lesotho were client states in all but name. Mozambique, moreover, was being pushed to the edge of political extinction by the depredations of the REMAMO. Botswana, Zimbabwe, and Zambia had lost much of their previous freedom to pursue independent regional policies. Namibia remained a domestic colony. Even Angola—Cuban troops and Soviet advisors to the contrary—had become firmly and decisively subject to the intruding tentacles of South Africa. In so extending its strategic reach, South Africa had demonstrated that it was stronger and could act more decisively in its own region in furtherance of its own interests than could any of the global powers. It had flexed its military muscle in ways that the Soviet Union could not. Its success showed, further, how readily the preferences of the West could be denied and the stipulations of the United States ignored.

After seven years of assiduous feints and attacks, and of covert reinforcing and refinancing of both the RENAMO and UNITA (and with some minor help from the United States and others regarding UNITA), South Africa had become sufficiently strong within its region to dictate, or at least strongly to affect, the political, economic, and logistical decisions of all of its near and distant neighbors. Acting with comparative impunity, and even extending its economic orbit to some of the offshore African islands, South Africa had achieved a number of striking strategic breakthroughs. Audaciously, it had seized the regional initiative in a manner that would have been unthinkable in the 1970s. In late 1986, for example, it was revealed that South Africa had purchased two converted Boeing 707 in-flight refueling tankers for its airforce. As a result, South African Mirage and Cheetah jet fighters could theoretically extend their attack perimeter to Nigeria, Cameroon, the Central African Republic, Uganda, and Kenya. Its usual regional sphere—Zaire through Malawi—could be reached with greater ease.[6]

South Africa's military men had successfully defended, and even extended, heir country's suzerainty. They mounted a broad-ranging and highly manipulative assault against the weak and weakened states around South Africa's periphery, and assailed the ANC, SWAPO, and their Soviet, East European, and Cuban backers, in their forward and then their rear redoubts (and even attempted a flawed attack on United States petroleum installations in Cabinda). They denied the anti-South African guerrilla movements zones of sanctuary in the larger nations of the region. They further employed economic and military coercion and political and economic persuasion to humble and sometimes to destroy states in the neighborhood which attempted to act autonomously in policy areas of concern to South Africa. In this manner, but in a pronounced form because of the unleashing of the RENAMO,

Mozambique, and to a far lesser extent Angola, have come under the dominant and lasting influence of South Africa.

It is self-evident that South Africa wants to make conditions as difficult as possible for the ANC which, in the mid-1980s, managed annually to infiltrate approximately 300 small cell-groups of armed saboteurs into South Africa. Each was capable of a small wave of bomb planting and grenade throwing, and of causing destruction in the cities, to military establishments, and along the country's border zones. Since the Soviet Union backs the ANC and SWAPO, and has always expressed hostility to apartheid, South Africa naturally opposes states which have demonstrated an affinity for or a relationship with the Soviet Union and other Marxist countries. But South Africa's policy of destabilization is more than a defensive reflex or a manifestation of unresolved historical and ideological hostilities. It flows from South Africa's determination to place its neighbors perpetually on the defensive in order to oblige them to focus their own aspirations inward rather than outward. Even Angola, distant and economically separate from South Africa, needed to be kept occupied in order to maximize South Africa's freedom of maneuver against SWAPO and the ANC. Moreover, an unharassed Angola might—South African reasoning asserts—encourage or permit surplus Cuban and Soviet attention and energies to be focused more directly than hitherto on South Africa. If their own internal problems were all absorbing, and internal chaos extreme, then the nations of southern Africa—Mozambique and Angola in particular—would leave South Africa and Namibia alone. Ultimately too, South Africa could by such means— by subtle and not-so-subtle, interference—demonstrate that black rule was a recipe for disaster, and that minority control had its validity. Like the regional bully that it is, South Africa has also attempted to pick on weak neighbors, even Mozambique, to demonstrate its might in order to keep all prospective challengers at bay.

This is an excessively cynical policy. Its benefit from South Africa's point of view is that it has weakened the ANC and SWAPO. Its cost can be denominated in the currency of international outrage and opprobrium or, even more expensively, in the determination of the Soviet Union to compete with South Africa at ever increasing levels. It is possible, too, that destabilization is a successful initiative only in the short run. Foreign critics, as well as politically influential white South Africans, suggest that the republic's most durable long-term security depends upon bolstering, not destroying, the stability of southern Africa as a whole, and of its fragile black-ruled nations individually and collectively. The prosperity of those nations—the argument of rationality proceeds—would deradicalize the cutting edge of black leadership, especially in countries like Zimbabwe. It would instead focus the attention of the leaders and their followers on issues of economic growth and on internal rather than external political struggles and adventures. If white South Africa were determined to maximize its own chances of avoiding an abrupt shift of power at home, then helping its neighbors to develop themselves to their fullest potential, and employing South Africa's vast regional economic leverage to help them to advance, would appear to make superbly good sense. Doing so in a cooperative manner would effectively deny outsiders, such as the Soviet Union, as well as radically minded and antagonistic insiders, opportunities to gain a significant position in or hold on neighboring nations. In other words, South Africa's benevolence could forge reciprocal ties with new or even old leadership cadres in the neighborhood, and thereby give South Africa enduring hegemony, in place of hegemony of a temporary and unpopular nature.

In the 1980s the leaders of white South Africa have obviously concluded that such a theoretically viable and ethically more acceptable policy is fraught with excessive risk. They have instead put their muscle behind a more aggressive and essentially subversive approach. They have decided that they can defend their nation's self-interest best by using the mailed fist instead of the velvet glove. By weakening the new black ruling groups, and by making their new countries and their fragile economies subject to steady undermining by South African-funded and armed initiatives and/or economic reprisals, the policy architects have seen South Africa gain strength while every other country in the region, and the SADCC members as a group, have become weaker.

The experimentation with and then the wholesale employment of destabilization as a strategic instrument has paralleled the growth within South Africa of the military, and has accompanied the enhanced involvement of the military in politics and national decision-making and the growth of power within the military establishment of the directorate of military intelligence. The reorganization of South Africa's formal machinery for strategic coordination, and the creation of the National Security Council has reflected and advanced that influence.[7] Given the influence of military planners and, especially, the intelligence community, on the council; the ties of the military to President Pieter W. Botha, for 13 years minister of defense before he became prime minister in 1978; the perception of increased danger to the regime in the aftermath of the Soweto riots of 1976-77; the achievement of independence by Angola and Mozambique in 1975; and the coming to power in Zimbabwe in 1980 of a revolutionary party that South Africa had strongly opposed, it is at least understandable that a defense force that had been humbled in Angola in 1975-76 should have sought an opportunity to determine external policy during the 1980s.

Since 1984, however, South Africa's hegemony within the region has been matched by a swelling crescendo of internal insecurity. More than 3,500 deaths, about 10,000 injured persons, and the wholesale arrest of about 30,000 detainees, including hundreds of children, have testified to the breakdown of law and order in the African townships. Also indicative of white South Africa's loss of full control in the African urban areas has been the successful refusal to pay rent of more than 1 million black householders. The tragic boycotts of schools and the periodic bans against black purchases from white-owned merchants, especially in Port Elizabeth, Port Alfred, and East London, have been the marks of turmoil. Most of all, in late 1986 and again in 1988, white South Africa acknowledged the seriousness of the urban revolt by proclaiming and strengthening successive states of emergency and by imposing press censorship.

Deteriorating security in the townships has, counterintuitively, produced no significant reorientation of South Africa's regional pretensions to power. There has been no diminution in the process of destabilization. Indeed, from 1984 to 1987 (even, especially, after Nkomati), South Africa escalated its support for both UNITA and the RENAMO, and struck often against its neighbors. Patrolling of the townships by the defense forces has not diverted from their activities those in military intelligence and the state security council who devised and have developed the forward movement of destabilization.

Other regimes beset by insurrection within might have been expected to focus exclusively on the restoration of order and thus to have abandoned or scaled down their bold, aggressive actions without. But regional dominance is regarded as basic to internal victory and intrinsic to white South Africa's survival. It comes cheaply, too, for its running costs are low (fixed emplacements having been amortized), and for the most part are not charged publicly to accounts subject to the established appropriations procedures of parliament. Thus the internal crisis has not diminished South Africa's quest for total control in the region. Indeed, it has accelerated as much because of turmoil within the country as despite that turmoil. It is still designed to counter the effectiveness of the ANC (and SWAPO) and to deter the appeal and success of Soviet and Cuban efforts. (Renewed Soviet and Cuban interest in the region paradoxically flows from the atmosphere of revolt—the seeming unconquerable resistance in the black townships.)

For all of these reasons, not least that South Africa retains the regional initiative both economically and militarily, lusophone southern Africa can expect no early release from South African bondage. South Africa intends to employ its logistical leverage within the region as a countervailing force to the imposition of extended sanctions from the West and, conceivably, from black Africa. The tighter the West pulls the putative economic noose around South Africa, the more South Africa will impose itself directly and indirectly upon its weak and endangered neighbors. Likewise, and again counterintuitively, the more those who protest violently within the townships are successful, the more South Africa will seek opportunities outside, in Angola, in Mozambique, and in other front line nations. If the ANC steps up its attacks against South Africa, or if the widespread popularity of the ANC in South Africa translates into obvious new support for the ANC among Africans in that country, then South Africa will intensify its punitive and preemptive strikes against its neighbors whether or not they connive with or back the ANC. The predatory role of South Africa within the region will not soon be eclipsed.

Since in 1988 there is no imminent sign of a Namibian settlement, and since UNITA and the MPLA show no signs of agreeing to form the coalition government that South Africa would like to sponsor, the war for Angola can be expected to continue and South Africa can be expected to strengthen its efforts on behalf of UNITA. Only an unexpected Soviet or Cuban military initiative could alter the Angolan equation and disrupt the stalemate that has so cleverly been engineered by South African military strategists.

Mozambique having suffered for several years from South African attention, will now suffer more. In 1987 South Africa, or at least the planners in its military intelligence directorate, sought to render the country totally ungovernable, before sponsoring a military victory by the RENAMO. Since the RENAMO lacks UNITA's legitimacy as an indigenous movement, an RENAMO victory would transform a supine near client into a puppet government. Thus South Africa senses a victory on the Mozambican front, and intends to be relentless.

Until that time (which may never come) when white South Africa is compelled to employ all of its energies in the defense of its heartland, when white resolve snaps, or when there is unanticipated external intervention of the preemptive kind, South Africa's large and powerful military machine should by 1988 reckonings, be able to cope with (if never to contain) its internal insurrection. It should also, and simultaneously, be able to continue to fuel the proxy wars in Angola and Mozambique and to support the overall program of regional destabilization. Its hegemony will remain in place, and Angola and Mozambique will be unable, barring a regime reversal, to escape the long arm of their white antagonists.

Notes

1. See Henry S. Bienen, "Economic Interests and Security Issues in Southern Africa," and Gavin Maasdorp, "Squaring up to Economic Dominance: Regional Patterns," both in Robert I. Rotberg et al., *South Africa and Its Neighbors: Regional Security and Self-Interest* (Lexington: D.C. Heath and Company, 1985), pp. 69-90, 91-136.
2. Robert I. Rotberg, "Decision Making and the Military in South Africa," in Rotberg, et al., *South Africa and Its Neighbors*, p. 17.
3. For the Soviets, see Kurt Campbell, *South Africa and Its Neighbors,* pp. 27-54 in this book; for Namibia, see Robert Legvold, "The Soviet Threat to Southern Africa," in Rotberg et al., *South Africa and Its Neighbors*, pp. 27-54.
4. "Chissano Rejects Talks with the Rebels," *Star Weekly*, 20 December 1986.
5. Chester Crocker, quoted in the *Washington Times*, 22 December 1986.
6. "SAAF Puts Half of Africa Within its Striking Range," *Star Weekly*, 29 November 1986.
7. See Robert I. Rotberg, "Decision Making and the Military in South Africa," in Rotberg et al., *South Africa and Its Neighbors*, pp. 13-26.

4: Soviet Policy in Southern Africa: Angola and Mozambique

BY DR. KURT M. CAMPBELL

1. Introduction: Soviet Policy in Southern Africa

The Soviet Union's continued involvement in the conflict-ridden politics of southern Africa is a subject of much interest and concern to the West. Since its dramatic entrance into southern Africa in 1975 to bolster the MPLA (*Movimento Popular de Libertação de Angola,* or Movement for the Popular Liberation of Angola) during the fractious Angolan civil war, the Soviet Union has played a central role in the military affairs of the region. While the counsel and pressure of both the United States and Britain have been heeded in various southern African capitals and boardrooms, only the Soviet Union, with its allies Cuba and East Germany, has made its influence felt and demonstrated its commitment on the battlefield.[1] Although Soviet attention and activities are directed to an assortment of governments and groups in the region, the lusophone states of southern Africa, Angola and Mozambique, are the Soviet Union's oldest surviving allies in black Africa, and have been the primary focus of Moscow's energies to date.

While there is a general consensus in the West about the desirability of challenging Soviet influence in southern Africa, there continues to be heated debate concerning the appropriate means to apply to check Soviet power.

Nowhere is this discord more acute than over Angola and Mozambique. Conservatives in the United States argue that Moscow has established military staging points in both countries to coordinate its final assault on South Africa through its proxy guerrilla front, the African National Congress (ANC).[2] Conservatives underscore the strategic significance of southern Africa's minerals and waterways and warn of the dire consequences should Moscow succeed in installing a Marxist government in Pretoria.[3] Accordingly, under the Reagan administration, the United States has moved to champion Jonas Savimbi's UNITA (*União Nacional Para a Independência Total de Angola*, or the National Union for the Total Independence of Angola) as part of a global effort to pressure the USSR's local clients and to create instability in the far-flung corners of the Soviet empire.[4] Even more conservative spokesmen advocate extending the so-called "Reagan Doctrine" to include Mozambique, but the administration has so far steered away from providing assistance to the MNR (*Resistência Nacional Moçambicana*, or Mozambique National Resistance, also known as RENAMO).[5]

Liberals, on the other hand, have tended to downplay the strategic East-West dimensions of the contemporary situation in southern Africa. What to do about apartheid in South Africa, rather than communism in Angola and Mozambique, currently tops the liberal agenda. There is a general fear, too, that to the extent the United States is drawn into anti-communist crusades in the region, America will promote, either by design or unwittingly, South Africa's policy of "regional destabilization." [6] Consequently, liberals have campaigned hard in opposition to military aid for UNITA, because of the obvious reliance of Savimbi on South Africa. They have also lobbied in favor of a more conciliatory policy toward Mozambique, with a view toward wooing the FRELIMO (*Frente de Libertação de Moçambique*, or Mozambique Liberation Front) government away from the Soviet Union. Liberals often point to the inability of the Soviet Union to meet the economic needs of its Third World allies and have actively promoted a more comprehensive strategy to lessen Soviet influence, relying on humanitarian aid, commercial incentives, and other forms of economic assistance.[7]

At the heart of the debate concerning U.S. policy toward both Angola and Mozambique is disagreement about (and general ignorance of) the Soviet Union's strategy and objectives in southern Africa. How have Soviet relations with the two lusophone states evolved since the collapse of the

Portuguese African empire? How committed is the Soviet Union to the survival and extension of socialism in southern Africa? How important to the Soviet leadership, ultimately, are developments on the southern tip of Africa? Is there any evidence of friction or discord in the Soviet Union's relations with Luanda and Maputo, respectively? This chapter will set out to answer these questions and in the process trace the twists and turns of Soviet policy toward these two states over the last decade.

Of course, Soviet attention and activities in southern Africa have not been confined to the two lusophone states, and indeed Soviet policy in the region has incorporated a diverse range of tactics. The hallmark of Soviet involvement, however, has been the provision of armaments and military training to various states and national liberation fronts. For instance, the Soviet Union continues to be the principal armorer of the African National Congress (ANC) and the South West Africa People's Organization (SWAPO), two organizations which seek to overthrow white minority rule in South Africa and Namibia respectively.[8] The Soviet Union has also provided some modest military support to Zambia and Botswana, two of the front line states confronting South Africa.[9]

Beyond military supply, the Soviet Union has demonstrated a desire to develop political contacts across the ideological spectrum and to play a major role in regional negotiations, commensurate with its status as a superpower.[10] The Soviets supported Joshua Nkomo's Zimbabwe People's Revolutionary Army (ZIPRA) during the Rhodesian civil war, only to witness Robert Mugabe's Zimbabwe African National Liberation Army (ZANLA) faction emerge after the British-sponsored Lancaster House elections as the new leadership of Zimbabwe. Initially, Mugabe displayed a clear preference for political and commercial links with the United States and China, but as relations between Washington and Harare have soured, largely because of discord over South Africa, the Soviet Union has moved to improve relations with Zimbabwe.[11] There has been no dramatic rapprochement between Moscow and Harare, to date, but since Mugabe's visit to the Soviet Union in late 1985 there has been a gradual upgrade of contracts and exchanges. Indeed, there has been considerable speculation that Zimbabwe would purchase sophisticated fighter aircraft from the Soviet Union.[12]

Furthermore, the Soviet Union tried unsuccessfully to participate in the British-organized negotiations over Rhodesia and the American-brokered talks concerning Namibia and Angola, but Soviet diplomats were denied entry and access to both of these consultations. As a result, the Soviet Union was a vociferous critic of the Lancaster House agreement and has, until very recently, fervently opposed Assistant Secretary of State Chester Crocker's complex diplomacy in Namibia.

South Africa offers the greatest long-term promise for Soviet strategy, but currently poses the most critical challenge to Moscow's efforts in southern Africa. Due to the Soviet Union's long-term military support of the fighting wing of the ANC, *Unkhonto We Sizwe* (the Spear of the Nation), the Soviet Union is assured of a role in determining South Africa's future.[13] However, the present leaders of Afrikanerdom have followed a policy of regional destabilization against Mozambique and Angola, with commando-style attacks and air raids on important military and economic targets coupled with major military support for anti-government rebel groups in each country, Jonas Savimbi's UNITA and the shadowy guerrillas of the MNR, respectively.[14] Consequently, the Soviet Union has directed most of its resources in the region toward bolstering these two outposts of socialism in the region against South African-orchestrated attacks.

In dramatic contrast to the war by proxy between South Africa and the Soviet Union is the discreet and fabulously profitable relationship between them for the marketing of gold, diamonds, and other precious minerals. Through an accident of politics and geology, these two enemies possess much of the world's supply of many strategic minerals. Yet, despite official hostility, the Soviet Union and South Africa manage to conduct a secretive and mutually beneficial partnership in international mineral markets.[15] For instance, DeBeers Corporation in South Africa pays the Soviet Union just under a billion dollars a year for its supply of gem-quality diamonds.[16] In an ironic twist, this lucrative pact to keep mineral prices high has not stopped the Soviet Union from criticizing South Africa's Western trading partners. This has allowed the Soviet Union to have its cake, by maintaining a covert marketing relationship with South Africa, and eat it too, with its propaganda attacks on the United States for doing business with apartheid. This commercial liaison between the Soviet Union and the Republic of South Africa is all the more surprising given the general lack of Soviet economic involvement or humanitarian assistance to its Marxist allies in the surrounding region.

Soviet policymakers, to date, have been generally content to exacerbate gingerly the existing tensions in South Africa, while cautiously avoiding having a major stake in the ongoing turmoil. For example, the Soviet Union has stepped up its public diplomacy and propaganda against South Africa, but there is no evidence of a substantial increase in military supply to or training for ANC guerrillas. Several senior Soviet spokesmen have spoken recently about the Soviet Union not seeking to "fan the flames" of the internal conflict inside South Africa. As mentioned above, Soviet attention and activities appear to be channeled more toward defending its regional allies in southern Africa, Mozambique and Angola. Although the Soviet Union has concentrated its efforts on consolidating, rather than expanding its position in southern Africa, this objective has surely proven to be much more vexing and elusive than Soviets anticipated. With this brief review of Soviet activities in the region as a whole completed, the remainder of this chapter will be primarily devoted to making a close examination of the rise and fall of Soviet fortunes in Angola and Mozambique over the last decade. In conclusion, we will examine Moscow's ongoing reassessment of its Third World role and responsibilities and what this might mean for the future of Soviet policy in southern Africa.

2. Angola: A Demonstration of Soviet Resolve

The era of Soviet involvement in southern Africa began, in a fundamental sense, during the earliest days of the Angolan civil war. The military position of the MPLA in late October 1975 was precarious. After waging a successful campaign to strike out from its natural base around Luanda and establish control in the majority of the provincial capitals of Angola, the MPLA was confronted by a coalition of rival liberation movements. These included the FNLA (*Frente Nacional de Libertação de Angola*, or Front for the National Liberation of Angola) and UNITA, fighting alongside the South African army. An armored column of nearly 2,000 South African troops had crossed Angola's southern frontier from Namibia, and had attacked MPLA positions in the port cities of Benguela and Novo Redondo. While the three nationalist groups had a history of mistrust and competition, dating back to before the collapse of the Salazar Caetano regime in April 1974, the overt South African incursion into Angola transformed not only the situation on the battlefield but the nature of the conflict as well.

The Soviet Union had provided modest political, ideological, and military support to the avowedly Marxist MPLA since the early 1960s. Soviet commentators tended to trace the origins of the MPLA back to the emergence of the Angolan Communist Party in October 1955, and viewed the MPLA as the only legitimate liberation organization in Angola.[17] Soviet assistance was provided to the MPLA in the period preceding the military coup in Lisbon, even though the three movements devoted as much of their energy to fighting one another as to resisting the Portuguese colonialists.[18] Each of the rival movements had received support from a host of international donors, but by 1974, only the People's Republic of China, the United States, the Soviet Union, and Cuba were involved directly in the Angolan civil war. Although the Soviet Union stepped up its military support to the MPLA at the beginning of 1975, Soviet leaders had reasons for optimism that the MPLA would assume uncontested power in Luanda without a massive military commitment from the Soviet Union and its allies.[19] Yet, the introduction of the South African Defense Forces (SADF) into the conflict set the scene for what was to be the most dramatic Soviet military initiative in Africa to date.

At the time of independence, November 11, 1975, Dr. Agostinho Neto, the president of the MPLA, announced the establishment of the People's Republic of Angola. Earlier, toward the end of October, in responseto advancing opposition forces and the deteriorating security of the fledgling regime, the Soviet Union had stepped up appreciably its arms shipments to the beleaguered country.[20] Although there was considerable uncertainty in Soviet policy toward Angola during the initial period of the civil war (the Soviet Union on at least two occasions temporarily suspended support for the MPLA due to discord within its ranks), once the survival of the MPLA was threatened, the Soviet Union committed its resources and prestige to the preservation of the regime.

Soviet airlifts and ships transported thousands of Cuban troops and tons of heavy weaponry to Luanda. In the period between November 1975 and March 1976, approximately 20 ships and 70 flights deposited their contents of men and arms in Angola.[21] Five separate supply routes have been identified by which the Soviet Union delivered its cargoes. Soviet An-22 transport planes flew to Maya Maya, near Brazzaville, where materials were shipped to MPLA strongholds north of Luanda. Other An-22 transports undertook direct flights from airfields in the southern Soviet Union to Luanda or Henrique de Carvalho, refueling in Guinea, Algeria, or Mali. Soviet cargo ships delivered small arms to Dar es Salaam in Tanzania, to Pointe Noire in the Congo, or to Guinea, where they were then ferried to collection points in territory controlled by the MPLA.[22]

The logistical, diplomatic, and military dimensions of the Soviet operation to bolster the MPLA required excellent planning and execution. Indeed, the joint Cuban/Soviet military venture alone demanded considerable coordination. By February 1976, 12,000 Cuban troops had reached Angola and, as they joined the battle against the rival factions, were armed with Soviet-supplied T-34 and T-54 tanks, armored personnel carriers, MIG-21 fighters, antitank missiles, BM-21 rocket launchers, SAM-7 missiles, and AK-47 automatic rifles. The weapons provided by the Soviet Union proved well suited to turning the tide of the struggle. The BM-31 rocket launchers, nicknamed "Stalin Organs," played a devastating role in the civil war, decimating the FNLA army marching on Luanda.[23]

In the final and decisive phase of the war, between December 1975 and April 1976, the MPLA with its socialist allies went on the offensive. The South African advance was halted 150 miles south of Luanda. The SADF force suffered serious casualties and several soldiers were taken prisoner before retreating to sanctuary in Namibia. The FNLA, after its encounter with Soviet-supplied "Stalin Organs" at the "Battle of Death Road," was completely demoralized and ceased to be a factor in the civil war. Jonas Savimbi's UNITA rebels fought well against the joint MPLA/Cuban force in the south but were ultimately outgunned and outnumbered and fled to camps in Ovamboland.

Thus, with the military equipment and advisers provided by the Soviet Union and soldiers sent by Cuba, the MPLA was able to cling to power in Luanda. The Soviet Union garnered significant political dividends from its investment in the Angolan civil war, while the United States and China terminated their commitments to the FNLA and UNITA at the height of the conflict. The United States managed not only to alienate its local allies— South Africa and the FLNA— in the conflict, but incurred the wrath and mistrust of black Africa as well because of its association with South Africa in the conflict.[24] South Africa's entrance into the war exonerated the Soviet involvement in the eyes of black Africa, and led to the United Nations' recognition of the MPLA as the legitimate government of Angola.

The reasons for the Soviet decision to intervene militarily in Angola have been debated by Western scholars and statesmen since the initiation of

Operation Carlotta (the Cuban name for the military operation to bolster the MPLA). Some have argued that Sino-Soviet rivalry and Soviet desires to score an ideological victory in the developing world inspired the Soviet actions.[23] Others contend that the primary adversary of the Soviet Union in Angola was the United States, and that the American failure in Vietnam, coupled with domestic troubles arising from the Watergate scandal, emasculated United States power and shifted the "global correlation of forces" in favor of the Soviet Union.[26] Still others claim that Soviet moves in Angola were based on regional rather than international factors, and marked a clear recognition of the strategic value of southern Africa's minerals and waterways.[27] Finally, there is a body of opinion which believes Soviet motivations were complex and can be attributed not to just one, but to some combinations of the above facts.[28] Perhaps this last "correlation of political forces" provides the best explanation regarding Soviet actions.

Regardless of the rationale for Soviet actions, it may be noted that Soviet involvement in the Angolan civil war signalled a new phase in the Soviet Union's relations with Africa. It marked the dramatic entrance of the Soviet Union into what Tanzanian President Julius Nyerere in the 1970s termed the "second scramble for Africa."[29] The success of the Angolan campaign prepared the way for a greater Soviet role in determining the future of southern Africa. In addition, the Soviet Union's forceful entry into a region where the United States was principally engaged ushered in a new era in superpower competition in the Third World. The Soviet Union's capacity and willingness to project force into a country far from its own borders and with little relevance to Soviet security brought forward a whole set of uncomfortable questions about the future of Soviet-American relations in such regions. Finally, the Soviet incursion into Angola ushered in a period of heightened concern in the West about the effectiveness and future of Soviet foreign policy in southern Africa.

Soviet policy in Angola has followed a pattern established by the forceful entry of the Soviet Union and Cuba into the Angolan civil war. In the more than ten years since the Soviet decision to bolster the MPLA against challenges from rival national liberation movements and from the South African army, the Soviet Union's military involvement in and commitment to the preservation of the ruling MPLA regime has increased substantially—some would argue dramatically. Currently, there are approximately 30,000 Cuban troops serving in Angola along with nearly 1,000 military advisers from the Soviet Union.[30] The Soviet Union has provided a wide array of sophisticated military equipment to Angola, including a squadron of MIG-23 fighters, MI-24 Hind attack helicopters (termed the "most effective counter-insurgency platform in the world"), an air-defense network south of the Benguela railroad using SAM-8 missiles, and an assortment of battle-tested tanks, artillery pieces, and logistical/communications equipment. Western intelligence estimates of total Soviet military investment in Angola are more than $3 billion, of which $1 billion arrived during 1987 alone. (Ironically, most Soviet equipment and personnel have been paid for by the sale to Chevron, an American oil company, of petroleum from the Cabinda enclave.[31])

Although Soviet military support has been instrumental in securing the MPLA's control of the capital, Luanda, and of the vital oil-producing Cabinda enclave, the Soviet Union has been frustrated in the struggle to defeat Jonas Savimbi's UNITA movement. After suffering defeat in the civil war, UNITA retreated to the bush of Ovamboland in southernmost Angola and northern Namibia. Yet South Africa moved to rearm and train Dr. Savimbi's forces in the late 1970s, and in the late 1980s UNITA was perhaps the most decisive factor in Angolan politics. UNITA's forces conduct operations in the majority of Angola's 17 provinces and Dr. Savimbi enjoys almost unparalleled popularity among American conservatives.

After several years of indecisive skirmishes between the Angolan army and UNITA's troops, often operating with South African air cover and logistic support, the MPLA leadership moved in August 1985 to launch a major offensive against Savimbi's base, the so-called provisional capital of Jamba near the border with Namibia. This operation coincided with a series of high level meetings between Soviet and Angolan officials. While visiting Moscow, from August 8 to 10, 1985, Angolan Minister of External Affairs A. Van Dunem met with Soviet Foreign Minister Eduard Shevardnadze. Both parties reaffirmed the principles of the October 8, 1976 Treaty of Friendship and Cooperation which stipulates that the Soviet Union will come to the assistance of Angola in time of crisis.[32] After several months of supply and reinforcements, in late August the Angolan army launched "Operation Party Congress" against UNITA strongholds around Mavinga and Cuito Cunavale in southern Angola. Soviet officers were reliably reported to have been involved in the operation, possibly serving at the regimental level. South

Africa intervened on behalf of UNITA and unofficial reports indicate that after several days of intense fighting, both MPLA and UNITA forces sustained heavy casualties.[33] Despite the magnitude of the clash, neither side was able to deliver a decisive blow.

This 1985 battle between the MPLA and UNITA signaled a new phase in the complex diplomacy involving Angola, Namibia, South Africa, and a host of international actors. Specifically, it marked a return to the battlefield after several years of intense negotiating at the bargaining table. (There were, of course, important military campaigns during these high level meetings, principally the battle of Cangamba in August 1983, but international attention remained focused on diplomatic developments.) Beginning with the appointment of Chester Crocker as Assistant Secretary for African Affairs in 1981, and the subsequent enunciation of a comprehensive American strategy to bring about Namibia's independence and the removal of Cuban troops from Angola, southern Africa has been the scene of some of the most intense dialogue and diplomacy in recent history, with Crocker and his associates "shuttling" throughout the region. Angola established discreet high level contacts with both the United States and South Africa, and the pace of the Soviet Union's official communications with Cuba and Angola also increased. The Soviet Union, ever wary of United States diplomatic maneuverings, sought to block any regional settlement in southern Africa along *Pax Americana* lines. The Soviet Union suffered a potential setback for its regional strategy of diplomatically isolating South Africa from the front line states with the signing of the Lusaka accord between South Africa and Angola on February 16, 1984.[34]

The Lusaka accord called for the staged withdrawal of the South African army from established positions in southern Angola in exchange for Angola's assistance in preventing SWAPO insurgents from entering the area. The agreement, following South Africa's "Operation Askari" which sent nearly 10,000 soldiers into southern Angola, was an attempt by Angolan officials in Luanda to bolster its faltering position in the southern half of the country. The Soviet Union correctly perceived that the south African invasion (which went ahead even after Soviet diplomats warned South Africa) and the subsequent pact between its principal regional ally and its acknowledged foe was a direct challenge to the Soviet Union's standing as a superpower and as an important player in sub Saharan politics. An official Soviet statement declared that

Pretoria's attack on Angola was an extension of United States imperialism and that such "aggression cannot go unpunished." [35] *Pravda* also noted that joint efforts between the Soviet Union, Angola, and Cuba had been inaugurated to "strengthen the defense capability, independence, and territorial integrity of Angola." [36]

Although in January 1982 the Soviet Union had launched a 10-year $2 billion economic aid program to Angola and in 1983 had delivered approximately $800 million worth of military hardware, a new level of Soviet commitment to the beleaguered MPLA regime was reached in 1984. Official Soviet statements and scholarly publications reflected a concern that Pretoria was acting on behalf of Washington to challenge the Soviet Union's position in the region. [37] Perhaps most revealing was a statement concerning the contemporary political situation in southern Africa made by the late CPSU General Secretary Konstantin Chernenko on March 29, 1984, to the effect that "no one has the right to turn back the pages of history." This was interpreted by Western analysts as underscoring Moscow's belief that the United States is intent on rolling back Soviet gains made in the Third World during the 1970s. [38] (In retrospect, Soviet leaders anticipated the objectives of the Reagan Doctrine long before its enunciation.)

This hardening of the Soviet Union's resolve in Angola coincided with the spate of domestic upheaval in South Africa which began in late 1984. Chester Crocker's nimble and delicate diplomacy between the many and diverse actors in southern African politics received harsh public exposure and criticism. The centerpiece of Crocker's efforts had been aimed at achieving Namibia's independence, but the overriding priority in Western political forums became the dismantling of apartheid in South Africa. In the greater debate about the merits of disinvestment in Western business, academic, and government circles, the status of the Angola/Namibia negotiations dropped from the scene. This, coupled with the emergence of a much more aggressive policy of regional destabilization sponsored by Pretoria, undercut Crocker's effectiveness as an overseer of regional diplomatic efforts and caused South Africa and Angola (and by association the Soviet Union) to take a harder line in the negotiations. Despite an optimistic public face by Crocker and his State Department staff that there continued to be "movement" in the private proceedings, it appeared from early 1985 that the complex diplomacy was dead in the water. [39]

Before the decisive battles of Operation Party Congress in late 1985, there was much speculation concerning the Soviet position in Angola (and about what a comprehensive settlement in southern Angola might look like). Had the Soviet Union's standing been eroded by Angola's decision to negotiate with Pretoria? Had changes in the ruling MPLA Politburo strengthened or weakened Moscow's hand? Would the Soviet Union approve of negotiations between the MPLA and UNITA? Had the Soviet Union made any firm claims about the "irreversibility" of socialist trends in Angola? And how did Soviet and Cuban objectives in Angola compare (or diverge)? Yet, with developments shifting dramatically from the field of negotiation to the field of battle, much of this speculation had become irrelevant. The Soviet Union's role as armorer to the MPLA could not be discarded, and with the struggle in Angola entering a crucial stage, its position had if anything become more entrenched and unbending.

The battle lines in Angola were further drawn with the declaration of the so-called "Reagan Doctrine" to counter Soviet imperialism in the Third World. In his October 24, 1985 address to the United Nations, President Reagan denounced forcefully Soviet expansionism in the Third World and outlined a regional peace initiative to resolve conflicts in Afghanistan, Angola, Cambodia, Ethiopia, and Nicaragua.[40] However, Reagan made clear that these trouble spots were a direct "consequence of a Marxist-Leninist ideology imposed from without," and the United States would be prepared to assist anti-communist forces in each of the five countries in their struggles against Soviet domination. In keeping with the mood to challenge Soviet adventurism, the United States Congress in 1985 approved the provision of $250 million for covert military aid to the "mujahideen" rebels in Afghanistan. Then in 1986, the Congress appropriated $100 million in military supplies and training for the Contra guerrillas in Nicaragua.[41]

The most serious test for the Reagan Doctrine to date is in Angola. The way was paved for American assistance to UNITA rebels with the repeal of the Clark amendment in July 1985. (The Clark amendment prevented the United States from providing covert support to the FNLA and UNITA during the Angolan civil war.) This development was soundly condemned by Soviet commentators and many speculated (correctly) that it marked a decision by the Reagan administration to provide military support for UNITA.[42] The movement to provide either overt or covert military assistance to the charismatic Savimbi, while greeted coolly by Africanists at the State Department, gathered momentum in late 1985 and peaked in early 1986 with the much awaited visit of Savimbi to Washington. Savimbi was accorded a reception worthy of a head of state. He met with President Reagan and Secretary of State Shultz, and was the keynote speaker for the annual Republican dinner in Washington. At the end of Savimbi's visit to the United States, many American officials went on record as saying that some form of military support, either an open program with congressional approval or, if necessary, a clandestine operation conducted by the CIA, would be forthcoming.

In March 1986, the Reagan administration announced that Savimbi's forces would receive "Stinger" surface-to-air missiles to combat the MPLA's attack helicopters. (The United States also promised to send TOW anti-tank weapons for use against Soviet-supplied tanks and armored vehicles.) UNITA received further support in September 1986 when Congress appropriated $15 million dollars worth of covert assistance. The Reagan administration announced in late 1987 its intention to offer a further $15 million to Savimbi's movement.[43] Much of the equipment shipped to UNITA forces by 1988 has been delivered via a secret air base in Zaire. Several reports actually suggested that Oliver North had journeyed to Savimbi's base, the so-called provisional capital of Jamba, to help coordinate arms deliveries. The supplying of Savimbi raised some concern in the United States due to UNITA's reliance on South Africa for supplies, logistical support, military training, intelligence, and air cover. Further, the American debate concerning support for Savimbi became more acrimonious and divisive because of the controversy surrounding American policy toward South Africa. Nevertheless, in late 1988 it appeared that the United States would continue to offer clandestine military support for UNITA's campaign against the Marxist MPLA.

By late 1986 South Africa, too, was poised to escalate the brush fire war in Angola. In 1986 Armscor, the government arms corporation, announced the development of the "Cheetah" fighter plane, an upgraded version of the Mirage III. There were also several indications that South Africa might be on the verge of deploying a ground launched cruise missile. Both weapon systems had the capability of attacking the Soviet missile and radar installations in southern Angola, which in 1988 denied South African air supremacy north of the Benguela line.[44]

With the United States moving to bolster UNITA's position in Angola in the face of serious MPLA buildup, and with the Soviet Union firm in its resolve to back the military campaign to defeat Savimbi, in 1987 the stage was set for an indirect superpower confrontation in southern Africa. During the summer dry season, beginning in July, the MPLA launched a second ambitious offensive against UNITA strongholds around the southern town of Mavinga. Under the direct command of Soviet General Konstantin Shaganovitch (who arrived in Angola in 1985 and is said to be the highest-ranking Soviet officer ever to have been posted outside of Europe or Afghanistan) and his aide General Mikhail Petrov (a counterinsurgency specialist), a large battle group of 12,000 Angolan and Cuban troops with Soviet advisors at the brigade level marched south from positions along the Benguela line. The combined forces set off in August 1987, moving very slowly—only about three to five kilometers a day. This time, UNITA forces were in the countryside around the unified battalions, and during the long march south were able to harass supply lines and pursue a successful hit and run strategy. The United States Department of Defense estimates that the MPLA took over 1,000 casualties in August and September while UNITA lost no more than 150 guerrilla fighters. Again—as in 1985—the MPLA, along with its Cuban troops and Soviet advisors, was forced to withdraw in disarray, leaving behind valuable equipment. This operation was a complete failure for the Soviets.[45]

In a purely military-tactical sense, the Soviet-supplied strategy of large-scale armored attacks across great distances was vulnerable to both South Africa's and UNITA's strengths. For such a strategy to prevail, air superiority, mobility, and surprise are all necessary preconditions. The MPLA enjoyed only the last during Operation Party Congress in 1985, and none of the three during the most recent offensive. The war plans provided by the Soviet Union were expensive, both in terms of equipment and lives lost. While by 1988 the level of fighting and the amount of military supplies sent into Angola had increased dramatically, there was no indication that either side could win this war.

Yet, at the same time that fighting between the two sides increased, the correlation of economic and political forces in the region became more confusing. The United States government was providing military support to anti-government rebels, while American oil companies were providing Angola with the necessary capital to pay for Soviet and Cuban assistance. (The Soviet Union actually had a trade surplus with Angola of just under $100 million per year between 1981 and 1984.) South Africa had forcefully committed its military resources to the Angolan campaign, while DeBeers ran Angola's diamond mines in northern Angola. The Soviet Union and South Africa are political and military archrivals in the region but maintain a mutually profitable pact to market diamonds and gold. In the midst of all this confusion of shifting alliances and hidden agendas, one thing appears certain for the immediate future in Angola. There are likely to be important moves and developments on the battlefield in addition to any movement at the negotiating table. This ensures that Soviet interest and involvement in Angolan affairs will remain salient.

3. Mozambique: Testing the Limits of Soviet Power

Soviet relations with Mozambique since independence in many ways mirror what has transpired in Angola, but Soviet involvement in Mozambique has not been as substantial as in Angola. Before the collapse of the Caetano dictatorship, the Soviet Union, together with China, provided modest military assistance and qualified diplomatic support to FRELIMO. Unlike the MPLA in Angola, FRELIMO went unchallenged, at least initially, by rival liberation movements and was able to assume power without massive assistance from the Soviet Union or Cuba. However, in 1977, Mozambique signed a twenty-year Treaty of Friendship and Cooperation with the Soviet Union, and FRELIMO transformed itself into an orthodox "Marxist-Leninist vanguard party" along Soviet lines. (For instance, FRELIMO's organizational structure includes a central committee and a politburo, which is largely responsible for policy formulation and direction.) [46] Mozambique thus joined Angola as one of the Soviet Union's more important Third World allies to emerge in the late 1970s.

In 1978, Soviet leaders had cause to believe that the local factors had shifted in their favor. As the "second wave" of national liberation wars was sweeping southern Africa, Soviet Africanists remained hopeful that, following FRELIMO's victory in Mozambique, Nkomo would emerge as the undisputed leader of Zimbabwe and would install a pro-Soviet government in Harare (then Salisbury). Even by 1978, the Soviet Union and its allies—East Germany and Cuba—were busy shaping Mozambique's internal political system, assisting in party organization, ideological education, propaganda coordination, and the training of the internal security police.[47] Mozambique began receiving substantial military assistance from the Soviet Union in the same year, and Machel served as an outspoken supporter of Moscow's foreign policy line on a host of international issues wholly unrelated to southern African politics.[48] As Rhodesia's conflicts shifted from the battlefield to the negotiating table, the Rhodesian-sponsored attacks of the MNR against FRELIMO tapered off accordingly. South Africa, uncertain and profoundly concerned about these political developments to the north, chose to remain aloof for the time being. In short, the Soviet Union and Mozambique had reason for optimism about the future.

However by 1986, not even a decade later, Mozambique was in shambles—the result of a concerted South African policy to destabilize the country, combined with a lethally incompetent Marxist economic system. As early as 1982, all ten of Mozambique's provinces were besieged by MNR guerrillas that were armed, trained, financed, transported, and supplied by South Africa. The South African military and intelligence élite openly boasted that the South African Defense Forces (SADF) could topple Machel's government in 48 hours if they chose to do so.[49] Mozambique, once a fervent supporter of the ANC, expelled ANC personnel from Maputo after signing the Nkomati accord with South Africa. Mozambique also suffered a terrible drought and severe flooding but did not receive the high profile humanitarian assistance that both the United States and the Soviet Union had given to Ethiopia. As a consequence, there were chronic shortages of staple goods and starvation became prevalent in much of Mozambique. The Soviet position in Mozambique suffered as a result, and official relations have shown clear signs of strain in recent years. Soviet military and economic personnel in Mozambique have been largely confined to the capital since the RENAMO attack on the Murrua mine in Zambezia Province in 1983 that killed two Soviet technicians. Currently, the Soviets stationed in Mozambique behave more as prisoners than as protectors of the faltering regime.

Mozambique's plummet into turmoil was not the direct result of Soviet actions, but Soviet inaction has undoubtedly contributed to Mozambique's decline. Indeed, the Soviet Union demonstrated its inability or unwillingness to deliver two crucial things in Mozambique—economic assistance and military security. Although it is not surprising that the Soviet Union has done little to promote development, its failings in defending the Mozambican revolution are surprising, given Soviet prowess and experience in security-related fields.[50] A review of Soviet activities in both the political-military and economic spheres reveals serious shortcomings in assistance and underscores the Soviet Union's desire to avoid an open-ended commitment in Mozambique.

Certainly the most important article of the 20-year Friendship Treaty between the Soviet Union and Mozambique concerns military assistance. Since independence, the Soviet Union has provided Mozambique with the bulk of its armaments, including tanks, armored vehicles, artillery pieces, surface-to-air missiles, and some fighter aircraft. Approximately 200 Soviet advisors helped to transform Machel's guerrilla forces into a conventional army. However, even with Soviet weaponry and the Soviet-trained army, Mozambique was ill-equipped and ill-prepared to deter direct South African aggression or to combat the RENAMO's insurgency campaign. Almost immediately after Zimbabwe's independence, the South African Department of Military Intelligence (DMI) took over from its Rhodesian founders as the patron of the MNR. The DMI took this ragtag band of disgruntled Portuguese expatriates, disaffected tribal groups, and former FRELIMO members, and molded them into a brutally effective guerrilla organization.[51] FRELIMO's army was unable to contain the growing insurgency, and the MNR proceeded to blow up the Beira-Mutare pipeline and storage tanks, destroy roads, bridges, and rail lines, and generally wreak havoc throughout Mozambique.[52]

To compound the deteriorating security situation, in January 1981 South African warplanes attacked a purported ANC compound outside of Maputo. The Soviet-supplied MIG-17s and the ineffective air defense system around Maputo were little match for South African air power. The Soviet Union's immediate response to the raid was to issue a statement from the Soviet ambassador in Mozambique, Valentin Vdovin, warning that the Soviet Union would come to the aid of FRELIMO if South African forces ever again crossed Mozambique's borders.[53] To underscore the warning, one cruiser and three smaller ships of the Soviet Indian Ocean squadron visited Maputo and Beira two weeks after the attack. It subsequently came to light that this was only a routine "show the flag" visit, not prompted by the South African raid.[54]

However, in the summer of 1982, Soviet and Mozambican officials held a series of high level meetings to discuss the deteriorating internal security situation. For example, in May, Soviet Defense Minister Ustinov, Marshal Nikolai Ogarkov, and Admiral of the Fleet Sergei Gorshkov hosted the visit to Moscow of Mozambican Chief of Staff General Sebastião Mabote.[55] The following month, General Aleskei Yepishev, chief of the main directorate of the Soviet Army, toured a number of defense installations in Mozambique and declared that Moscow was prepared to offer further assistance in combatting the RENAMO rebels.[56] Finally, after a meeting between Machel and Marshalls Ogarkov and Sergey Sokolov at Brezhnev's funeral, Nikolai Zotov, head of the main directorate for foreign military assistance of the general staff, flew to Mozambique to offer specific recommendations concerning techniques for waging a counterinsurgency war.[57]

During the same period, there were also persistent rumors that Cuban troops from Angola would be flown to Mozambique to assist in the fight against the REMANO. This rumor gained credence after a flurry of diplomatic exchanges between senior Soviet and Cuban officials in late December 1982. For instance, Raul Castro met with Soviet General Secretary Yuri Andropov to discuss the problematic security situation in southern Africa.[58] These pointers were enough to compel South African foreign minister Pik Botha to warn Cuba that a move to introduce combat troops into Mozambique would not be tolerated.[59] Likewise, Deputy Undersecretary of State for African Affairs Frank Wisner advised Machel not to "internationalize" the war.[60]

Perhaps because of these warnings, Cuban military aid was not forthcoming and Soviet material support to combat the spreading insurgency increased only moderately, if at all. (Some sources suggest that the dollar value of Soviet military deliveries was actually lower in 1982 and 1983 than during 1978 and 1979.[61]) Furthermore, in May 1983 South African jets again bombed a suspected ANC training facility located outside Maputo to underscore Mozambique's vulnerability. It is likely that during this period the Mozambican leadership determined that the country must look beyond the Soviet bloc for military assistance. One Western commentator noted that "Soviet weapons—with the exception of a handful of MIG-21s, MI-24 helicopter gunships, and some SAM-7s—were out-of-date and costly, a fact not lost on the Mozambicans. Moreover, there was growing dissatisfaction with the quality of the conventional military training provided by Eastern Bloc advisers, which proved ineffectual against the MNR guerrillas." [62] This led Mozambique to seek Portuguese help in fighting counterinsurgency warfare. As part of an April 1982 agreement between Lisbon and Maputo, Portugal stepped up its supply of military equipment and started training élite elements of the Mozambican army.[63] Of course, the March 1984 Nkomati accord with South Africa was primarily motivated by a desire to improve the security situation, but when diplomacy with Pretoria failed, Mozambique looked to the United States, the United Kingdom, and even Zimbabwe for military aid. Although a move to provide Mozambique with $1.2 million worth of "nonlethal" military equipment and training was defeated in the United States Congress,[64] bilateral military cooperation between Mozambique and Zimbabwe proved relatively successful.[65] Moreover, British officers began to train small elements of Mozambique's army in Inyanga, Zimbabwe.[66] Despite these efforts, the security situation became increasingly dangerous and in 1988 Mozambique hovered perilously close to total collapse.

FRELIMO's situation was further challenged by the death of its first president. On October 19, 1986, a Tu-134 jet with a Soviet crew crashed into the South African mountainous border area killing President Machel and ten of his closest advisors. The circumstances surrounding the crash have remained a mystery, but many in black Africa are convinced that South Africa engineered the accident. Machel was succeeded by Joaquim Alberto Chissano, who had been foreign minister since independence in 1974. The Soviet Union has maintained good relations with the new Chissano government, but Chissano himself appears to look more to the West rather than to the East for economic assistance. While the Soviets have encouraged both Angola and Mozambique to pursue commercial contracts with the West, the Soviet Union has been more cautious on the military front.

Soviet reaction to Mozambique's diversification of military contracts has been mixed, ranging from general uneasiness over renewed ties with Portugal to open dissatisfaction about the precedents set by Nkomati. However, Soviet concern has not been enough to spur the Soviet Union into providing a more substantial commitment to Mozambique's survival.

On the economic front, the Soviet Union has also demonstrated its desire to avoid a major stake in Moazmbique's development.[67] By one estimate, the Soviet union provided Mozambique with only $175 million worth of economic assistance between 1978 and 1982.[68] Soviet allies, including East Germany and Romania, have extended trade credits and supplied technical advisors, but the general lack of Soviet assistance has been criticized by senior officials in Maputo. Furthermore, in 1980 Mozambique requested entry to

CEMA, the socialist trading community, but was granted only observer status because its level of economic development was so far below member states. As a result, Mozambique has since the early 1980s sought closer economic ties with the West and with South Africa.[69] However, since 1984 the Soviet Union has stepped up moderately its economic assistance to Mozambique in response to that country's growing discontent. For instance, the Soviet Union rescheduled Mozambique's external debt, donated 9,000 tons of fish, increased oil supplies "on favorable terms," and provided greater humanitarian assistance to drought victims.[70] Nevertheless, the Soviet Union's relations with Maputo have no doubt suffered because of the lack of Soviet economic investment in Mozambique.

4. What Future for Soviet Power in Angola and Mozambique?

Conspicuous in its absence from Mikhail Gorbachev's speech to the Soviet Union's 27th Party Congress held in Moscow in February 1986 was any serious mention of Soviet policy in the Third World. When consideration was given to Soviet foreign policy, in an agenda otherwise dominated by domestic issues, it was focused primarily on the central areas of contention with the United States, such as arms control. This decision largely to ignore the Soviet Union's activities in the Third World contrasts with the experience of the last party congress in 1981, presided over by an ailing Leonid Brezhnev, when there was significant discussion about the Soviet Union's "internationalist" duty to promote revolutionary trends in the developing world. Indeed, ever since Khruschev's dramatic speech to the 1956 party congress, the twists and turns of Moscow's policy in the Third World have been prominent in the ritualized party proceedings.

Given recent developments, it is perhaps surprising that the Soviet Union's current plight in the Third World did not attract greater comment. The Reagan Doctrine called for a forceful new policy to champion anti-Soviet insurrections in Afghanistan, Nicaragua, Ethiopia, Cambodia, and Angola. In keeping with the administration's desire to challenge Soviet gains in the Third World made in the 1970s, Congress has provided covert military assistance to a collection of anti-Soviet guerrilla organizations. This trend in American policy reflects a dramatic shift in Soviet fortunes in the developing countries of Latin America, Asia, and Africa. Traditionally, the Soviet

Union has gained influence through its sponsorship of national liberation movements intent on undermining the old colonial order.

First under the aegis of the Communist International, later through the provision of weapons and guerrilla training, and finally through the direct involvement of Soviet armed forces, the Soviet Union has championed the goal of national liberation in its foreign policy. However, with several of its local allies, including Angola and Mozambique, currently besieged by domestic rivals and hostile powers, the Soviet Union now finds itself in the unusual and unenviable position of seeking to bolster, rather than to topple, unpopular or ineffective regimes. This transition from an insurgent to counterinsurgent power represents a dramatic reorientation for the Kremlin.[72]

Given these pressing concerns, what accounts for the lack of dialogue on the whole issue of Soviet involvement in Third World crisis areas? Since Gorbachev's rise to the party leadership in March of 1985, his overriding preoccupation has been to increase the operational effectiveness of the internal Soviet system. During his first year in power, Gorbachev spoke sparingly about possible new directions for Soviet policy in the Third World, and in this respect the party conference was merely a continuation of high-level silence on the issue. However, it is becoming increasingly clear that the long-term future of Soviet involvement in the developing world has come under serious review.[73] There are clearly thinly veiled debates among Soviet élites about what the ultimate responsibility of the Soviet Union in the Third World should be, with many arguing for a lower profile in the far-flung corners of the globe.

While this so-called "reassessment" of Soviet actions in the Third World has gathered momentum under Gorbachev, it actually began during Yuri Andropov's brief tenure as general secretary. His most important statement on the Third World came in his speech to the Central Committee plenum in June 1983. Andropov declared that: "It is one thing to proclaim socialism as one's aim and quite another to build it. For this, a certain level of productive forces, culture, and social consciousness are needed. Socialist countries express solidarity with these progressive states, render assistance to them in the sphere of politics and culture, and promote the strengthening of their defense. We contribute also, to the extent of our ability, to their economic development. But on the whole, their economic development, just as the entire social progress of those countries, can (of course) be only the result of the work of their peoples and of a correct policy of their leadership." [74]

More and more, Soviet theorists, political commentators, and party leaders are arguing that the Soviet Union should attend to its own economic development, rather than devoting badly needed resources to underdeveloped Third World clients, particularly in Africa. Instead, the Soviet Union is looking more to better off Third World states to expand trade and bilateral relations on a purposefully non-ideological basis.[75] Indeed, among many Soviet writers, there is an underlying pessimism about the revolutionary potential of sub-Saharan Africa and growing sentiment that developments there are peripheral to Soviet interests. Furthermore, Soviet publicists have demonstrated a growing awareness that the Soviet Union's adventurism in the Third World undermined détente and increased superpower tension.[76] Soviet spokesmen and scholars are exploring the concepts of "interdependence" as part of this new approach to the Third World.[77] This realization has led to Gorbachev's support—at least in public—for negotiated settlements in Asia, the Middle East, and southern Africa. This stated willingness to engage in regional dialogue was given substance in southern Africa when Valdillen Vasev, the head of the East and southern African department of the ministry of foreign affairs, who met with Chester Crocker in May 1985 and subsequently traveled to Africa to hold high level discussions in Zimbabwe, Zambia, Mozambique, and Ethiopia.[78] Recent movement in the international diplomacy over Namibia and Angola underscores this newfound Soviet commitment in negotiated settlements for regional disputes. [Indeed, Soviet diplomats have played a crucial role behind the scenes in the ongoing negotiations between Cuba, Angola, South Africa, and the United States.]

Yet there has been no suggestion whatsoever of an eventful Soviet-American rapprochement over regional disputes, and Gorbachev himself has given no indication that he is prepared to abandon Soviet forays in the Third World. While there have been no new Soviet initiatives during Gorbachev's short tenure, the Soviet Union has continued to concentrate its energies on providing military assistance to faltering Marxist regimes in the developing world. For instance, since 1985, Nicaragua has received Hind MI-24 helicopter gunships from the Soviet Union. The Soviets have also upgraded Angola's radar network and provided more sophisticated surface-to-air missiles. In addition, Nicaragua, Angola, Vietnam, and Ethiopia have each undertaken large-scale military operations against rebel forces, often with Soviet military advisers involved in the planning and execution of the campaigns. In many of these countries, where Gorbachev has inherited commitments, the Soviet Union has persevered and even slightly stepped up its military support. [79]

Recent Soviet actions in Angola and Mozambique pose no exception to this general trend. Gorbachev has taken special care to improve relations with Maputo and Luanda. By 1988 he had hosted President Machel twice and Chissano once in Moscow and had met with President Dos Santos no less than three times since March 1985. Yet, there continued to be areas of disagreement and discord in both relationships. The persistent Soviet refusal to expand its economic and commercial activities continued to be a source of consternation, particularly in Mozambique. Moreover, in the late 1980s, the Soviet Union was taking 75 percent of the fish catch from the territorial waters of Angola and Mozambique, even while both countries were suffering from serious food shortages.[80]

For their part too, the Soviets had some hesitations and reservations. Measured against Soviet military support for the MPLA in Angola and for FRELIMO in Mozambique, the Soviet Union has received only modest strategic and political returns. While the Soviet Union has acquired basing facilities in Angola for long-range reconnaissance flights over the South Atlantic to monitor Western shipping, and while Soviet ships are allowed port calls in Maputo and Luanda, both Mozambique and Angola had, until 1988, resisted Soviet requests for naval surface ship or submarine bases.[81] On the political front in 1985, Mozambique, instead of supporting the Soviet Union, abstained in the United Nations vote condemning the Soviet invasion of Afghanistan, which was taken as a sign of Mozambique's increasing interest in strengthening political and economic ties with the West.[82]

After reaping the rewards from its forceful entry into southern Africa in the late 1970s, the Soviet Union is now bearing the burdens of a global empire. Indeed, although the Soviet Union has demonstrated an ability to project power and establish influence in southern Africa, it has had difficulty maintaining a foothold in Angola and especially in Mozambique due to the increasingly treacherous politics of the region. As a consequence, the Soviet Union has made no claims about the "irreversibility" of socialist trends in either country. The Soviet Union has little more at stake in southern Africa than its prestige and a desire to play a role in a region on the periphery of world politics. In terms of geographical ranking (which is admittedly of dubious value), southern Africa is a distinctly secondary consideration in the formulation and execution of Soviet foreign policy, ranking in importance after Europe, Asia, the Middle East, and even North Africa.

Yet, given the history of Soviet and Cuban military resolve in Angola, it is not unreasonable to assume that the Soviet Union will continue to persevere there, even in the face of challenges from UNITA, South Africa, and the United States. However, it is in Mozambique that the limits of Soviet power and reach are most apparent. Mozambique is the "weakest link" in the chain of fledgling and faltering Marxist regimes in the Third World, and is the most likely candidate for a counterrevolutionary coup or a further slide into domestic turmoil. What ultimately transpires in Mozambique will probably be more influenced by South African military policy and Western commercial assistance than by Soviet power and influence.

Notes

NB: Sections of this chapter have been adapted from a forthcoming *Adelphi Paper* entitled "Southern Africa in Soviet Foreign Policy" with the permission of the International Institute for Strategic Studies.

1. An important exception here is the Reagan administration's move, beginning in early 1986, to arm Jonas Savimbi's UNITA movement.
2. For instance, see the report of Senator Jeremiah Denton in *The Role of the Soviet Union, Cuba, and East Germany in Fomenting Terrorism in Southern Africa,* Hearings before the Subcommittee on Security and Terrorism, Committee on the Judiciary, United States Senate Washington, D.C.: Government Printing Office, (1982), pp. 2-8.
3. Robert J. Hanks, *The Cape Route* Cambridge, Massachusetts: Institute for Foreign Policy Analysis, (1981); W.C.J. von Rensburg and D.A. Pretorius, *South Africa's Strategic Minerals: Pieces on a Continental Chess Board* Johannesburg: Valiant, (1977); W. Scott Thompson and Brett Silvers, "South Africa in Soviet Strategy," in Richard E. Bissell and Chester A. Crocker (eds.), *South African Into the 1980s* Boulder: Westview, (1979), pp. 142-44.

4. See Richard H. Shultz, Jr., "Countering Third World Marxist-Leninist Regimes: Policy Options for the United States," in *Third World Marxist-Leninist Regimes: Strengths, Vulnerabilities, and U.S. Policy* (Cambridge, Massachusetts: Institute for Foreign Policy Analysis, 1985), pp. 111-25.

5. There is, however, a growing sentiment among U.S. conservatives to include support for the MNR (Renamo) as part of the Reagan Doctrine. See Allen Isaacman, "Chissano's Friends and Enemies," *Africa Report.* (September-October 1987), pp. 48-50.

6. For a discussion of regional destabilization, see Kenneth W. Grundy, *The Militarization of South African Politics* (Bloomington: Indiana University Press, 1986), pp. 19-34; Steven Metz, "Pretoria's 'Total Strategy' and Low Intensity Warfare in Southern Africa," *Comparative Strategy,* vol. 6, No. 4 (1987), pp. 437-70.

7. See Michael Clough (ed.)., *Reassessing the Soviet Challenge in Africa,* Policy Papers in International Affairs, No. 25 (Berkeley, California: Institute for International Studies, University of California, 1986).

8. See David E. Albright, "The Communist States and Southern Africa," in Gwendolyn M. Carter and Patrick O'Meara (eds.), *International Politics in Southern Africa* (Bloomington: Indiana University Press, 1982), pp. 3-44.

9. See Peter Vanneman and W. Martin James III, *Soviet Foreign Policy in Southern Africa: Problems and Prospects* Pretoria: The Africa Institute of South Africa, 1982), pp. 34-53.

10. See David E. Albright, "New Trends in Soviet Policy Towards Africa," *CSIS Africa Notes,* No. 27 (April 1984), pp. 2-8; S. Neil MacFarlane, *Soviet Intervention in Third World Conflict* (Geneva: Programme for Strategic and International Security Studies, Graduate Institute of International Studies, 1983), pp. 26-50; The recent Soviet interest in regional negotiations was also underlined by Soviet General Secretary Mikhail Gorbachev in *Perestroika: New Thinking for Our Country and the World* (New York: Harper and Row, 1987), pp. 173-90.

11. For a good overview of recent Soviet diplomacy towards Zimbabwe, see Michael Clough, "Moscow and Africa: A 1986 Balance Sheet," *CSIS Africa Notes*, No. 55 (March 21, 1986); Glen Frankel, "Moscow's Gains in Africa," *Washington Post* (May 25, 1986).

12. See Kurt M. Campbell, "The Case of the MIGs and Zimbabwe's New Soviet Tilt," *Christian Science Monitor*. (May 7, 1987).

13. See Kurt M. Campbell, *Soviet Policy Towards South Africa* (London: Macmillan, 1986).

14. For a discussion of the new, aggressive thrust of South Africa's regional policy, see Philip H. Frankel, *Pretoria's Praetorians* (Cambridge, England: Cambridge University Press, 1984), pp. 71-123.

15. See Kurt M. Campbell, "The Soviet-South African Connection," *Africa Report*, Vol. 31. No. 2 (March-April 1986), pp. 72-75.

16. For some background discussion of these clandestine commercial dealings, see Eduard J. Epstein, *The Diamond Invention* (London: Hutchinson, 1982); Timothy Green, *The World of Diamonds* (London: Weidenfeld and Nicolson, 1981).

17. On this point, refer to John A. Marcum, *The Angolan Revolution: The Anatomy of an Explosion* (Cambridge, Massachusetts: MIT Press, 1969), pp. 28-29.

18. See John A. Marcum, *The Angolan Revolution: Exile Politics and Guerrilla Warfare* (Cambridge, Massachusetts: MIT Press, 1978).

19. As early as 1970, *Strategy Survey* (International Institute for Strategic Studies) rated the MPLA as the most effective guerrilla organization in Portuguese Angola.

20. Jiri Valenta, "The Soviet-Cuban Intervention in Angola, 1975," *Studies in Comparative Communism*, Vol. II (Spring/Summer 1978), pp. 3-9.

21. For an excellent account of Soviet military and diplomatic initiatives in Angola, see Bruce D. Porter, *The USSR in Third World Conflicts* (Cambridge, England: Cambridge University Press, 1984), pp. 147-81.

22. *Ibid.,* p. 161.

23. John Stockwell, *In Search of Enemies: A CIA Story* (New York: Norton, 1978), p. 214.

24. For an account of American concern about these issues, see Nathaniel Davis, "The Angolan Decision of 1975: A Personal Memoir," *Foreign Affairs*, Vol. 57 (Fall 1978), pp. 109-24.

25. See, for instance, Colin Legum, "The Soviet Union, China, and the West in Southern Africa," *Foreign Affairs*, Vol. 54 (Summer 1976), pp. 45-62.

26. See Arthur Jay Klinghoffer, *The Angolan War: A Study of Soviet Policy in the Third World* (Boulder: Westview, 1980).

27. These sentiments are more prevalent among conservative and South African commentators. See Peter Vanneman and Martin James III, "The Soviet Intervention in Angola: Intentions and Implications," *Strategic Review* (Summer 1976).

28. See Larry C. Napper, "The African Terrain and U.S.-Soviet Conflict in Angola and Rhodesia," in Alexander L. George (ed.), *Managing U.S.-Soviet Rivalry* (Boulder: Westview, 1983), pp. 155-85.

29. Cited in Jiri Valenta, "Soviet Decision-Making on the Intervention in Angola," in David E. Albright (ed.), *Communism in Africa* (London: Indiana University Press, 1980), pp. 94-95.

30. See the section on Angola in *The Military Balance: 1987-1988* (London: International Institute for Strategic Studies), p. 120.

31. See John D. Battersby, "Angola Lags in Drive on U.S.-Backed Rebels," *New York Times* (September 14, 1987); William Claiborne, "In Angola, It's Getting Harder to Tell the Good Guys from the Bad," *Washington Post Weekly* (October 26, 1987); Robert M. Press, "Soviets Lead Angola Buildup," *Christian Science Monitor* (April 7, 1987).

32. For a careful review of Soviet diplomacy in the region during this period, see Peter Clement, "Moscow and Southern Africa," *Problems of Communism*, Vol. 34. No. 2 (March-April 1985), pp. 29-50.

33. For a useful comment on the yearly "dry season offensives," see "Angola's War Clouds," *Economist* (October 10, 1987), pp. 39-40.

34. Martin Lowenkopf, "Mozambique: The Nkomati Accord," in Michael Clough (ed.), *Reassessing the Soviet Challenge in Africa,* pp. 60-64; Winrich Kuhne, "What Does the Case of Mozambique Tell Us About Soviet Ambivalence Toward Africa?" *CSIS Africa Notes*, No. 46 (August 1985), pp. 3-6.

35. The TASS statement is cited in Clement, "Moscow and Southern Africa," p. 35.

36. *Pravda* (January 13, 1984).

37. Y. Tarabrin, "Afrika v Globalnoi Strategii Imperializma," *Mirovaya Ekonomika i Mezhdunarodnye Otnosheniya,* No. 2 (February 1982), pp. 25-37; A. Urnov, "Alyans Vashington-Pretoriya i Afrika," *Mirovaya Ekonomika i Mezhdunarodnye Otnosheniya,* No. 3 (March 1982), pp. 56-66.

38. For an insightful look at the Soviet response to the Reagan administration's more forceful regional diplomacy, refer to Francis Fukuyama, *Moscow's Post-Brezhnev Reassessment of the Third World,* Rand Report R-3337-USDP (February 1986), pp. 76-82.

39. For a good account of Crocker's complex regional diplomacy, see Christopher Coker, *The United States and South Africa: Constructive Engagement and Its Critics* (Durham: Duke University Press, 1986), pp. 154-78.

40. See Stephen S. Rosenfeld, "The Guns of July," *Foreign Affairs* (Spring 1986), pp. 700-705; William R. Bode, "The Reagan Doctrine," *Strategic Review* (Winter 1986), pp. 23-27.

41. Refer to Raymond W. Capson and Richard P. Cronin, "The Reagan Doctrine and Its Prospects," *Survival* (January/February 1987), pp. 40-55.

42. See the TASS report, "Sharp Criticism," *FBIS Africa* (July 16, 1985), which was reprinted from *Izvestia.*

43. Kurt M. Campbell, "The Wars of the Reagan Doctrine," *Boston Globe,* December 7, 1987.

44. Helmoed-Romer Heitman, "Angola: Crucial Confrontation Ahead," *Jane's Defense Weekly* (October 24, 1987), pp. 950-51.

45. Ibid.; Peter Younghusband, "Rebels Crush Major Attack by Cuban-Led Angola Forces," *Washington Times* September 30, 1987.

46. Allen and Barbara Isaacman, *Mozambique: From Colonialism to Revolution* (Boulder: Westview, 1983); Barry Munslow, *Mozambique: The Revolution and Its Origins* (London: Longmans, 1983).

47. Thomas Henriksen, *Mozambique: Revolution and Counter-revolution* (Westport: Greenwood, 1983).

48. For instance, Machel strongly supported the Soviet position in the Euromissile debate during 1982-83.

49. See Simon Jenkins, "Destabilization in Southern Africa," *Economist* (July 16, 1983).

50. Fukuyama, *Moscow's Post-Brezhnev Reassessment of the Third World*, pp. 71-74

51. Richard Leonard, *South Africa at War* (South Africa: Donker, 1983), pp. 89-94.

52. See Simon Jenkins, "Meanwhile in Mozambique," *Economist* (March 30, 1985); Phyllis Johnson and David Martin (eds.), *Destructive Engagement* (Harare: Zimbabwe Publishing House, 1986).

53. See Peter Clement, "Moscow and Southern Africa," p. 40.

54. Seth Singleton, "The Shared Tactical Goals of South Africa and the Soviet Union," *CSIS Africa Notes*, No. 12 (April 26, 1983).

55. *Krasnaya Zvezda,* May 27, 1982.

56. *Kraznayz Zvezda,* June 6, 1982.

57. Peter Clement, "Moscow and Southern Africa," p. 40.

58. *Ibid.*

59. See John de St. Jorre, "Destabilization and Dialogue: South Africa's Emergence as a Regional Superpower," *CSIS Africa Notes,* No. 26 (April 1984).

60. For a good discussion of American policy towards Mozambique during this period, see Coker, *The United States and South Africa,* pp. 232-34; Jonathan Steele, "Mozambique's Quandary," *Guardian* (January 13, 1983).

61. See *World Military Expenditures and Arms Transfers 1972-1982*, United States Arms Control and Disarmament Agency (ACDA) (Washington, D.C.: Government Printing Office, 1982), p. 80.

62. Winrich Kuhne, *Nkomati and Soviet Africa Policy in the Mid-18980s: The End of Ideological Expansion?* (Ebenhausen, Germany: Stiftung Wissenschaft und Politik, 1985), p. 12.

63. See Shirley Washington, "Portugal's New Initiatives," *Africa Report,* No. 27 (November-December 1982); Richard Timsaar, "Portugal Offers Military Aid to Former African Colonies," *Christian Science Monitor* (November 17, 1982).

64. For details about the blocked attempt to send aid to Mozambique's military, see B. Drummond Ayres, Jr., "U.S. Plans to Aid Mozambique Army," *New York Times* (January 17, 1985).

65. See "Rebel Base Captured by Joint Zimbabwe-Mozambique Strike," *Christian Science Monitor* (September 14, 1985); Norman McQueen,

"Mozambique's Widening Foreign Policy," *World Today,* No. 40 (January 1984), pp. 22-28.

66. See "War Aid for Mozambique: British Spit and Polish," *New York Times* (May 18, 1986).

67. The Soviets' general disinterest in extending large aid and economic subsidies to impoverished Third World states is alluded to in Elizabeth Kridl Valkenir, "New Thinking About the Third World," *World Policy Journal* (Fall 1987), pp. 651-74.

68. Cited in Francis Fukuyama, *Moscow's Post-Brezhnev Reassessment of the Third World*, p. 71.

69. David Lamb, "Mozambique Moving Closer to the West," *International Herald Tribune* (November 16, 1984); Joanmarie Kalter, "Mozambique's Peace with South Africa," *Africa Report,* No. 29 (May-June 1984), p. 21.

70. Philip R. Nel, "Continuity and Change in Soviet Policy Toward Southern Africa," Unpublished text, Institute of Soviet Studies, University of Stellenbosch, South Africa (1985).

71. This point, along with other Soviet explanations for their general reluctance or inability to extend further economic assistance, is discussed by Francis Fukuyama, *Moscow's Post-Brezhnev Reassessment of the Third World*, pp. 48-61.

72. This is detailed by Mark Katz, "Anti-Soviet Insurgencies: Growing Trend or Passing Phase?" *Orbis* (Summer 1986), pp. 365-91.

73. For an analysis of recent Soviet writings on Third World issues, see Jerry F. Hough, *The Struggle for the Third World: Soviet Debates and American Options* (Washington, D.C.: Brookings Institution, 1986).

74. Andropov's speech appears in full in "Rech' General'nogo Sekretariya Ts. KKPSS tovarishcha Yu. V. Andropov," *Kommunist*, No. 9 (1983), pp. 6-9; for a useful background to this address, see Curtis Keeble, "The Roots of Soviet Foreign Policy," *International Affairs* (London) Vol. 60, No. 4 (Autumn 1984), pp. 571-75.

75. "Moscow's Third World Game," *Newsweek* (March 23, 1987), p. 34; Bill Keller, "Soviet, in a Shift, Expands Contact with the Third World," *New York Times* (May 25, 1987).

76. Ye. Primokov, "New Philosophy of Foreign Policy," reprinted from *Pravda* in *FBIS* (July 14, 1987), pp. CC5-CC10; Thomas J. Zamostny, "Moscow and the Third World: Recent Trends in Soviet Thinking," *Soviet Studies*, Vol. 36, No. 2 (April 1984), pp. 231-38.

77. Arguments about a new "global interdependence" and a need for super-power crisis prevention regimes can be found in V. Zhurkin, *Global Problems of Mankind and the State* (Moscow: Progress Publishers, 1985).

78. This is described in Philip Nel, "Soviet Policy in Southern Africa," *Soviet Revue,* Institute for Soviet Studies, University of Stellenbosch, Vol. 3, No. 2 (March-April 1987).

79. For interesting reviews of the areas of continuity and change in Soviet policy in the developing world, see Alvin Z. Rubinstein, "A Third World Policy Waits for Gorbachev," *Orbis,* Vol. 30, No. 2 (Summer 1986), pp. 355-64.

80. Jonathan Marshall, "Russia's Africa Flop," *Inquiry* (September 1982), p. 17.

81. J. Marcum, "Angola," in G. Carter and P. O'Meara (eds.), *Southern Africa: The Continuing Crisis* (Bloomington: Indiana University Press, 1979), pp. 193-94.

82. Elaine Sciolino, "UN, 122-19, Asks Troop Pullout in Afghanistan," *New York Times* (November 14, 1985).

5: The Cuban Role in Angola

WAYNE S. SMITH

Ask the average American why Cuba is involved in Angola, Namibia, and to a lesser extent in the rest of southern Africa, and he will almost certainly respond that Cuba is there at the orders of the Soviet Union to play a troublemaking role. "Why else *would* it be there?" he will ask. "After all, Cuba is only a small Caribbean island. What possible interests could it have so far from home?"

In fact, Cuba has interests and objectives of its own in southern Africa. It is there to pursue them, not to play a troublemaking role—though in the very act of pursuing them, it may of course create problems for other countries, including the United States. Further, it is there not on Soviet orders but because it wants to be.

Rationale for Cuban Involvement

Cuba has historical ties of blood and culture with Africa. As much as 40 percent of the Cuban population is of African ancestry and Cuba would not be Cuba without the influence of African music, religion, and myths. Since the earliest days of the Cuban Revolution, these ties, this heritage, have been glorified. And since those earliest days also, the new government has been involved on the African continent. Cuba felt a close bond of kinship with the Algerian revolution against France which coincided with Castro's revolution to overthrow Fulgencio Batista. Almost as soon as he had won, Castro began providing small amounts of military assistance to Algerian freedom fighters. Upon their victory, Cuba was one of the first countries to establish relations with the new government in Algiers, and in 1963, Cuba sent a small military contingent to fight on Algeria's side in the first Algerian-Moroccan war. The next year, Ernesto "Ché" Guevara visited most of the so-called progressive countries in an effort, joined by Ahmed Ben Bella's Algeria, to set up an alliance of progressive states to fight against Western imperialism, first in the Congo and then throughout the continent. Nothing came of the alliance (if only because Ben Bella was overthrown in 1965), but it was during this tour that Guevara established the first links between Cuba and Agostinho Neto's Popular Movement for the Liberation of Angola (MPLA), which was then struggling against Portuguese colonialism. By 1965, Cuba was supplying arms and advisers to the MPLA. By 1965 also, Guevara was back in Africa, this time to set up an anti-Western guerrilla group in the Congo—what was to have been the first step in the alliance he and Ben Bella had envisaged the previous year. He failed and shortly went off to fight and die in Bolivia. Once undertaken in 1965, however, Cuba's commitment to the MPLA in Angola remained constant.

Cuba's interest in Africa did not, of course, stem simply from its own African heritage; rather, from the earliest days of the Revolution, Castro saw that Cuba's natural milieu—and his best stage—was the Third World. Very quickly, then, Cuba put itself forward as a Third World country. In a 1959 speech to the United Nations General Assembly, for example, Foreign Minister Raul Roa emphasized that while Cuba was by history and tradition part of the West, as it now for the first time had the freedom to choose an independent foreign policy, it intended to do just that. It no longer accepted the inevitability of choosing between East and West. There were now other paths and other solutions. Cuba's paths and solutions were those of the other Latin American countries and of the peoples of Africa and Asia. Cuba, he said, was one of them.[1]

Cuba was one of the founding members of the Non-Aligned Movement (NAM) in 1961. It was a forum much suited to Castro's charismatic style and he quickly became one of its most active leaders. Indeed, playing a major role on the world stage as a leader of the Third World—a leader of the same prestige and preeminence as Nasser, Nehru, and Tito—was obviously all along one of Castro's most cherished objectives.[2]

Seen against this background, it becomes clear that another interest Cuba sought to pursue in Africa was the enhancement of its leadership position within the NAM, and the Third World generally. Cuba did not see itself simply as a small Latin American country; rather, its vision of itself was as a major actor in the Third World, one with alliances in Africa and the Middle East as well as with the socialist world. And indeed, its ability to project its military and political influence into far corners of the globe did set it apart from most other Third World countries and also assured it an unquestioned place at the head table. Cuba took its "internationalist duty" seriously. It was indeed devoted to the idea of promoting world revolution against the imperialist enemy. But it was equally important for Cuba's political position within the Third World that it be seen as occupying a vanguard position in that struggle. Hence, its ideological drives served its more practical political objectives, and the latter also helped fuel the former.

It should be remembered that during the decade of the sixties, Castro played a relatively independent role in the NAM, in Latin America and in Africa— often to the great distress of the Soviet Union. In 1961, he had associated himself with the Soviets, but as Castro saw it, that did not mean he had to take orders from them, or even to accept their interpretation of Marxist/ Leninist doctrine. On the contrary, he declared in a speech on October 3, 1965 that the world Marxist movement was not the Catholic Church; there was no Rome and no Pope. Each communist party was autonomous and would decide for itself how Marxism could best be applied in its particular country. There was no doubt as to how Castro intended to apply it: he would pursue a radical path. He insisted that revolution could only be made through the barrel of a rifle and insisted also that it was the duty of all progressive states (read, especially the Soviet Union) to come to the aid of national liberation movements. The very idea of coexistence between East and West was anathema to him. The only way to deal with the imperialists, said Castro, was with rifle in hand.

But all this was at direct odds with the Soviet approach. After the 1962 missile crisis, Moscow sought détente with the West. It cautioned against armed struggle in most emerging countries and was itself unwilling to provide national liberation movements with the sort of unstinting support Castro thought was in order. This led to sharp tensions between Cuba and the Soviet Union. By 1965, both Castro and Ernesto "Ché" Guevara were openly expressing their disgust with the soft Soviet line. Guevara called the Soviets "Marxist revisionists," and Castro (in 1967) rejected Soviet formulae for Latin American revolution, stating that he would ignore questions of affiliation with the world communist movement in his dealings with Latin American revolutionaries.[3]

Needless to say, given this open dispute with the Cubans over tactics and objectives, it would not have served Soviet purposes to encourage them to involve themselves in Africa during the decade of the sixties. That would have been simply to spread the dispute to another continent and to invite further embarrassment to Moscow. Soviet and Cuban policies, moreover, seemed to respond in very different ways to the same phenomena. The fall of Ben Bella in Algeria and Nkrumah in Ghana, as well as the defeat of progressive forces in the Congo, caused the Soviets to scale back their expectations, and their activities, in sub-Saharan Africa during the latter part of the sixties. But as we have seen, Cuban involvement and commitment became more intense after 1965. Moscow and Havana were marching in opposite directions.

The most intense Soviet-Cuban disagreements over tactics began to dissipate near the end of the decade. Guevara's defeat and death in Bolivia symbolized, at least for the time being, the failure of the guerrilla tactics so favored by Castro. This failure, plus pressure from Moscow, brought Castro around to the acceptance of more moderate, and safer, Soviet popular front tactics in Latin America. This greater harmony was reflected in the NAM as well. While during the sixties Castro had used the NAM as a forum to criticize and dispute Soviet positions, during the seventies he used it to push the idea of a natural alliance between the socialist camp and the anti-imperialist countries of the Third World.

Cuba in Angola: Specific Objectives

In Angola, however, Havana and Moscow remained at odds. Cuba's support for the MPLA was total and unwavering. The Soviet approach on the other hand continued to reflect Moscow's growing disenchantment. By 1972, the Soviets had begun drastically to reduce their support and by the end of 1973 it had been cut off altogether. Agostinho Neto and Castro got along famously. Both were revolutionaries and nationalists first, Marxists second. The Soviets, however, found it difficult to work with Neto and obviously would have preferred a more malleable ally.[4]

As Portuguese rule began to collapse in 1974, all interested outside powers were backing one or more of the three national liberation groups: (a) the United States, Zaire, and the Chinese People's Republic supported Holden Roberto's National Front for the Liberation of Angola (FNLA); (b) the Soviets and Cubans backed the MPLA—though Soviet support as of the end of 1974 was mostly moral; and (c) Jonas Savimbi's National Union for the Total Independence of Angola (UNITA) was supported by South Africa and the Chinese—United States support for UNITA beginning only in 1975.

As it became increasingly clear that the Portuguese would soon pull out, these three groups were in competition—and often bloody competition—to control the government of the new nation. The Portuguese, with problems enough back home, simply wished to wash their hands and withdraw. In an effort to prevent chaos following their departure, however, they did, in January of 1975, bring the three contending factions together in Alvor, Portugal, and persuade them to agree to share power in a tripartite transitional government until elections could be held in November of that same year. This came to be called the Alvor agreement.

One would have expected the United States to throw its support behind this agreement, which offered the best hope—perhaps the only hope—that Angola's transition from colony to nationhood might be accomplished without a full-scale civil war and without major outside intervention. In fact, however, shortly after the Alvor agreement was signed, the National Security Council's 40 Committee (which oversaw clandestine CIA activities) authorized the transfer of some $300,000 in covert aid to Holden Roberto. United States-supplied arms also began flowing to Roberto through Zaire. The purpose of this aid became immediately apparent. In the words of John Stockwell, then head of the CIA's Angola Task Force: "In February of 1975, encouraged by Mobutu and the United States, Roberto moved his well-armed forces into Angola. In one instance in early March they gunned down 50 unarmed MPLA activists. The fate of Angola was then sealed in blood." [5]

The United States, then, was instrumental in shattering the Alvor agreement. This turned out to have been a grave error. Nor was it one forced upon us by the other side. As Stockwell emphasizes, both the MPLA and the UNITA had given evidence of intending to honor the agreement. So had the Cubans and the Soviets. Both the latter, however, now moved quickly to counter the United States move. They were certainly aware that the United States, as well as Zaire and Peking, were behind Holden Roberto's offensive. They saw no reason to give us a free hand. Hence, in March of 1975 the Soviets resumed shipments of arms to the MPLA, and in June the Cubans sent some 230 military advisers of their own to help the beleaguered MPLA. This new assistance shifted momentum toward the MPLA and by July it had expelled FNLA and UNITA forces from Luanda and was holding its own on other fronts.

It is important to note that United States and Chinese support to the FNLA not only provoked increased Soviet and Cuban support to the MPLA, it also served as a catalyst to bring the policies and objectives of the two into a much closer harmony. The two retained their own points of view and they did not always act in concert even after February of 1975, but it is at least safe to say that from that point forward, there was a greater coordination between them than had previously been the case.

In response to the reaction of Moscow and Havana, the United States again upped the ante. The 40 Committee in July authorized larger amounts of covert support (some $32 million in all as a very conservative estimate) to Roberto, and now to Savimbi as well. The CIA also began recruiting mercenaries to fight in support of Roberto, and sent CIA advisers to serve with his forces. And on August 9, 1975, South African forces intervened for the first time, crossing into Angola and occupying the Cunene hydroelectric project. At the same time, South Africa opened training camps in Namibia and southern Angola for FNLA and UNITA forces.

The MPLA, concerned over South Africa's intentions, asked first the Soviet Union and then Cuba for increased assistance, including military advisers. Moscow was unwilling to go beyond the supply of arms. Havana had no such reservations; in late August and September, several hundred additional Cuban military personnel were sent to Angola.[6] Whether these were regular line forces or whether they served simply as advisors is still a debated point. Whatever the case, their number was small and their arrival was clearly a response to the earlier commitment of South African forces. Their presence was immediately felt and enabled the MPLA to stabilize its position. It was not able to go over to the attack, but it could now hold its own.

Stabilization of the fronts in itself created a critical problem for Washington and Pretoria. If the situation remained unchanged, independence day— November 11, 1975—would find the MPLA still in control of Luanda and thus in a position to declare itself to be the new national government. This neither Washington nor Pretoria was prepared to accept. Hence, both opted for a dramatic new effort to oust the MPLA. On October 14, the South Africans crossed into Angola in force and launched an all-out drive on Luanda. South African helicopter gunships and armored units swept the demoralized MPLA before them. The way to Luanda seemed open.

The United States obviously knew in advance that the South Africans were going to invade. Indeed, according to John Stockwell, the chief of the CIA's Angola Task Force at the time of the invasion, there was close liaison between the CIA and the South Africans.[7] Subsequently, "high officials" in Pretoria claimed that their intervention in Angola had been based on an "understanding" with the United States.[8] No documentary evidence of such an understanding has yet been produced, but it is striking that, as South African armored units and artillery poured into Angola, the Ford administration voiced not a word of protest or even concern.

If, as suggested by Stockwell (who certainly ought to know), the United States aided and abetted the South African invasion of Angola, it thereby committed a crucial error—and one even more irreparable than its earlier decision to overthrow the Alvor agreement. For, once the conflict—or at least the international perception of it—was transformed from one of a fight among competing Angolan factions to one of a struggle between racist South Africa and the MPLA, Cuba, as another Third World state, could not lose politically by going all-out to the assistance of the MPLA.

Thus, in response to desperate appeals from the MPLA, Cuba first airlifted the State Security Special Forces Battalion to Luanda and then dispatched additional forces by sea. The arrival of these units immediately turned the tide in favor of the MPLA, enabling its forces to stop Holden Roberto at the battle of Quifangondo and to slow the South African advance in the south—eventually, indeed, halting the South Africans altogether.

Between November 8, 1975, when the first plane-loads of Cuban troops arrived, until March of 1976, when the war was virtually over, as many as

30,000 Cuban troops were deployed to Angola. The decision to send them, it should be emphasized, was made by the Cubans themselves. It was the Cubans, along with MPLA commanders, who directed the conduct of the war. Even Soviet logistical support for the Cuban intervention had its limits. The rapid deployment of Cuban troops in November was critical for the MPLA's survival, yet the Cubans had to use the best available aircraft then in their own inventory—outdated Britannias already in the air almost 20 years. Surely, had the Soviets wished to support the Cuban deployment by supplying air transport, they could have had safer and more modern aircraft in Cuba within 48 hours. But no such effort was made. Indeed, it was not until January of 1976 that the Soviets began to provide transport aircraft, and even then only because United States diplomatic pressures had successfully denied the Cubans landing rights in several countries, making the continued use of Cuban commercial air transport impossible.[9]

Further confirmation that the deployment of its troops to Angola was Havana's own idea comes from no less a source than Arkady N. Shevchenko, the Soviet Under Secretary of the United Nations who defected in 1978. Describing a 1976 conversation with senior foreign ministry official Vasily Kuznetsov, he relates that: "Kuznetsov told me that the idea for the large-scale military operation had originated in Havana, not Moscow. It was startling information. As I later discovered, it was also a virtual secret in the Soviet capital. Certainly, Western analysts had assumed that the Soviet Union ... had called on its Caribbean ally for what proved to be crucial assistance."[10]

That Cuba had taken the initiative in coming to the MPLA's defense did not, of course, mean the Soviets were *opposed* to such a course of action. They would not have so responded themselves, nor would they have suggested the Cubans do so. By Moscow's calculations, the risks were too great, the gains insufficient. But if the Cubans themselves were determined to run the risks and pay the cost in lives, Moscow would at least give its tacit blessing. At first, that was all it did give. Only later did it begin to provide large-scale logistical support for the Cuban expeditionary force.

If not at Moscow's behest, why *did* Cuba intervene in Angola? Strangely, Western policymakers, mesmerized perhaps by Metternichian or Mahanesque theories, seemed unable to answer. Cuba could hardly be after raw materials, they noted; it had little industry and thus little demand for them.

Nor could it be after warm-water ports or access to the Cape. It did not, after all, even have a distant-water navy.

All true enough, but Castro *was*—had always been—interested in winning political influence, and in that sense Cuba's intervention was perfectly consistent with the policies and objectives it had pursued in Africa since the early years of the Revolution. Perhaps more than any move Cuba had made in Africa, its intervention to save the MPLA from the South Africans enhanced its leadership credentials in the Third World, and in Africa itself. Cuba was suddenly—if briefly—seen as a major Third World power to which other progressive but weaker governments could turn in times of trouble. If Castro had cherished the dream of playing the kind of role on the world stage once virtually reserved for great powers, this was too perfect an opportunity to pass up. All the constellations were aligned. The MPLA was the sort of progressive force with which Cuba could identify. The enemy, South Africa, was the embodiment of everything the other emerging countries, and especially those in Africa, were struggling against. And, finally, while the Soviets were themselves unwilling to risk much in Angola, they were not *opposed* to Cuban risk-taking. Thus, Castro doubtless calculated, if Cuba could save the day in Angola, that would strengthen its bargaining power with Moscow. Cuba would have advanced the cause of socialism and thus would be in a strong position to ask for better terms of trade and increased assistance from Moscow. Cuba would not have gone in for that reason alone, but it was at least an attractive secondary consideration.

Finally, Cuba won for itself a special place—a partnership—in Angola, and by extension in southern Africa.

Some United States policymakers were quick to aver that Cuba's intervention proved (1) that efforts to negotiate with Castro were futile, and (2) that he was more interested in troublemaking abroad than in improving relations with the United States. The Ford administration, they pointed out, had indicated an interest in improving relations and had opened confidential talks with Havana to explore the possibilities. Castro had responded by going into Angola.

This, of course, was a self-serving and rather exculpatory view. As I have maintained in other writings: "Rather than proving that dialogue and efforts at pragmatic problem solving with the Cubans availed us nothing, the Angola case demonstrated the exact opposite: we almost certainly would have been better off if we had backed the Alvor agreement and discussed the situation frankly with the Cubans and Soviets, advising them that we intended to keep hands off and warning that they should do the same. *That* might have worked. The Soviets were pursuing a policy of détente with us, to which they obviously attached considerable importance. Angola, on the other hand, was a low-priority area for them. Cuba too was interested in improving relations with us—though certainly not at any price. Both might have kept hands off *had we also shown restraint.* But we did not—far from it. What was needed was sound diplomacy, but what we got instead from our government was an irresponsible military operation that backfired badly." [11]

Rationale for Continued Cuban Presence

Cuba came to the assistance of the MPLA against South Africa in 1975 with a view to winning political influence. It remains in Angola 13 years later for the same reason. A special relationship with the Angolan government has long since been assured, but Angolan security has not. South Africa remains a constant threat. And as Cuba's image was enhanced by its defeat of South African forces in 1975, so would its credibility—and self-respect—be diminished if it now let Pretoria and its local ally, Jonas Savimbi, destroy the MPLA government. It is determined to prevent that.

It is in pursuit of Angolan security also that Cuba has become involved with the question of Namibian independence. Since 1976, Cuba's position had been quite clear: Cuban troops were in Angola to defend the latter against South Africa and its Angolan surrogates (meaning Savimbi). They could be withdrawn if UN Resolution 435 (calling for Namibian independence) were honored and South African troops withdrawn.

Cuba, then, has always acknowledged linkage between the presence of its troops in Angola and the independence of Namibia, but its equation is the reverse of South Africa's. Cuba says that Namibia must be independent and free of Pretoria's forces before its own troops leave Angola. Pretoria on the other hand insists that Cuban troops must be out of Angola before it pulls out of Namibia and honors Resolution 435.

The gap between the two positions would not be insurmountable if there were a real interest on both sides in a solution. For its part, Cuba did in 1980 indicate a disposition to consider the possibility of a simultaneous and phased withdrawal, i.e., contingents of Cuban troops would leave Angola as specified contingents of South Africans were removed from Namibia. [12]

In 1984, Cuba and Angola put forward a variation of the phased withdrawal scheme. Under this plan, all Cuban troops would first be pulled back to positions north of the 13th parallel and then, in a subsequent stage, to those north of the 16th parallel. Most of them were then to have been returned to Cuba. Retirement north of the parallels and then to Cuba would of course have been triggered by the phased withdrawal of South African troops from Namibia and Pretoria's stated agreement to respect Resolution 435.

Unfortunately, this proposal was never seriously discussed with the Cubans—or, for that matter, with the Angolans. Perhaps the plan was not satisfactory in all details, but it was at least movement in the right direction and ought to have been pursued. The South Africans, however, had not the slightest interest in it. Any possibility that an arrangement could be negotiated at that point was obviated when in May of 1985, in blatant violation of a cease-fire worked out by the United States, South Africa sent a commando team into the far north of Angola to blow up a Gulf Oil facility.

If there has been a single insurmountable obstacle to a negotiated solution in southern Africa, it has not been Cuba's attitude or position, or Angola's; it has been, rather, South African intransigence. Pretoria has not wished to give up Namibia. It has aimed to keep the so-called Front Line States off balance and on the defensive. It has therefore wanted an end to the fighting in Angola no more than it wanted a settlement in Namibia. In fact, the one effectively blocked the other. By keeping Savimbi attacking the MPLA, South Africa furthered its aim of hanging on to Namibia.

Unfortunately, for ideological reasons, the Reagan administration had until now put the shoe on the wrong foot. It has named Cuba as the intransigent party and sided with South Africa. Thus, when South African troops invaded Angola in force in 1981, the United Kingdom and France voted for a United Nations resolution calling for their immediate withdrawal. The United States vetoed the resolution and continued to insist that *Cuban* troops be withdrawn from Angola.

Then, in 1986, the Reagan administration began providing material and financial support to Jonas Savimbi, thus entering into a de facto alliance with South Africa. One can hardly imagine greater folly. Such an undertaking serves to help South Africa perpetuate the fighting in Angola. It is a prescription for continuing the turmoil and bloodshed, not for ending them. No peaceful solution is possible so long as this joint United States-South

African effort continues. And, finally, it undermines United States relationships with black Africa.

Perhaps in response to the harder United States line followed since 1981, Cuba also adopted a less forthcoming approach—for the time being at least. To his earlier and more reasonable conditions for Cuban withdrawal from Angola, Castro in Janauary of 1985 seemed to add a new one: the end of apartheid in South Africa.[13] Whether this was intended as a trial balloon or to suggest a calculated change in Cuban policy, it proved ephemeral. By 1987, senior Cuban officials were insisting that all Castro had meant to suggest was that the Front Line States, including Angola, could not feel secure so long as apartheid endured in South Africa. Cuba's position, then, if it had in fact ever changed, now came back to what it was in 1984, i.e. Cuban troops can be withdrawn when Namibia is given its independence and the South African threat to Angolan security has ended. In fact, Cuba's position—and that of Angola—may even have softened. In February of 1988, the United States for the first time sat down at the same negotiating table with the Angolans *and* the Cubans to discuss the situation. During these conversations, the former two emphasized that they were willing to contemplate the withdrawal of *all* Cuban troops from Angola, provided the South Africans fulfilled the usual conditions. Previously, Cuban and Angolan formulae, such as the one put forward in 1984, had envisaged the retention of a small number of troops—apparently to guard the oil facilities in the Cabinda enclave.

The fact that the United States was for the first time willing to discuss the matter with the Cubans suggests that its position may be softening a bit also. The key question remains: Is South Africa really willing to give up Namibia?

Other Indications of Cuban Moderation

Conventional wisdom aside, Cuban actions in southern Africa have frequently not fallen within the category of "troublemaking." In 1978, for example, Cuba offered to cooperate with the United States in defusing the crisis caused by the second invasion of Shaba province by Katanganese exiles living in Angola. The United States rather rudely rebuffed these overtures, but Castro demonstrated his seriousness of purpose by going ahead with a joint operation with the Angolan government to disarm the Katanganese and move them away from the border. Subsequently, also, he played a key role in bringing about an easing of tensions, and even a certain rapprochement, between Angola and Zaire.

In 1978 and 1979, Cuba urged the South West African People's Organization (SWAPO) to accept Western proposals for a settlement in Namibia. Also, in 1979, it supported the Lancaster House agreement leading to independence for Zimbabwe, where it has, ever since, maintained a low profile. Contrary to expectations, finally, Cuba has resisted the temptation to become militarily involved in Mozambique, even though the attacks of the South-African-backed guerrillas against the FRELIMO government have given it ample provocation to do so.

Possibilities of A U.S.-Cuban Accord

To be sure, the presence of some 30,000 Cuban troops in Angola is of concern to the United States. In the final analysis, indeed, it would serve no one's interests to turn Africa into a cockpit of superpower struggle, and given that Cuba is the ally of one of the superpowers, the presence of so many of its soldiers in southern Africa could easily lead in that direction. The removal of those forces is a perfectly legitimate United States objective. But the United States must understand that Cuba itself has a legitimate objective in Angola: assuring Angolan security. Only when that problem is addressed frankly and effectively can progress be made toward Cuban withdrawal. Providing for an independent Namibia is an integral part of the problem, and will also be an integral part of any future solution.

The United States and Cuba may be on opposite sides of the ideological barricades in southern Africa but, if analyzed dispassionately, their interests and objectives are seen to be reconcilable. Cuba wants an independent Namibia. So does the United States. The fact that Cuba supported the earlier Western recommendations, moreover, suggests that inevitably distinct preferences as to Namibia's future form of government are not unbridgeable.

Cuba wants a secure Angola. That ought not to be unacceptable to the United States. An Angola—albeit a socialist Angola—at peace with its neighbors, with its civil conflict resolved, and with its doors open to Western economic influence, would in fact serve the long-term United States interest in regional stability.

The United States wants Cuban military forces to withdraw. Cuba is prepared to withdraw them, so long as the two conditions above—neither of which is unacceptable to the United States—are fulfilled.

Where then is the sticking point? Unfortunately, it would seem not to reside so much in Cuba's policy as in United States failure to appreciate its own policy interests and how best to address them. Hopefully, that is changing. The talks begun in February of 1988 have continued. As of this writing, the outline of a settlement appears to be taking shape.

Notes

1. *Revolución* (Havana) 25 September 1959.
2. See my discussion of this point in Wayne S. Smith, *Castro's Cuba: Soviet Partner or Nonaligned?* (Washington, D.C.: The Woodrow Wilson Center for Scholars, 1984),. pp. 7-9.
3. *Ibid.* pp. 18-22.
4. William M. LeoGrande, "Cuban-Soviet Relations in Africa," in *Cuban Studies* (January, 1980), pp. 8-9.
5. John Stockwell, *In Search of Enemies: A CIA Story* (New York: W. W. Norton, 1978), p. 68.
6. John Marcum, *The Angolan Revolution: Exile Politics and Guerrilla Warfare, 1962-1976* (Cambridge: MIT Press, 1978), p. 443.
7. Stockwell, op. cit., p. 188.
8. Marcum, "Lessons of Angola," in *Foreign Affairs* (April, 1976), p. 422.
9. LeoGrande, op. cit., p. 13.
10. Arkady N. Shevchenko, *Breaking With Moscow* (New York: Alfred A. Knopf, 1985), p. 272.
11. Wayne S. Smith, *The Closest of Enemies: A Personal and Diplomatic History of the Castro Years* (New York: W.W. Norton, 1987), pp. 97-98.
12. Cuban officials discussed this possibility with me when I was chief of the U.S. Interests Section in Havana. The conversations were fully reported to Washington but, so far as I know, never elicited any response.
13. See Castro's report to the Third Congress of the Cuban Communist Party, published along with other Congress documents in January of 1986.

6: Learning From Adversity: The Mozambican Experience

GILLIAN GUNN

By virtually any criteria, Mozambique has become one of the most beleaguered countries in the world. A guerrilla war rages over virtually its entire territory; one third of its population hovers on the brink of famine; it enjoys the dubious distinction of having one of the world's worst child mortality rates; its annual debt service obligations far exceed yearly foreign exchange earnings; and large chunks of its transport network are in ruins.

In the West, the deterioration of Mozambique had traditionally interested only a small number of scholars, relief agencies, and policymakers. But recently Mozambique has begun to matter, and for a very simple reason. Mozambique lies next to a country of considerable importance to the West which seems to be entering a phase of prolonged crisis: the Republic of South Africa. This has several consequences.

Because Mozambique shares a porous border with its powerful southern neighbor, whoever rules the territory has the ability to facilitate or hinder efforts to resolve the crisis within the Republic. Mozambique can, for example, restrict or aid infiltration of guerrillas seeking to overthrow apartheid by force, and use its leverage as a potential transit route and refuge to encourage or discourage guerrilla groups' negotiations with Pretoria. Since antiapartheid violence began to escalate in 1984, these Mozambican capacities have received growing attention from Western analysts.

Second, Mozambique's potential as an alternative to South Africa's transport routes has grown in importance since the Republic began to manipulate its own transport facilities in retaliation against rising pressure of international sanctions. Since four of the potential beneficiaries of the Mozambique route—Zambia, Zaire, Botswana, and Malawi—have good relations with the West as a whole, and one, Zimbabwe, has good relations with

Europe (though ambivalent relations with Washington), Mozambique's transport routes are receiving a larger portion of policymakers' time.

Agreement that Mozambique is important, however, does not necessarily produce a consensus about the policies the West should pursue towards it. Judgments about policy are always subjective and, in this case, have become increasingly entangled in ideology. In recent years, Mozambique has joined Angola, Nicaragua, Cambodia, and several other countries that are viewed by one segment of the political spectrum primarily as a battleground in the anti-communist struggle. This group argues that given the "Marxist" orientation of the party currently ruling Mozambique, and its historic connections with the Soviet Union, the forces of RENAMO (the *Resistência Nacional Moçambicana* or Mozambique National Resistance, also known as the MNR*) seeking its overthrow should be aided. This is in the expectation that, once in power, the RENAMO forces would take a more accommodating attitude towards the West than the present government. In concert with such a policy, or as a separate option, it is held that current United States economic aid to Mozambique should be cut, so that the United States would not be aiding a Marxist government. Others contend that in light of recent overtures by Mozambique to the West, continued or even increased United States aid is the best means of decreasing Eastern bloc influence in that country and boosting Western influence.

Yet Mozambique is more than a theater of operations in the cold war; it is also part of the conflict in southern Africa that is fueled by the struggle for power between the races in South Africa. Policy toward Mozambique needs to be grounded in an understanding of the historical process which led that country to its present situation and of the role Mozambique has played in the wider regional context.

PRE-INDEPENDENCE

Mozambique's pre-independence experience falls into two distinct phases, before and after Premier Antonio Salazar came to power in Portugal.

Pre-Salazar

As far back as the early 15th century, Mozambique's chief attraction for foreigners was the access it provided to neighboring territories. The area first

---

*This organization was originally known by its English acronym MNR, reflecting its Rhodesian heritage, In the mid-1980s it began using the Portuguese acronym RENAMO, in order to appear to be indigenous to Mozambique. The use of the term RENAMO in this chapter is not intended to reflect a judgment concerning its legitimacy, but merely to reflect the present most commonly used title.

entered the world economy as a transit point for Muslim traders. When the Portuguese arrived there in the late 15th century they found an already thriving commercial network. Portugal was mainly interested in Mozambique as a provisioning point for ships en route to the Far Eastern spice sources, but the wealth of an inland empire also caught its attention. In 1525 Portugal wrested control of the port of Sofala, now known as Beira, from the Muslim traders. After almost another century of intermittent warfare, the Portuguese forced the rulers of Monomotapa and Malawi into alliance with Lisbon. Portugal ruled the territory from Goa, and considered it part of Portuguese India.

In the mid-18th century, labor shortages in the new world triggered a new economic activity: the slave trade. More than one million Mozambicans were eventually exported as slaves. They were mainly drawn from the northern part of the territory.[1] Portugal outlawed slavery in 1836, but even towards the end of the century slaves were still Mozambique's major export.[2] The slave trade severely disrupted the northern Mozambican economy by removing the strongest individuals from the country.

As the 19th century drew to a close, Portugal faced another crisis in Mozambique—rival colonial ambitions. At the 1884-85 Conference of Berlin the "Great Powers," and in particular the United Kingdom, rejected Lisbon's claim to Mozambique, and decreed that "pacification" and "effective control" were prerequisites for recognition as a colonial power. Because it was predominantly a trading nation with a feudal agricultural economy, Portugal lacked capital to develop an economic infrastructure within Mozambique, as the French and British were doing in their colonial territories. This hindered establishment of "effective control" and "pacification." The situation was further complicated at the turn of the century by the outlawing of slavery, the mechanism by which Portugal exerted leverage on the indigenous aristocracy.

Thus a new four-pronged Portuguese strategy was devised, by which Lisbon: (1) increased military campaigns against recalcitrant hinterland regions; (2) began to rent out large tracts of Mozambican territory to wealthy foreign firms in "concession agreements"; (3) replaced the slave trade with the hiring out of Mozambican workers to the emerging industrialists of the neighboring anglophone colonies of Southern Rhodesia and South Africa, and; (4) encouraged neighbors to direct more traffic through Mozambican ports.

The predominantly British, French, and German companies which took up the concessions encountered difficulty obtaining African workers, so an

1899 native code provided for forced labor, a practice that continued until the 1960s.[3] Local chiefs who refused to enforce the labor regulations were replaced with *regulos* (Portuguese appointed chiefs).

The practice of hiring out Mozambican workers to neighboring countries, began with the 1901 treaty between Portugal and South Africa's Witwatersrand Native Labour Association (WNLA). This treaty gave the WNLA labor recruitment rights in southern Mozambique in return for commissions paid to the colonial administration, and provided for one half of each worker's salary to be paid direct to the colonial government in gold, calculated at a discounted exchange rate. This permitted the government to pay the Mozambican worker the outstanding half of his wages in paper currency, and sell the gold on the international market at a profit. Revenue from gold re-sale became a major source of income for the colonial administration. In southern Mozambique, mine wages provided Africans eight times the sum earned by selling cash crops,[4] which tied the region's economy more to South Africa than to Lisbon.[5] The 1901 treaty also provided that, in return for the supply of cheap labor, Pretoria would divert a set percentage of its trade to the port of Lourenço Marques. By 1917, fees earned from this transport service accounted for one third of Mozambique's income.[6]

Similar relationships were established with other neighbors. The 1914 "Tete Agreement" permitted the British colony of Southern Rhodesia to recruit 25,000 Mozambican workers each year[7] and, following Cecil Rhodes' 1899 completion of a railroad linking Southern Rhodesia with the Mozambican coast, the port of Beira became that territory's most direct rail link with the outside world.[8] Another rail line linking Nyasaland (now Malawi) with Beira was completed in 1922.[9]

These agreements permitted South Africa and Southern Rhodesia economically to colonize southern and central Mozambique respectively, while Portugal remained the middleman.

While this four-pronged strategy assisted Portugal in "pacifying" and "controlling" Mozambique, the colony's economy still did not thrive, particularly after depression struck. Portugal's *Commercial and Colonial Journal* for 1923 agreed that "the financial situation of the province of Mozambique and the conditions in which the economic life takes place, are greatly embarrassing."[10]

From Salazar to Armed Struggle (1926 to 1964)

This was the situation in 1926 when a right-wing coup toppled Portugal's republican government. In 1928 Antonio Salazar became minister of finance, rose to the post of prime minister four years later, and began to formulate his conservative/nationalist policies under the rubric of the *Estado Novo* ("New State"). In Portugal he sought to encourage indigenous industrialists and reduce British economic penetration. Similarly, he hoped to halt the process of Mozambican economic integration with the economies of non-Portuguese colonial powers, and to mobilize the territory's resources for Lisbon's benefit with greater efficiency.

One of Salazar's earliest moves was to rephrase labor laws in deference to international public opinion, while making implementation of those regulations more rigorous. Thus in 1928 forced labor laws were repealed, but a 1930 *Regulamento do Trabalho dos Indigenas* (Regulation of Work of the Natives) obligated virtually all *indigena* (native) African men to perform six months of "contract labor" per year, for either a private employer or for the state. *Regulos* helped the Portuguese enforce regulations,[11] and only migrant workers with contracts in neighboring states, and *assimilados* (assimilated persons) were excused from labor obligations. To attain the status of *assimilado*, an African had to read and write Portuguese, earn wages from a trade, and acquire "Portuguese cultural habits." Salazar put few resources into African education, and by the early 1960s less than one percent of Mozambique's African population was "assimilated."[12]

In 1928 Salazar also ordered all *indigena* females to cultivate cotton and sell it to Portugal at sub-market prices. This secured a cheap supply of raw cotton for the metropolitan country's fledgling textile industry, which Salazar also promoted by prohibiting textile manufacturing in Mozambique. Forced rice cultivation followed in 1942.

Attempts to avoid labor or crop-growing obligations were punished with beatings and sentences to terms of unpaid penal labor. As inefficient as the Portuguese economy was at developing modern forms of production, it evolved extremely efficient police methods.

While such measures ensured more effective extraction of African labor for the benefit of Portugal, they did not reduce penetration of the Mozambican economy by foreign firms. Salazar therefore placed restrictions on foreign investment in the territory, and by 1941 had ended most of the concession agreements. He also encouraged Portuguese peasants and entrepreneurs to emigrate to Mozambique and take over the role of supervising of labor. This strategy also had the advantage of reducing the numbers of impoverished peasants in Portugal.

The numbers of Portuguese arriving in Mozambique increased markedly from 1950 onwards, but the agricultural settlements they established were economically unsuccessful, partly because the relatively poor colony mainly attracted immigrants from the lowest rungs of Portuguese peasant society, who often had only rudimentary agricultural skills. The colonizing failures resulted in most of the 150,000 Portuguese who arrived in Mozambique between 1950 and 1973 congregating in the cities, which in turn reduced job opportunities for non-whites. The poor educational level of the colonists (in 1955 only one third of Mozambique's Portuguese residents were literate),[13] led them to monopolize low-skill jobs that in British and French colonies were usually held by Africans. The overabundance of unskilled urban whites also distorted Mozambique's colonial bureaucracy, for red tape increased to provide clerical employment. (Salazar's refusal to delegate power further encouraged a passive rubber stamp mentality within the bureaucracy.)

While Salazar made vigorous attempts to reduce non-Portuguese domination of agriculture and industry, he left existing transport and labor agreements with foreigners intact, for they helped finance Mozambique's trade deficit with Portugal, which tripled from 1950 to 1960.[14] Throughout the Salazar period, about 100,000 Mozambicans per year worked legally in South Africa, and an equal number went to Southern Rhodesia.

By the early 1960s Salazar had accomplished one of his two goals: he was better mobilizing Mozambique's resources for Lisbon's benefit. He was not, however, significantly reducing the colony's integration with non-Portuguese powers.

Portugal's Response to African Resistance

Lisbon's policies changed as African protest against Portuguese colonialism escalated in the mid- and late 1960s (as will be described below). However, the reforms did not go far enough to stem the unrest, and eventually strengthened the links between Mozambique and the southern African region at the expense of ties with Portugal.

One of the first Portuguese responses to rebellion was officially to abolish forced labor and crop cultivation, and to promise to construct more schools and health posts. However, none of these policies was vigorously implemented. Then in 1965, as the cost of military conflict with African nationalists mounted, Portugal lifted the restrictions on foreign investment. The most important new investment was made in 1966 by an international consortium of British, United States, South African, French, West German, and Italian capital in the Cabora Bassa Dam project in Tete province. The dam was to provide electricity for Mozambique and South Africa. In addition, Lisbon hoped the lake created by the dam would form a physical barrier against guerrilla penetration of southern Mozambique. South African firms also invested heavily in Mozambique. In 1973 South Africa replaced Portugal as the main exporter to Mozambique, and—after Portugal and the United States—South Africa was Mozambique's third most important export market.[15]

Portugal also turned to Western nations for loans, military material, and diplomatic support. President Kennedy was initially reluctant to get too close to Lisbon, but threats to end United States access to the Portuguese-controlled Azores base in the North Atlantic caused Washington to reverse its stand. West Germany and France provided significant loans to Lisbon, and in 1971 the Nixon administration committed $435 million of Export-Import Bank money to Portugal in return for Lisbon's agreement to extend United States access to the Azores until 1974.

Portugal also attempted to create a class of Africans who would identify with Portuguese interests. Africans were recruited into the secret police and the army, and by the early 1970s over 10,000 black troops were fighting in Mozambique's northern provinces.[16] A new black bourgeoisie was also encouraged, educational opportunities were opened up for some, and a token Mozambican black became a member of the Portuguese Assembly. By the early 1970s, more than 100,000 Mozambicans were cooperating in one way or another with the Portuguese.[17]

And of course there was a military component to Portugal's strategy. In 1966 the army began to gather Africans into *aldeamentos* (village settlements), modeled on the "strategic hamlets" established by the United States in Vietnam. This, Lisbon hoped, would cut off guerrillas from contact with the peasant population, and reduce their influence.[18]

The Evolution of FRELIMO

The economic and political environment described above led to an upsurge in black protest in the late 1950s and early 1960s. The peculiar nature of Portuguese relations with Mozambique affected the character of the evolving movements in two ways. First, Portugal's labor export policies exposed Mozambican workers to the more politically mobilized populations of neighboring anglophone states, and inspired them to form Mozambican independence organizations in Southern Rhodesia, Malawi, and Kenya. Second, Portuguese restrictions on African education meant that, unlike radical movements in many other Third World countries, Mozambique's nationalist leadership was generally not exposed to Marxist-Leninist theory in the early days.

The independence movements operated in exile until the UN Trust Territory of Tanganyika under British administration (now a component part of Tanzania) gained independence in December 1961, and offered a secure base for infiltration into northern Mozambique. The three movements then joined together in June 1962 to form FRELIMO (*Frente de Libertação de Moçambique,* or Mozambique Liberation Front) and set up offices in the Tanganyikan capital of Dar es Salaam. The presidential post went to Eduardo Mondlane. Mondlane had become Mozambique's first African to earn a doctoral degree. His studies had been funded by American charitable organizations, and he had married a white American.

The influence of anglophone African independence movements was evident in FRELIMO's strongly nationalist platform, adopted at its first congress held in September 1962. It called for "installation of a democratic regime based on total independence," declared all Mozambicans would be equal, promised to "transform Mozambique from a colonial and underdeveloped country into an economically independent country,"[19] declared FRELIMO would collaborate with all countries "on the basis of mutual respect for national sovereignty," promised to "forbid foreign military bases," and pledged "non-adhesion to a military bloc."[20] The only hints of radicalism were the confirmation of solidarity with all "anti-imperialist forces in the world,"[21] and an expression of "indignation ... against all countries which supply Portugal and help maintain its regime."[22]

Western relations with FRELIMO at the time of its founding were quite cordial. The Ford Foundation in the United States provided $100,000 for the Mozambique Institute, established in Dar es Salaam to educate FRELIMO youth, and the CIA is rumored to have also contributed funds. However, within a year relations began to deteriorate as, responding to Portuguese pressure, the United States reduced support. Mondlane told Kennedy in 1963: "Friends of freedom and democracy cannot comprehend why the United States does not move to the forefront in this struggle for freedom."[23]

FRELIMO also began to prepare for armed struggle. In 1963 it infiltrated trusted members into the country to begin "politicizing" the peasants and secured military assistance from an unusual mix of backers, including the Organization for African Unity (which recognized FRELIMO as the sole legitimate liberation movement in Mozambique), Algeria, Egypt, Israel, China, and, the Soviet Union.

Relations with the Soviet Union, however, were somewhat tense. A FRELIMO activist has since commented: "The USSR took a condescending view towards us, saw us 'country bumpkins.' They did not believe we were capable of launching a successful guerrilla struggle."[24] Relations with China were warmer but still ambivalent. Mondlane visited Peking in 1964, and was attracted by the Maoist idea that the peasantry was a sufficient base for launching a guerrilla struggle. He was, however, unenthusiastic about the cultural revolution. FRELIMO therefore tried to avoid taking sides in the Sino-Soviet dispute.

Armed actions finally began on September 25, 1964. Raids in the provinces of Tete, Zambezia, Niassa, and Cabo Delgado were supposed to occur on the same day, but only in Cabo Delgado, most easily penetrated from Tanganyika, were they effective.

It soon became apparent that the vagueness of FRELIMO's policy pronouncements concealed intense internal conflicts on exactly what the front was fighting for. Decisions could be avoided in the conference hall. But once significant chunks of territory fell under FRELIMO's control and had to be administered, they could no longer be postponed.

Broadly speaking, FRELIMO divided into two camps. One group, led by the FRELIMO chairman for Cabo Delgado province, Lazaro Nkavandame, defined the enemy as colonialism, and wanted independence, without significantly changing the existing social and economic structures. The faction associated with Mondlane, in contrast, gradually came to define the enemy both as colonialism and the economic system "which exploited the peasants." If FRELIMO was to penetrate further into Mozambique, this faction argued, peasants would have to feed the fighters, conceal them from the authorities, and act as an intelligence network. If FRELIMO alienated the peasants, such support would not materialize. Therefore Mondlane and his colleagues began to advocate policies which put the peasants interests first, and adopted phraseology which sounded more and more like socialism.

The conservative/radical split eventually became evident in virtually all aspects of FRELIMO policy:

• The conservatives advocated retention of the structure FRELIMO had borrowed from the anglophone parties in neighboring states, which made guerrillas subservient to political authorities. The radicals advocated merging political and military roles, arguing that the guerrillas were the key link with the peasantry and had to have a say in policymaking.

• Nkavandame played on the northern Makonde ethnic group's longstanding fear of domination by southerners, making much of the fact than many FRELIMO military leaders came from the south.

• The conservatives saw whites as the enemy, while the radicals said the economic system was the problem.

• The Nkavandame group wanted to employ peasants to work in FRELIMO-controlled fields, and make a profit for the war effort by paying laborers with low-value consumer goods. Mondlane's group wanted to collectivize production and "equitably distribute profits."

• The Nkavandame group advocated urban warfare, partly because it would be more easily controlled by FRELIMO's political authorities. The Mondlane group believed Portuguese military strength in the cities would doom any FRELIMO uprising, and advocated a "prolonged people's war" based in the countryside.

• Nkavandame favored retention of traditional tribal social relations. The Mondlane group wanted to mobilize all energies for the war effort, and, seeing the female half of the rural population as an untapped resource, called for the emancipation of women, and the abolition of brideprice, child marriage, and polygamy practices—changes which threatened the power of the chiefs.

• The conservatives believed that secondary school studies at FRELIMO's Mozambique Institute should be geared towards securing foreign scholarships, and that graduates were too valuable to be risked in guerrilla warfare. Mondlane's group wanted the Institute's courses to concentrate on skills useful for the conduct of the liberation struggle, and insisted students return to Mozambique without pursuing university level training.

From the time of FRELIMO's founding, its leaders had cultivated "consensus" decision making, which concealed these conflicts. Disagreements were aired during long secret meetings, in the hope a consensus would emerge, and little was said publicly about the divisions. However, the conflict finally broke into the open in the movement's 1968 Second Congress. Mondlane arranged for the proceedings to be held inside Mozambique, in Niassa province—"liberated territory" controlled by his faction—rather than in Dar es Salaam or Cabo Delgado, where the Nkavandame group enjoyed support. The congress resulted in an almost total victory for the Mondlane "revolutionary" line.

At the congress the tone of FRELIMO's foreign policy switched from the regretful disillusionment with the West, exemplified by Mondlane's 1963 remarks to Kennedy, to defiance. The congress documents declared: "This struggle integrated itself in the world movement for the emancipation of the people," and "The socialist countries ... give us more help than any other peoples."[25] China, the Soviet Union, Bulgaria, Czechoslovakia, Hungary, East Germany, North Korea, and Cuba were listed as suppliers, in that order. While thanking Western humanitarian organizations and the Scandinavian governments for their support, the Second Congress resolutions lambasted the United States, West Germany, France, the United Kingdom, Italy, Belgium, and Japan "for the military, financial and moral support which they give to the colonial-fascist Portuguese government."[26]

While the Second Congress resulted in the radical faction's victory on paper, it did not yet mean victory on the ground, for Nkavandame still controlled Cabo Delgado. Following the death of a Mondlane envoy, apparently at the hands of the conservative faction, Nkavandame was stripped of party responsibilities in January 1969. A month later Mondlane was assassinated. It was not clear if the parcel bomb he opened had been sent by the Portuguese, or by Nkavandame's group, or was the result of cooperation between the two forces.

Mondlane's death triggered a replay of the factional dispute, but by May 1970 the radicals again emerged victorious. Samora Machel was elected president, and Marcelino dos Santos received the vice presidential post. Machel originally had been trained as a nurse, and at the time of Mondlane's death was secretary of the department of defense and one of the military men who most strongly advocated socialist style policies as the best way of gaining peasant support. Dos Santos, a mestizo (person of racially mixed ancestry) educated in France, was of similar political persuasion, but his ideas were more influenced by book learning than were Machel's.

Factionalism more or less under control, FRELIMO moved to increase military pressure on the Portuguese. In 1968 FRELIMO had re-started operations in Tete province and, with Machel at the helm, the guerrillas now intensified actions in the hope of delaying the Cabora Bassa Dam project sited in that province. In 1970 Portugal retaliated with Operation Gordian Knot, designed to recapture Cabo Delgado and divert FRELIMO resources from Tete. FRELIMO suffered major casualties, but had neutralized the Portuguese offensive by the end of 1970.

Nonetheless, the experience convinced FRELIMO it needed more military supplies, and in 1971 Machel began to make the rounds of socialist countries, visiting the Soviet Union, Bulgaria, Romania, the German Democratic Republic,[27] and China. Peking's support for FRELIMO subsequently increased substantially. In the period from 1970 to 1974, China reportedly provided 80 percent of FRELIMO's weapons,[28] and Chinese officers began to give regular training in FRELIMO's Tanzanian camps.

Possibly to please its socialist country backers, FRELIMO's anti-West rhetoric increased even more in this period, and an ideological element entered its writings. A 1971 FRELIMO article said, "This enmity [between FRELIMO and the West] has even deeper roots [than the fact that the West was supporting Portugal] which lie in the contradictions between our ultimate aims on the one hand and the very nature of their society on the other. Thus capitalist society is characterized by the principle of exploitation of man by man ... yet we fight to put an end to these very evils in our own country!" [29]

FRELIMO then increased the amount of territory it controlled in Tete and by July 1972 was able to use the Tete bases to launch operations in the central Manica and Sofala provinces, which contained crucial transport links susceptible to sabotage. However, FRELIMO was never able to control these provinces and, from 1973 until the April 25, 1974 coup which brought down the Portuguese government, the tempo of FRELIMO territorial conquests slowed. On the eve of the coup, the FRELIMO and Portuguese armies were at a standoff, controlling the northern and southern thirds of the country respectively, and disputing the central third.

The Origins of RENAMO

FRELIMO consolidation in Tete and penetration of Manica and Sofala caused consternation in neighboring Southern Rhodesia, (called simply Rhodesia from 1964 on). That territory's white minority government, which unilaterally declared independence from Britain in 1965, feared FRELIMO presence in the border area would permit infiltration of Robert Mugabe's Zimbabwe African National Union (ZANU) guerrillas, referred to as the Zimbabwe African National Liberation Army (ZANLA), who sought to establish majority rule in Rhodesia. Therefore in early 1971 small numbers of Rhodesian troops began to operate in Tete with the Portuguese.[30] Rhodesia's Central Intelligence Organization (CIO) head, Ken Flower, says that at an August 1972 meeting with Marcello Caetano (who had succeeded Salazar in 1968), the CIO "offered to develop an internal resistance movement in Mozambique" to combat FRELIMO, and that Caetano approved. However, the operation stalled because of rivalry between the CIO and Portugal's General Security Directorate (DGS).[31]

According to journalists David Martin and Phyllis Johnson, in March 1974, after ZANLA infiltration into Rhodesia from Tete had escalated, the organizations overcame their mutual distaste and "agreed to start a clandestine movement directed jointly by the CIO and DGS to operate against FRELIMO and ZANLA."[32] On April 24, 1974, the day before the Portuguese coup, Flower met with DGS head Silva Pais in Lisbon to finalize logistical details.[33] The movement was later to become RENAMO.

Conclusion

Thus, on the eve of the coup which removed the Caetano regime from power, the basic dynamics of the forces which would condition the options of any independent Mozambican government were already in place.

(1) Portuguese policy had integrated Mozambique's economic structure more closely with the neighboring territories of South Africa and Rhodesia than with Lisbon.

(2) FRELIMO had adopted a socialist vision for post-independence Mozambique, but had started on this path in reaction to Mozambican conditions, not in reaction to foreign ideological indoctrination.

(3) The internally-generated shift towards socialism had been consolidated in the late 1960s and early 1970s by external dynamics. Western countries,

in FRELIMO's view, supported Portugal's military operations, while socialist countries aided, in differing degrees, the FRELIMO operations. As the battle intensified, FRELIMO began to adopt the ideological trappings of its benefactors, adding a foreign element to its policies, which overlaid, and seemed compatible with, the indigenous socialism already developing in the movement.

(4) Portuguese policy of ignoring the educational needs of Africans, and preserving even the lowest rungs of the Mozambican modern economy for Portuguese settlers, meant that Mozambique's African population had not acquired the skills necessary for running an independent country.

(5) Three developments had created the conditions for the growth of an armed dissident movement should FRELIMO gain power. First, factional fighting had led a number of middle and low level ex-FRELIMO members to feel they had been badly treated. Second, the leaders of the defeated conservative movement stood ready to mobilize this anti-FRELIMO sentiment. And third, Rhodesian intelligence had started to formulate the mechanism to organize and arm these elements.

INDEPENDENCE AND AFTER
The Transition

At 10:45 p.m. on the night of April 24, 1974, Lisbon radio broadcast a popular song, "And After the Goodbye," giving a signal to a group of young officers, calling themselves the "Armed Forces Movement" (MFA), to launch a coup against the government of Marcello Caetano. Wearied by 15 years of battling independence movements in Portugal's African colonies, and convinced victory was impossible, the MFA wanted an immediate end to the bloodshed.

The coup was successful and, after a delay caused by internal divisions in the new Portuguese government, Lisbon signed an independence agreement with FRELIMO. On September 7, 1974 in Lusaka, Zambia, Mário Soares, Portugal's foreign minister, and Machel agreed to a ceasefire, arranged for a FRELIMO-dominated transitional government to take office on September 25, 1974 and scheduled full independence for Mozambique under FRELIMO for June 25, 1975.

The following day, September 8, 1974, a right wing Mozambican group called "FICO" (Portuguese for "I Stay") staged an abortive coup in Lourenço

Marques[34] and called for a Rhodesia-style UDI (Unilateral Declaration of Independence). Africans rioted in response, and Machel called for calm in broadcasts from Dar es Salaam.[35] Portuguese troops eventually took back the facilities occupied by FICO, and on September 25 the transitional government took office. A Machel protégé, Joaquim Chissano, headed the transitional government, apparently because FRELIMO wanted Machel's time free for grass roots political activity.

A month later the violence cycle started again when white commandos killed some FRELIMO members and the black townships exploded in violence. Several dozen whites were killed before the transitional government restored order, and Portuguese citizens began to leave the country in droves, over half departing by independence in June 1975. They took virtually everything movable with them, sabotaging what remained.[36]

The unrest during the 14 months between the Portuguese coup and independence could have made Mozambique vulnerable to interference by the region's white minority regimes. In the event, little materialized, but seeds for future problems were planted.

South Africa took a wait-and-see attitude towards FRELIMO, partly because Pretoria believed the economic leverage it wielded over Mozambique would leave Machel with little choice but to accommodate its interests.[37] Also, South Africa's President Balthazar Johannes Vorster was pursuing a "détente" policy with African states in 1974-75, and feared intervention in Mozambique might damage his image. Thus, in August 1974 when Mozambican whites asked South Africa's consul general in Lourenço Marques (renamed Maputo after independence) for assistance in resisting FRELIMO, he refused.[38] According to FRELIMO sources, the whites then approached South African Minister of Defense P.W. Botha, and he agreed to back them, but the plan was sabotaged by the head of South Africa's Bureau for State Security (BOSS), General H. J. van den Bergh, who believed left-wing Portuguese soldiers would come to FRELIMO's defense.[39] Chissano then had extensive meetings with South African diplomat Brand Fourie in the closing months of 1974, during which time "Mozambique leant over backwards to establish good relations." [40]

Rhodesia's reaction to FRELIMO was quite different, possibly because of FRELIMO's pre-coup commitment to ZANLA. Thus when 55 black and white ex-Portuguese soldiers crossed into Rhodesia in June 1974, they were taken to an isolated military camp for training and possible re-infiltration into Mozambique.[41]

The United States was ambivalent, despite the efforts of Donald Easum, then assistant secretary of state for African affairs. Easum met with Machel in Dar es Salaam in October 1974, indicating his interest in building a new United States relationship with Mozambique. After listening to Easum's presentation, Machel stated he was "prepared to let bygones be bygones" and said he would arrange for Easum to visit Maputo. Several weeks later Easum, who was still traveling in southern Africa, met for an entire morning in Maputo with Chissano and members of his cabinet. Chissano stressed Mozambique's critical economic and relief needs. Easum revealed he had already set up a working group in Washington to study the ways in which the United States might be helpful. He promised to expedite the work of the group when he returned to Washington and indicated that the next step might be a visit to Mozambique by a team of experts to study the situation on the ground. When Easum returned to Washington, he found his proposal for assistance to Mozambique had been shot down by Secretary of State Henry Kissinger, who said any U.S. aid to Mozambique should be given to Portugal to administer since the United States wished to encourage the more conservative faction of the Portuguese regime. Easum was unsuccessful in his efforts to argue his case directly before Kissinger, who had already decided to try to find some other assignment for his activist assistant secretary.[42]

FRELIMO was confused by the United States position. "We made concrete proposals to the United States," Chissano later said. "We never received an answer. We think the United States was concerned about the manner in which we received independence, and our alliance with the socialist countries." [43] Neither the United States nor West German consul was subsequently invited to the independence day ceremonies.

United States unease with FRELIMO was no doubt exacerbated by Machel's high profile visits to East Germany, Bulgaria, Romania, China, and North Korea in late 1974 and early 1975,[44] his Independence Day declaration of "ideological solidarity" with the socialist countries,[45] and FRELIMO's Independence Proclamation promise to "progressively apply ... the just principle of to each according to his work and from everyone according to his ability." [46]

The Learning Process (1975-1982)

During the first seven years of independence FRELIMO went through a painful three-phase learning process, moving gradually from radicalism to a realization that reform would be necessary.

1975-1977: The Radical Era

The success of radical policies in generating peasant support during the war, and Eastern bloc encouragement, led FRELIMO to institute socialist policies in a number of spheres immediately after independence. Within six months it had nationalized education, the medical and legal professions, funeral services, all houses not used by their owners as family residences, and land. FRELIMO did not, however, immediately nationalize all "means of production," as classic Marxist theory demanded.

White reaction to the measures that were introduced, however, gave FRELIMO little choice but to "intervene" in many sectors it had not yet planned to nationalize. By the first anniversary of independence, Mozambique's white population had fallen from 200,000 to 20,000.[47] Because Africans had been excluded from responsible positions, employees of abandoned enterprises were unable to take over the management functions. Farms, shops, and workshops ceased operation, and wages were not paid. FRELIMO therefore appointed state managers for derelict enterprises, started to convert abandoned estates into state farms, and began a network of state-run "People's Shops" to replace the departing Portuguese traders. FRELIMO subsequently argued that if the whites had not left so fast, or if indigenous private managers had been available to take their place, FRELIMO would not have nationalized the economy as fast as it did.

Many of the state manager posts went to the few non-African FRELIMO members, again because of the dearth of trained blacks. Even in the top ranks of the government, non-blacks received a large number of the ministerial posts, as they had the requisite educational qualifications. And among the blacks who received high posts, a disproportionate number were southerners who had enjoyed slightly éasier access to education than their more isolated northern colleagues.

In 1976 the economic situation deteriorated. The north was hit by drought, the south by floods, and FRELIMO's closure of the border with Rhodesia in compliance with mandatory UN sanctions began to lose the nation more than $100 million per year in transit fees and migrant worker remittances.[48] In 1976 Machel also increased support for ZANLA,[49] channeling arms to the guerrillas, and providing them with refuge in the border area.

Rhodesia's prime minister, Ian Smith, responded briskly, starting a series of direct raids on Mozambique which by the end of the war had caused $300 million worth of destruction.[50] He also began to build the fledgling anti-FRELIMO guerrilla movement which had been started just before the Portuguese coup. The Rhodesian CIO recruited a Mozambican refugee, André Matade Matsangaiza, to head the new organization. "André" had served in FRELIMO's forces from 1972 to 1974, worked at a quartermaster's store after independence, and was then sent to a "re-education center" after being accused of stealing a Mercedes car. He escaped and in 1976 made his way to Rhodesia, where he was picked up by the CIO. In 1977 André went back into Mozambique to free colleagues from his old re-education camp and bring them to Rhodesia—a recruitment technique his organization was to use frequently in the future.[51] Afonso Dhlakama soon became André's deputy in the organization, eventually to be named RENAMO. Various reports claim that Dhlakama was an ex-Portuguese army soldier, or, conversely, that he was a FRELIMO officer who, like André, had been sent to a re-education camp, and escaped.

A CIO officer later described the Rhodesian strategy at this time in the following terms: "The MNR gave a cover for Rhodesian operations and, from initial intelligence-gathering operations, moved on to getting recruits and then on to the offensive, disrupting roads and rail links and making it harder for FRELIMO to support ZANU."[52] A CIO/MNR radio station was established in July 1976 to beam into Mozambique.[53]

These actions convinced FRELIMO it needed a conventional army to defend itself against Rhodesia. Machel discovered his prior main arms supplier, China, simply did not have the arms industry to provide the heavy weaponry Mozambique now wanted. Consequently military supplies from the Soviet Union began to increase. The Soviet Union supplied a SAM air defense system to protect the capital and other strategic locations, as well as tanks, artillery and military training. FRELIMO paid for these arms partly with hard currency, and partly by agreeing to let Soviet ships trawl Mozambican waters, the catch being counted against the debt.

The Soviet/FRELIMO relationship still was not warm, however. FRELIMO refused to give the USSR the base facility it desired, and

Chissano reportedly "chided the Soviet ambassador for pressuring Mozambique on the issue" during a diplomatic reception at the end of 1975.[54] Mozambique's constitution supported "the principle of turning the Indian Ocean into a non-nuclear zone of peace,"[55] which would exclude the Soviet Union as much as the United States. FRELIMO also secretly diverted some Soviet weaponry to ZANLA.[56] This displeased Moscow, as ZANLA had close relations with the Chinese, and Moscow favored a rival Rhodesian guerrilla movement based in Zambia. The Soviet Union, for its part, was well aware of the close Machel-Peking links prior to independence, and classified Mozambique as a "Marxist-oriented" country rather than a fully Marxist-Leninist state. Thus the quality of the equipment provided was frequently below that supplied to other Soviet allies, and Mozambique was often required to pay in hard currency. Nonetheless, in 1977 Mozambique did sign a 20-year Treaty of Friendship with the Soviet Union. Non-military agreements with the Soviet bloc were also signed just after independence. The most common were barter deals in which Mozambique traded agricultural produce, coal, and cotton for industrial equipment and vehicles.

Relations with the West were fairly frigid during this first period. A ban on United States economic assistance to Mozambique did little to warm relations.[57] However, the Scandinavian countries provided a $55 million grant for agricultural development[58] and Sweden provided major bilateral assistance.

FRELIMO's radical course was crystalized at the February 1977 Third Party Congress. The meeting: (1) made FRELIMO a vanguard party, thereby accepting an important element of Marxist orthodoxy; (2) declared the "working class" to be the "leading force" in society (even though Mozambique had virtually no working class); (3) gave the state wide-ranging responsibility for planning and running the economy; (4) gave state farms priority in agricultural production, and; (5) called for closer ties with the socialist countries.

Shortly after the congress, FRELIMO nationalized Mozambique's insurance industry, its main oil refinery, most banks,[59] the country's only coal mine, and the processing, transportation, and marketing of cashews, cotton, sugar, copra, and rice.[60] Unlike many of the 1975-76 "interventions," the majority of these nationalizations were not responses to owner desertion, but were ideologically motivated.

By the end of 1977 FRELIMO was drifting away from the traditions it had developed in the guerrilla war. Instead of developing ideology from experience, a process which at least ensured some link between policy and reality, it began to impose ideology upon reality.

1978-1980: "This Isn't Working"

In the two years following the congress, the foregoing policies combined with external events to plunge the Mozambican economy into a severe crisis. The balance of payments fell from its 1976 surplus of $41 million down to a 1978 deficit of $244 million, and an even more serious $360 million deficit in 1980.[61] By the latter year, food was accounting for half of Mozambique's consumer goods imports.[62] Gradually FRELIMO began to realize some policy adjustment would be necessary.

Some of the deterioration was caused by events beyond FRELIMO's control. South Africa's 1977 decision to reduce use of Mozambique's transport network and to cut the number of Mozambican workers employed in the Republic by two-thirds,[63] combined with its 1978 decision to stop paying part of laborer's remittances in discounted gold,[64] ate into foreign exchange reserves. According to a South African source close to the issue, Pretoria's policy shift was due to "political interference from the [South African] right wing."[65] Following the June 1976 Soweto riots, and the flight into exile of thousands of young blacks, the right was worried Mozambique might help the Soweto rebels reinfiltrate into South Africa as ANC guerrillas. The rightward shift in foreign policy was then consolidated by the 1978 replacement of the architect of the "hands-off" policy, Vorster, with Minister of Defense P.W. Botha, who shared many of the right's concerns.

Other factors partially beyond FRELIMO's control—sanctions against Rhodesia and Salisbury's military retaliation—also contributed to Mozambique's economic problems.[66] From 1978 to April 1980, when Rhodesia became the independent state of Zimbabwe, the sanctions continued to deprive Mozambique of transport and labor remittances, while the tempo of direct Rhodesian attacks escalated. Rhodesia-sponsored RENAMO activity also increased, though it was responsible for only a small portion of the total destruction. In 1978 RENAMO had grown to about 500 members, and Rhodesia established a rebel base inside Mozambique on top of the Gorongosa mountain.[67] The 1979 death of "André" and internal RENAMO acrimony about Dhlakama's succession hampered the rebels' activities, but the group nevertheless began to receive modest support from South Africa.[68]

FRELIMO's policy decisions were also responsible for much of the economy's problems. The ideologically motivated emphasis on mechanized state farms, for example, was disastrous. After the departure of the Portuguese, the country simply did not have the management experience or craftsman skills to run them. Inappropriate equipment was imported and not maintained, unsuitable crops were planted, and inputs arrived at the wrong times. It came to cost more foreign exchange for a state farm to produce a ton of grain than it would have cost simply to import the crop.[69]

FRELIMO's treatment of the private peasant sector was perhaps even more damaging. The sector traditionally produced 80 percent of Mozambique's agricultural output, and cultivated 94 percent of the land.[70] But individual peasants received virtually no credit and little fertilizer, seed, or equipment. Poor organization of the state buying organizations, low (state-controlled) prices for crops, and a shortage of consumer goods in rural People's Shops further discouraged production. Peasants who joined cooperatives, as FRELIMO encouraged, fared only a little better.

FRELIMO was slow to respond to the negative impact of its policies for a number of reasons. First, because of the shortage of trained personnel, FRELIMO did not dismantle the colonial machinery after independence, but tried instead to convince ex-colonial bureaucrats to adopt the party's goals. FRELIMO's 1977 decision to increase state control therefore meant it handed control of the economy to a bureaucracy which retained Portuguese inefficiencies, had a rubber-stamp mentality, and lacked initiative. Second, Portuguese cultural influence led many FRELIMO cadres consciously or unconsciously to aspire to the urban *assimilado* lifestyle, and to shun tasks associated with the rural *indigena* status.

Nonetheless, FRELIMO did slowly begin to realize something was wrong. In 1980 the state began to sell off many small businesses, including the People's Shops, and, while state farms retained top priority, plans were introduced to decrease their average size. FRELIMO promised to increase support for the family (i.e. peasant) sector, raise prices for crops, and supply more consumer goods to peasants.

The re-thinking affected foreign economic policy as well. Mozambique began to realize that the socialist countries were unable or unwilling to provide capital and technology, and that the West was the only alternative source. Thus from 1978 to 1980 Mozambique signed loan and aid agreements with the United Kingdom, the Netherlands, Italy, France, Canada, Portugal, and Greece, received an Exim Bank credit from the United States,[71] and in 1980 hosted a foreign investment promotion conference. However, Mozambique still resisted membership in the International Monetary Fund and favored membership in Comecon (an economic association of Communist countries, comparable to the European Common Market). In foreign economic policy, as in the internal sphere, change was coming, but slowly.

In foreign diplomatic initiatives FRELIMO's shift to pragmatism progressed faster, partly because a historic opportunity was presented. In 1979 Britain's Prime Minister Margaret Thatcher convened the Lancaster House Conference, hoping to get a negotiated settlement to the conflict in Rhodesia, which was still technically a British colony. The scheme her diplomats devised included a ceasefire, restriction of combatants to camps, and elections to be run by the British. ZANU leader Robert Mugabe feared a British "trick." Machel, however, was acutely aware of the war's cost to Mozambique, and strongly urged Mugabe to agree. Since Mugabe was dependent upon Mozambican bases, he had little choice but to comply. Machel's role was deeply appreciated by the British government. Machel, in turn, was pleased by Britain's handling of the eventual elections, which resulted in a Mugabe victory and an end to the war which had so drained Mozambique.

So, by 1980, FRELIMO was in a poor economic state, partly because of external factors, but also due to implementation of inappropriate policies. As the costs became apparent, Machel took cautious steps to adjust his internal economic strategy, while also taking bolder measures to rid Mozambique of the costs associated with the Rhodesian war. As the year drew to a close, FRELIMO was highly optimistic about the future.

1980-1982: "Something Must be Done"

By 1980, logic suggested that FRELIMO was now over its troubles. In the event, however, the worst was still to come.

First, reform was still resisted by the bureaucracy. Despite FRELIMO's promises to reduce state farm sizes and allocate higher priority to the peasant sector, the 1981-1990 plan envisaged the reverse. It stressed large projects, called for "accelerated development of state farms on a basis of large areas and mechanization,"[72] planned major investment in heavy industries, and allocated only one quarter of agricultural investment to cooperatives.[73] Even though the reformers said it could not be implemented, and instead began to draw up a more realistic three-year plan, covering the years from 1980 to 1982, the total supply of consumer goods to the rural population fell by one quarter,[74] and, in the event, by 1982 one half of all peasant production was being sold on the black market.

The confusion thus created was caused by the reformers' battle against bureaucratic inertia. Within the bureaucracy were officials with material interests in maintaining the status quo, as well as East European-trained economists, familiar only with the conventional socialist model. Party directives were simply not carried out by the government apparatus. To rectify this, in 1981 two ministers were relieved of their posts and given responsibility for strengthening the party structure.[75] Meanwhile, Machel began a major anti-corruption drive.[76]

The economy also suffered from the impact of the world recession. In 1982 the average price of exports fell by 11 percent while the price of imports rose 3 percent.[77] Interest rates shot up, and by early 1983 foreign debt payments had fallen five months behind. Furthermore, in 1982-83 Mozambique's southern provinces received only one half their normal rainfall.

FRELIMO hoped to solve some of its economic problems by obtaining major assistance from the socialist countries, as well as private investment from the West. Neither materialized to the degree FRELIMO expected. In December 1981, Moscow turned down Mozambique's request to join Comecon,[78]—apparently being reluctant to incur the additional costs for an "unreliable" ally. Perhaps to make up for this, when Iraq told FRELIMO in 1983 that it would no longer be able to supply oil at below market prices, the Soviet Union agreed to provide oil at a price linked to a rolling average of the market price.[79] However, socialist country aid was still far below the level Machel had hoped for. Western investment was little better, and by 1983 the only significant new Western investment was in oil exploration in Cabo Delgado. Economic relations with the West also were damaged when FRELIMO announced in 1981 that it had discovered a CIA espionage ring operating in Maputo, and expelled a number of United States diplomats. The United States responded by leaving the ambassadorial post in Maputo vacant, and, according to FRELIMO sources, refusing Mozambique permission to purchase United States agricultural equipment and Boeing 707s.[80]

A new factor also entered the Mozambique equation at this time: South African military aggression. Mozambique's relationship with the Southern African Development Coordination Conference (SADCC) and the African National Congress (ANC) led Pretoria to take up destabilization where Rhodesia had left off.

The SADCC was formed by the leaders of Angola, Botswana, Lesotho, Malawi, Mozambique, Swaziland, Tanzania, Zambia, and Zimbabwe in the spring of 1980. These leaders realized that Zimbabwean independence removed a sanctions barrier from central southern Africa, increasing opportunities for regional economic cooperation while reducing dependence on South Africa. The transport sector received top priority, and plans were drawn up to rehabilitate the Beira railroad, as well as the road and oil pipeline facilities running from Zimbabwe to the Mozambican coast, which had lain derelict since Machel closed the border in 1976. A functioning "Beira Corridor" would permit Zambia, Botswana, Zimbabwe, and Zaire to divert freight from South African ports. This did not fit with South Africa's "constellation of states" plan, which envisaged close economic links between the Republic and the whole region.

Mozambique's role in the SADCC alone, however, probably would not have triggered major South African aggression. It was FRELIMO's support for the ANC which tipped the balance. Machel officially forbade the ANC bases in Mozambique, and FRELIMO/ANC relations were sometimes strained by perceived ANC condescension, as well as by differences in the analysis of South African conditions. But in the "anything is possible" euphoria surrounding the Lancaster House agreement, Machel began to "look the other way," and ANC infiltration into South Africa increased.

South Africa reacted even before the infiltrations escalated significantly. In March and early April 1980, on the eve of Rhodesian independence, Pretoria transferred RENAMO's radio station, personnel, and equipment to a base in northern Transvaal province.[81] Seven months later it began to airlift RENAMO guerrillas and equipment into Mozambique. By early 1983, RENAMO was operating in nine of Mozambique's eleven provinces, was disrupting railroad traffic on the Zimbabwe-Maputo and Zimbabwe-Beira lines, had destroyed 1,000 rural shops, had kidnapped more than 40 foreign technicians, killing 4, and was stealing or destroying an estimated one quarter of the normally marketed grain.[82]

South African support obviously was responsible for much of the RENAMO's success, but FRELIMO also aided the rebels' advance. Its loss of contact with the countryside, and the rural food and consumer goods shortages caused by its policy errors, facilitated RENAMO recruitment and made peasants less willing to risk retaliation by reporting the guerrillas' presence. FRELIMO's policy of press-ganging young men into the military encouraged some to go over to RENAMO. The excesses of the East German-trained FRELIMO security forces in the late 1970s, which Machel exposed and criticized in 1981, had generated a population of former re-education camp internees with a grudge against the party. FRELIMO's curtailing of chiefs' authority, and administrative reliance on southerners, whites, and mestizos further gave RENAMO an opportunity to tap ethnic and regional emotions. The fact that the majority of top RENAMO leaders came from Mozambique's central region—the area most accessible to the original Rhodesian recruiters—gave the group an additional weapon in putting the regional argument to inhabitants of the central provinces.

And by early 1983 RENAMO was not only getting support from South Africa. Its top leadership had close links with Portuguese industrialists who had lost their property to FRELIMO nationalizations. Funding, as well as staff for RENAMO's external offices, came from Lisbon. RENAMO also convinced some Islamic countries to provide support, on the grounds that FRELIMO was repressing the Islamic religion popular in the northern part of the country. Right-leaning West German political parties, always concerned about governments linked to East Germany, also began to express interest in RENAMO following Dhlakama's visit to Bonn in late 1980.[83]

One major factor, however, worked against RENAMO's interests: its own brutality. The organization's behavior hampered the development of true popular support. Rape and the severing of breasts, ears, and lips in retaliation for non-cooperation became common.[84] RENAMO's inability to articulate a coherent political platform, beyond anti-communist rhetoric, also lessened its chances of developing firm grassroots support.

South Africa also directly attacked Mozambique. On January 30, 1981, South Africa raided ANC houses in the Maputo suburb of Matola;[85] in October, road and railway bridges over the Pungue River near Beira were sabotaged;[86] in November the marker buoys for Beira port were destroyed;[87]

and in December 1982 the oil storage depôt at Beira was sabotaged, causing more than \$20 million dollars worth of damage.[88]

South African manipulation of its economic ties with Mozambique, already begun in 1977, continued. In March 1981, South Africa blocked all cargo going to Maputo for two weeks.[89] Between 1979 and 1983, South African traffic through Maputo fell from 4 to 1.5 million tons.[90] In 1982 Pretoria expelled 12,000 Mozambican farm laborers working in the Eastern Transvaal.[91] Despite this economic hostility, in 1982 Machel decided not to boycott South Africa, estimating it would cost Mozambique over \$100 million per year in lost revenue.[92]

FRELIMO's military response to the South African aggression was at first slow. FRELIMO had long assumed it was most vulnerable to a conventional invasion by Rhodesia and/or South Africa, and concentrated on appropriate training and equipment, generally supplied by the Soviet Union.[93] However, as the war progressed it became clear that Mozambique needed an anti-guerrilla capacity, and in 1982 Machel adjusted his strategy accordingly. He appointed FRELIMO officers with experience in the "Independence War" as commanders for all affected provinces and instructed them to study ways to generate more party support in the countryside. Militias that had been disbanded after Zimbabwean independence were re-formed, and veterans from the liberation war were sent to train new commando units. Machel did not abandon the build-up of conventional defense, however, and in 1982 Zimbabwe sent in 1,000 troops to start guarding the Beira line.[94]

As the war worsened, Machel also began cautiously to explore the possibility of negotiations with South Africa, and in December 1982 ministers from both sides met at the border town of Koomatiport.[95] Their talks made little progress, but a visit by United States Assistant Secretary of State for African Affairs Chester Crocker to Maputo in January 1983, in which he implied Washington might be willing to pressure Pretoria to cease destabilization, convinced Machel this route was still worth exploring.[96]

In the last weeks of 1982 and early 1983 FRELIMO also addressed the issue of the slow pace of economic reform. Machel's provincial military commanders were reporting that better serving of peasant needs was a crucial part of any anti-RENAMO military strategy. The military threw its weight behind the reformers and rekindled debate on a wide range of economic issues as the agenda for the Fourth FRELIMO Congress, scheduled for April 1983, was prepared.

By the eve of the Fourth Congress FRELIMO was just beginning to return to practices it had adopted in the early stages of its own guerrilla war, but had drifted away from after independence. First, it was once again re-integrating military and economic strategies at the party level, as it had in the bush. Second, the ability to respond to situations without pre-set ideological prejudices, which FRELIMO had let atrophy in the years since independence, was starting to return. And third, FRELIMO's early policy of flexibility in foreign diplomacy, exemplified by its pre-independence will-ingness to work with arch rivals, and which had flared back to life at Lan-caster House, began to be more consistently followed.

Pragmatism (1983-1987)

From the Fourth Congress in April 1983 onwards, FRELIMO embarked upon a series of remarkably pragmatic policy initiatives.

1983-1984: The First Initiatives

The first initiative came at the Fourth Party Congress in April 1983. All the failings of past FRELIMO economic policies were closely examined. Marcelino dos Santos's remarks were typical of the tone of the proceedings. "We are not bothering about manufacturing the hoe," he said, "because we are awaiting the arrival of the tractor we must import. We are distributing tinned beans, that cost foreign exchange, in a communal village that pro-duces beans and from which no one has bothered to collect surplus produc-tion. We overload the peasant with items he does not use, but do not pro-vide him with a lamp, cloth, a file, or a hammer. Nonetheless, we expect him to exchange his production for goods he does not need."[97]

The new policies announced at the end of the congress represented a major, but not complete, victory for the reformers. The congress gave agriculture top priority; promised peasants greater access to seeds, fertilizer, agricultural tools, and consumer goods; declared private farmers eligible for government support (though they would have to sell a portion of their production to the state); endorsed private shops (but subjected them to government "monitoring"); recognized the need to raise prices paid to producers; promised to shift invest-ment from big new projects to complete projects already started, and smaller scale new projects; praised the role of foreign capital; promised to break up large state enterprises into smaller units; pledged to reward good workers with salary increases; and called for decentralization of planning.[98]

The self-critical language of the congress proceedings indicated FRELIMO intended to pursue reform with maximum urgency. But, as in previous reform attempts, the urban bias of some party members interfered with implementation. For example, despite all the talk about the importance of the family sector, the Fourth Congress expected a 40-45 percent increase in its production over the following two years, while consumer goods to this sector were to increase only 20-23 percent. Priority in consumer goods was to go to "workers." [99] Concerns of those who feared loss of state control were also evident, particularly in the limits placed on private peasants and shopowners.

Implementation of the congress policies over the following twelve months was also hampered by the security situation and the weather. Goods and services simply could not be safely transported to many areas due to RENAMO sabotage of transport routes. The 1983 rains failed, and 1984 brought a combination of central/northern drought and southern floods. An estimated 350,000 people lost their crops in the floods, and the death toll from the drought was estimated at between 30,000 and 100,000.[100]

As the party sought to overcome these difficulties, it also continued the diplomatic initiatives started with South Africa in late 1982. At first discussions progressed slowly. A meeting between South African and Mozambican officials on May 5, 1983 in Koomatiport achieved little, and 18 days later South African jets bombed two Maputo suburbs in response to a bomb explosion in Pretoria which South Africa blamed on Mozambique-based ANC operatives.[101] South Africa also dropped nine tons of arms to a RENAMO base in August 1983.[102]

Machel concluded the only way to get South Africa to negotiate would be to convince the West to force Pretoria's hand. Throughout 1983 Mozambican ministers repeatedly visited Washington and stressed that FRELIMO viewed South Africa, not the United States, as the main enemy. They also implied Mozambican willingness to facilitate negotiations between the MPLA *(Movimento Popular de Libertação de Angola,* or Popular Movement for the Liberation of Angola) government in Angola and the United States government on withdrawal of Cuban troops from Angola, and also to mediate between the MPLA and the South African-backed UNITA (*União Nacional para a Independência Total de Angola*, or National Union for the Total Independence of Angola)—the guerrilla group seeking its overthrow. In October, Machel visited Portugal, France, Britain, Holland, and Belgium, where he was well-received.

The lobbying paid off. In November, the United States made a positive gesture by filling the vacant ambassadorial post in Maputo. When South African Foreign Minister Pik Botha visited Europe in November 1983, British Prime Minister Margaret Thatcher urged him to be more accommodating in negotiations with FRELIMO. United States diplomats also advised Pretoria that the level of destabilization was unacceptable.

The effect of Western pressure on South Africa was uneven, however, affecting the diplomats more than the military. Thus on October 17, and again on December 7, South Africa attacked ANC offices and residences in Maputo. But when Mozambican and South African diplomats met again in December 1983 in Mbabane, the capital of Swaziland, Pretoria dropped previous demands that FRELIMO recognize the South African homelands and expel all ANC diplomats as well as military personnel, requesting instead that economic links between South Africa and Mozambique be increased. Mozambique responded that it first wanted a guarantee South Africa would cut RENAMO aid. While discussions continued, both sides agreed not to increase aid to their guerrilla allies.

The ball was now rolling, and simultaneous meetings occurred on January 16 in Pretoria and in Maputo, at which working groups on security, tourism, Cabora Bassa, and economic matters were established. Further clarification of terms occurred at a February 20 meeting in Maputo, and at a March 2-3 meeting in Cape Town.[103] During this period the United States played a discreet behind-the-scenes role, urging the two sides to agree.

Finally, on March 16, 1984, with much ceremony, Machel and Pik Botha met on the banks of the Nkomati river and signed the Nkomati Accord. Both countries agreed to "refrain from interfering in the internal affairs of the other," to prevent the use of their territories for bases, transit or accommodation of guerrillas, not to make land, sea, or air attacks or sabotage operations, and to end radio broadcasting stations and telecommunications facilities for their respective guerrilla allies. The understanding was that the

ANC military would leave Mozambique, but that an ANC diplomatic mission would be permitted to remain.

The Nkomati Accord caused strains in a number of spheres. Machel departed from FRELIMO's tradition of consensus decision-making; he involved a small group of top officials in the negotiations, and informed the rest of the government only when the accord was almost a fait accompli. The South African government was similarly divided. Military intelligence had built a close relationship with RENAMO, and was reluctant to abandon its friends, while the Department of Foreign Affairs (DFA), possibly because of United States pressure, appeared enthusiastic about the accord. The signing also damaged FRELIMO's relations with the Soviet Union, as Moscow considered the deal unfortunate. It was also unpopular with the Front Line States, who were uneasy about the impact of the deal's economic aspects upon the SADCC's programs.

1984-1986: The Aftershocks

FRELIMO was in an optimistic frame of mind in March 1984. However, many of the post-Nkomati hopes were to meet the same fate as the post-Lancaster House expectations.

FRELIMO's first task after Nkomati was to control the ANC. The government asked that organization, which had responded to Nkomati by calling Mozambique a "South African Bantustan," to divulge its arms cache locations so that weapons could be safely shipped to another country. The ANC insisted it had no such caches. But South Africa gave FRELIMO intelligence on arms locations, and FRELIMO soldiers inspecting the indicated sites found large quantities of weapons. FRELIMO was furious and most ANC members were quickly put on planes out of the country. Only a small diplomatic delegation was allowed to remain, as provided by the accord.

South Africa appeared to comply with the accord equally rigorously. The RENAMO radio station was shut down, and a procession of South African businessmen passed through Maputo. South Africa seemed to be returning to Vorster's 1975 strategy; the manipulation of Mozambique/South Africa economic integration rather than the internationally embarrassing use of military force.

Machel was comfortable with this arrangement, believing that the greater interest South African businessmen had in Mozambique, the more pressure they would exert on Pretoria to live up to the Nkomati terms. Thus FRELIMO asked South Africa to employ 8,000 more Mozambicans in its mines in 1985,[104] direct more freight through Mozambican ports, buy more power from Cabora Bassa Dam at a higher tariff, and help rehabilitate Mozambican railways and port facilities. South Africa agreed to all the requests. Furthermore, South African farmers offered technical assistance and investment and hotel chains looked into rehabilitating Mozambican tourism.

Talks also began on South African/Mozambican military cooperation. FRELIMO requested arms and intelligence information on RENAMO arms caches and communication techniques. South Africa did not refuse, but was reluctant on all counts.[105]

An equally dramatic part of the immediate post-Nkomati period was the vigor of Western, and particularly United States, reaction. In April 1984, the ban on United States aid to Mozambique was lifted and, in July, Mozambique signed an agreement with the United States Overseas Private Investment Corporation, providing bilateral investment guarantees.[106] In September Mozambique became an IMF member, the United States authorized an $8 million bilateral aid program, and FRELIMO released a liberalized investment code. In the same period, the United Kingdom responded favorably to a FRELIMO request to start training Mozambican officers, and Mozambique's plans to join the EEC's Lomé Convention were confirmed.

However, the optimism was dampened by the deterioration of the military situation. Instead of decreasing, RENAMO activity escalated. The power line from South Africa to Maputo was cut, roads linking South Africa and Swaziland with Maputo were attacked, the road north from Maputo became dangerous. Attacks in the north of the country similarly increased, apparently launched from Malawi, and the railroad linking Malawi to the port of Nacala was cut. Refugees began to pour into the cities and neighboring countries.

Suspecting the South Africa military might still be aiding RENAMO, but hoping the attacks were simply RENAMO's last gasp, FRELIMO, with encouragement from South Africa's Department of Foreign Affairs (DFA), extended feelers for a negotiated solution. In May, a FRELIMO envoy had an inconclusive meeting in Frankfurt with RENAMO representative Evo Fernandes, a Portuguese citizen of Goan descent who had worked for Portuguese industrialist Jorge Jardim in Mozambique. The FRELIMO envoy offered an amnesty, but Fernandes demanded cabinet posts for RENAMO leaders, a government of national reconciliation, and a multi-party system.[107]

South Africa's DFA then arranged more meetings in Pretoria and, on October 3, Mozambican and RENAMO delegations stood in the same hall while Pik Botha read the "Pretoria Declaration." This (1) acknowledged Machel as president of Mozambique; (2) said armed activity in Mozambique must stop; (3) requested South Africa to play a role in implementaton of the declaration; and (4) established a commission to aid the implementation of the declaration.[108]

Then, in the midst of ceasefire negotiations, Fernandes apparently received a phone call instructing him not to sign anything until he travelled to Lisbon for consultations. A week later RENAMO announced that Machel was only recognized as president until elections could be held, and meanwhile the war would continue.

Two factors seem to be responsible for the failure of negotiations. First, as will be detailed below, RENAMO was indeed continuing to receive military supplies from the South African military, possibly without DFA knowledge, and therefore the pressure to cut a deal was less than it appeared. Second, South African diplomats wanted economic access to Mozambique and a cessation of ANC infiltration, and as they felt they were obtaining this, peace seemed acceptable. RENAMO's Portuguese patrons, however, wanted the return of nationalized property and an opportunity to re-establish their pre-independence lifestyle in Mozambique, and apparently urged RENAMO to refuse a deal until this was secured.

FRELIMO therefore turned back to the military option. In June 1985, Zimbabwe agreed to send a further 5,000 combat and support troops into Mozambique, while Tanzania agreed to train Mozambican recruits to fight in the northern provinces.[109] The newly arrived Zimbabwe troops took RENAMO strongholds relatively easily, but the FRELIMO troops which then occupied the re-won territory performed poorly. Reports of FRELIMO soldiers fainting from hunger, raiding villages for food, and melting into the bush when RENAMO approached, became rife. Coordination between the Mozambican and Zimbabwean troops was also poor, as some FRELIMO commanders felt humiliated by Zimbabwean aid, and feared that their neighbor had territorial designs on the Beira corridor.

Meanwhile, hopes for economic cooperation with South Africa dimmed. Most of the companies interested in investments were unable to provide finance and, given South Africa's pariah status, Mozambique's friends were not about to foot the bill. The South African government's political commitment to the economic link also declined, and South African rail traffic through Mozambique decreased by a third between 1983 and 1985.[110]

The improvement in United States-Mozambique relations also began to be thwarted by the American right. United States aid to Mozambique increased to $66 million in 1985,[111] and in the spring of that year the State Department requested permission to reprogram a small amount of military aid for Mozambique, to be spent on non-lethal equipment. Congress turned the request down and when the Department requested $1.15 million in non-lethal military aid and training for 1986, Congress made it contingent upon Mozambique holding elections. Furthermore, Congress restricted development aid to the Mozambican private sector.

A military and propaganda breakthrough then occurred in late August 1985 when Zimbabwe/FRELIMO troops overran RENAMO headquarters in Gorongosa. They discovered a RENAMO diary which showed South African military intelligence had delivered a large quantity of arms to RENAMO shortly before the Nkomati signing, and had promised Dhlakama aid would continue after the signing. Furthermore, the diary showed, the military had advised RENAMO not to accept FRELIMO's peace terms, and had bugged Foreign Minister Pik Botha's meetings with FRELIMO. A deputy of Pik Botha had flown to Gorongosa with South African military officers on three occasions after the Nkomati signing, while—also after the signing—South Africa had continued to train RENAMO, and had made repeated arms drops.[112]

On September 18 Pik Botha claimed the Nkomati violations were "technical," and were connected with Pretoria's attempts to get RENAMO to the negotiating table, as FRELIMO had requested. Machel was unconvinced, and suspended the Joint Security Commission which had been set up as a Nkomati watchdog. But he did not abrogate the agreement, saying Mozambique would continue to adhere to its side of the bargain.

Machel intended to use evidence of South African Nkomati violations to rally Western aid for Mozambique. The Gorongosa diaries were still hot news when Machel went on a scheduled visit to the United States, and met with President Ronald Reagan. Machel's mischievous sense of humor went down very well in Washington but events concerning Angola soon made it more difficult for the United States to respond to his appeals. In early 1986, UNITA leader Jonas Savimbi visited Washington and received red carpet treatment.

Within weeks a United States decision to aid UNITA in its fight against the MPLA government leaked to the press. The American right, which had already hampered State Department aid efforts for FRELIMO, began to talk about the need to extend the "Reagan Doctrine" to Mozambique in the form of RENAMO aid.

The right-wing lobbyists ran into problems over the second half of 1986, however, when internal RENAMO squabbling became public. Fernandes was demoted as part of RENAMO's attempt to present a more "black nationalist" rather than "white Portuguese" image and charges of embezzlement led to the expulsion of other officials. United States foundations backed rival RENAMO factions, and a new "political wing" of RENAMO was founded only to be disowned by Dhlakama. Domination of RENAMO leadership by members of the Manica tribe (from the center of the country) was rumored to be causing internal friction, and rival individuals repeatedly turned up in Western capitals, each claiming to represent the organization. Nonetheless, the right made the administration hesitate to push hard for aid to Mozambique.

While relations with the United States experienced these difficulties, relations with Europe remained good. In February 1986 the United Kingdom began training Mozambican officers in Zimbabwe, and later in the year Britain sold sophisticated rifles to the Mozambican army. However, Mozambican lack of finance, combined with concern that weapons might fall into the "wrong hands," prevented the British from meeting more of FRELIMO's arms requests.

A new element then entered the picture in the second half of 1986: sharply increasing violence in South Africa. Not only did Pretoria suspect Mozambique of aiding the ANC, but threats of new international sanctions triggered by the escalating violence made Pretoria redefine the whole Mozambique/South Africa relationship. The prospect of impending Western sanctions led Pretoria to seek to force all regional traffic though South Africa, so it could convincingly threaten to cut off the region's links with the outside world if sanctions were imposed. The Beira Corridor from Zimbabwe to the Mozambican coast thus took on a new significance, as it is the shortest non-South African route for Zambian, Zimbabwean, and some Zairean and Botswana traffic. This is the reason, FRELIMO believes, why RENAMO attacks on Beira began to increase in mid-1986. Many raids seemed to originate in Malawi, which Machel accused of facilitating continuing South African aid for RENAMO. In September Machel, Mugabe, and Zambia's Kenneth Kaunda urged Malawi President H. Kamuzu Banda to turn over to FRELIMO all RENAMO guerrillas located in his country. Banda responded by simply telling RENAMO to leave his territory. A reported 10,000 guerrillas flooded into Mozambique and began a rapid push towards the coast, apparently hoping to win access to a point from which sea resupply might be conducted.[113]

Tensions with South Africa hit a new high in early October when a landmine exploded in the Transvaal, not far from the Mozambican border, and Minister of Defense Magnus Malan warned, "If President Machel chooses terrorism and revolution, he will clash head-on with South Africa." Shortly afterwards, South Africa announced it would not recruit any more Mozambican workers, and would not renew the contracts of existing workers when they expired, cutting Mozambique's foreign exchange revenues by approximately one third.[114] Tensions escalated even further on October 17 when Mozambique's official news agency announced it had received private warnings of a South African plot to assassinate Machel.

Machel faced additional internal problems during these months. Young black FRELIMO cadres became restless, complaining about the monopolization of top posts by *"historicos"*—i.e. figures from the pre-independence era—and also pointing out the high proportion of mestizos in powerful positions. The dislocation of peasant populations by RENAMO activities, combined with the agricultural legacy of drought and mismanagement, brought the country to the brink of mass famine. In September Mozambique announced that it would be able to provide just over one third of the 715,000 tons of grain needed over the following 12 months. Its debt service ratio was up to 170 percent; the budget deficit was up to $250 million, and defense spending was accounting for 43 percent of total government expenditure.[115]

Clearly then, as Machel boarded a plane on October 19, 1986, on his way back from a meeting of the Front Line States in Zambia, Mozambique was in crisis. The relationship with socialist countries and internal FRELIMO unity had been shaken by the Nkomati signing, and yet Nkomati had not brought peace. Western countries had been impressed by the non-aggression pact, and were providing more aid, but for various reasons were having difficulty responding to all FRELIMO's needs. The relationship with South

Africa was as bad as ever, and the Mozambican people were suffering more than at any point in the past. Perhaps Machel was pondering these problems as his plane crashed into a South African hillside minutes before its scheduled arrival in Maputo.

The Chissano Era

Considering how bleak Mozambique's future appeared at Machel's death, the Chissano era that followed was surprisingly positive. Six months after assuming office, he had won FRELIMO some breathing space in both economic and security spheres, though the country still remained in deep crisis.

The selection of Foreign Minister Joaquim Chissano as Machel's successor went smoothly. FRELIMO sources say the party had agreed years before that Chissano should succeed Machel, and six days after Machel's funeral, FRELIMO's Central Committee ratified the choice. The new president had been Mozambique's foreign minister for 11 years, and was closely associated with both Machel's "opening to the West" and growing economic pragmatism.

Chissano's top priority upon taking office was to continue Machel's attempts to improve relations with neighbors, and Malawi was the first to receive attention. Chissano's task was rendered more difficult by Pik Botha's November 6, 1986 announcement that documents found in the wreckage of Machel's plane showed FRELIMO had been plotting, with the Zimbabweans, to topple Malawi's President Banda by aiding anti-government guerrillas and destroying bridges linking the landlocked state with the sea.[116]

Chissano denied the claim, and began intensive shuttle diplomacy between the Mozambican and Malawian capitals. On December 18, 1986 the two states signed an agreement aimed at "the physical elimination of armed banditry ... and ensuring utilization of Malawi's traditional routes to the sea." [117] There were some doubts whether Banda would live up to the deal, as similar agreements had been signed in the past to no avail. But in March 1987, Malawi prepared to send 300 soldiers into Mozambique to protect transport routes[118] and Banda was reportedly permitting FRELIMO forces to enter his territory, circle behind RENAMO elements, and force them into the waiting arms of Zimbabwean/FRELIMO units on the Mozambican side of the border.[119] "Malawi," Chissano said, "is on our side." [120]

Chissano's next priority was to obtain more aid from the Front Line States. He met with Mugabe at Victoria Falls on January 15, 1987,[121] and convinced his colleague to increase the number of troops committed to Mozambique. Shortly afterwards Zimbabwean forces began to operate outside the Beira corridor area, where they had previously been concentrated, and changed their tactics, both taking and holding territory. Tanzania was also persuaded to provide personnel, and by March 1987 at least 600 Tanzanian troops were operating in northern Mozambique.[122]

There was a price for this aid, however. The Front Line leaders wanted FRELIMO's forces to cooperate better with their allies. Partially in response to this request, and also because it was a move Machel had pledged to make shortly before his death, Mozambique's chief of staff, Col. Gen. Sebastião Mabote, was replaced by Lt. Gen. Armando Panguene, who had a better relationship with the Zimbabweans.

The increased aid from the Front Line states paid off. Between December 1986 and March 1987 Zimbabwe/FRELIMO/Tanzanian forces partially rolled back the RENAMO offensive. They retook much of Zambezia province, re-opened major highways, recaptured several towns, and retook a key railway bridge over the Zambezi River.[123] FRELIMO believes this thwarted a RENAMO attempt to secure a new supply route running from the coast up the Zambezi.

Chissano also devoted attention to that most powerful of neighbors, South Africa. Despite the timing and location of Machel's death, which implied South African complicity, FRELIMO initially was very careful to say the event occurred in "circumstances that are unclear." Analysis of the cockpit voice recordings subsequently revealed a possible phantom navigational beacon, that may have been activated to confuse Machel's Soviet pilots and cause the crash. But, as of spring of 1987, Chissano still said, "We do not know who planted that instrument. We must still continue the investigation."[124]

The South Africans were relatively well disposed towards Chissano, remembering his conciliatory attitude as leader of the 1974-75 transitional government. Immediately after taking office Chissano emphasized that he would continue to honor the Nkomati Accord, even though, he claimed, South Africa was not complying with its side of the bargain. He subsequently explained, "It is more difficult for South Africa to operate against us with the Nkomati accord [than] it would be ... without the ... accord."[124] He also insisted, as had Machel, that Mozambique would not impose economic sanctions on South Africa. And in early January 1987, when Pretoria asked Chissano to expel six ANC members it claimed were using Mozambican territory to plot sabotage within South Africa, he complied, even though this was just days before major celebrations to commemorate the ANC's 75th anniversary. South Africa responded to Chissano's conciliatory tone by offering to cut the contracts of only half the Mozambicans working in South Africa, rather than all of them,[126] and Chissano began to say there was no concrete evidence of current South African aid to RENAMO, only suspicions.[127]

Relations with neighbors somewhat under control, Chissano turned to internal government affairs. Machel had been planning a government reshuffle that would move the younger generation more to the fore, and retire some of the "historicos," which also would reduce the proportion of mestizos in the government's top ranks. Chissano had to move much more cautiously than Machel, as he was still consolidating his power. However, in mid-January 1987 he did make some changes. Minister of Health Pascoal Mocumbi was moved from his post to the vacant foreign minister's post, a change that was well received in Washington. Sergio Viera, the mestizo security minister, who incidentally had been less than enthusiastic about the Fourth Congress economic reforms, was removed from his post and assigned to teach at the party school. Armando Guebuza, the charismatic and outspoken former minister of the interior, viewed as a role model by those young black FRELIMO members who resented mestizo prominence in the government, was given the important post of minister of transport and communications.

The economy was the next area to receive Chissano's attention, and on January 30 he announced a series of measures: a 420 percent devaluation; rent hikes for urban dwellers; a 50 percent wage increase to help workers cope with the increased costs that devaluation would create; continued "liberalization" of prices for agricultural produce; a new wage policy designed to reward productive workers; new tax collection techniques; new price rises for a wide range of goods and services, mainly those used by the urban populations; and a "strict restriction on the issuing of new money" and credit controls.[128] Work also began on a new law to promote private investment by Mozambicans.[129]

Many observers interpreted these changes as Chissano's abandonment of socialist goals, but the new president insisted: "Our country has defined the construction of socialism as the objective of Mozambican society." [130]

The economic reforms came none too soon. In early 1987 the government admitted that Mozambique's debt service ratio had reached 200 percent,[131] and that 1986 commercial agricultural production had dropped by a fifth.[132] These statistics showed Mozambique urgently needed new financing. Discussions with the International Monetary Fund for a ten-year loan picked up momentum following the introduction of the new reforms.[133]

Chissano did not neglect relations with foreign countries in his first months in office. At first he seemed to have little good to say about the socialist states, and focused on the West. The U.S. Under Secretary of State for Political Affairs, Michael H. Armacost, visited Mozambique in mid-December 1986, and reportedly came away highly impressed with Chissano.[134] The United States senior deputy assistant secretary of state for African affairs, Charles Freeman, then visited Mozambique in March 1987, following a United States donation of an extra $50 million in food aid in February.[135] Britain was even more forthcoming. In January 1987, it agreed to double the number of Mozambicans entering its training program,[136] and in February it sent Minister of Cooperation Christopher Patten to discuss the possibility of increasing British aid to Mozambique by almost 50 percent.[137]

The Soviet Union, which had been overshadowed by these visits, then began to receive more attention. Three high-ranking Soviet delegations visited Mozambique in the first three months of 1987; in January the Soviet ambassador in Mozambique promised to continue to aid Mozambique "with no conditions"[138]; and in March the tenth anniversary of the Mozambique-Soviet cooperation treaty was celebrated with great fanfare in Maputo.[139]

Chissano stated his view on East/West alliances in an interview with the Italian news agency ANSA, saying: "Our relations with the countries of the East are based on the exact same principles as those with the West, respect for sovereignty and independence ... It will be necessary for the world to begin treating us as responsible adults and not as children. The United States and the Soviet Union have economic relations ... I do not see why we should not have relations with both blocs ... It was not our choice [to accept military assistance only from the Eastern countries] but it is a reality. We always said we were prepared to accept military aid but the Western countries had difficulties ... [T]here is only one thing to do for those countries which feel they are not well represented in Mozambique: Create the premise for increasing their presence here ... Our problem is not one of making a choice in the field on the basis of ideology." [140]

One major area in which Chissano did not launch major new initiatives was that of negotiations with RENAMO. Though he reaffirmed FRELIMO policy of clemency for RENAMO members who turn themselves in to government forces, he warned: "The continuation of the struggle, without pause, against armed banditry in our country constitutes the most sacred and fundamental of the tasks in this phase of our history. It is a struggle in which there can be no form of compromise." [141] Sources close to FRELIMO speculated that Chissano might be willing to negotiate with RENAMO, but only after rolling back their military operations more decisively and better sealing off their supply routes.[142] RENAMO similarly showed little enthusiasm for a peaceful solution. Some RENAMO officials expressed interest only in a "hand over of power," while others claimed RENAMO would offer a ceasefire and amnesty to FRELIMO in return for free elections and the expulsion of foreign troops.[143]

Another field in which Chissano refrained from action was that of extra-African military intervention. He, like Machel, is said privately to believe the MPLA made a mistake by having a long-term Cuban presence, and press reports claim Chissano turned down a Cuban offer of troops.[144]

By mid-1987, therefore, Chissano had several accomplishments to his credit. He had partially stabilized the relationship with South Africa, worked out a modus vivendi with Malawi, convinced the Front Line States to increase their military commitment to Mozambique, and apparently had succeeded in remaining in the good graces of the East and the West. On the home front, he had introduced major austerity measures which finally forced the urban population to bear some of the brunt of the country's economic difficulties, had reshuffled the government in a manner that slightly increased the power of blacks, and had retaken chunks of territory from RENAMO, albeit without turning the military situation firmly in FRELIMO's favor.

Most importantly, Chissano was continuing the thread started under Machel in 1983 of returning to the pre-independence FRELIMO practice of deriving policy from practical realities, rather than from ideological abstractions.

CONCLUSION

The preceding history permits two different types of conclusions. First, conclusions about how Mozambique came to its current predicament. Second, conclusions about what the United States should do about that current situation.

Mozambique's evolution

Mozambique's current predicament traces its roots to the days when the first foreigners landed on its shores. In the pre-independence period the underdeveloped state of the Portuguese economy resulted in the territory becoming economically colonized by Southern Rhodesia and South Africa, which were relatively prosperous. Moreover, Portugal's colonial policies limited African access to modern skills. Thus the 1974-75 Portuguese exodus left Mozambique extremely poorly prepared to face the challenges of independent existence.

The way FRELIMO has coped with those challenges has also been conditioned by its pre-independence experience. FRELIMO moved gradually from a nationalist program to a socialist one, with the evolution spurred initially by conditions of guerrilla struggle, and only secondarily by the encouragement of socialist foreign backers who themselves followed the socialist model. The advice of those supporters was taken particularly seriously, inasmuch as the advocates of the capitalist model, the West, seemed to ally themselves with Portugal's colonial policies.

The pre-independence regional situation also conditioned the post-independence options FRELIMO would face. The proximity of Rhodesia, and that regime's interest in preventing Mozambique from being used as a base by Rhodesian guerrillas, led to plans being laid for the creation of an anti-FRELIMO guerrilla force in the future. FRELIMO's own internal problems as it struggled with ideological questions in turn created a pool of potential future recruits for such an organization.

The effect of this legacy was clearly evident when FRELIMO took power in 1975. The success of the radical approach in generating peasant support during the war, the encouragement of foreign allies, and the absence of indigenous entrepreneurs to take over abandoned enterprises led the party to institute radical economic, political, and foreign policies. However, the new policies proved ineffective on all counts. South Africa manipulated economic ties with Mozambique; Rhodesia escalated destabilization actions; mother nature alternately inflicted drought and floods; and the pool of potential anti-FRELIMO recruits was enlarged. The leadership came to realize that changes would have to be made.

The process of returning to the pre-independence habit of deriving policy from actual conditions began in the late 1970s and early 1980s. The turning point came when the military men, responding to the worsening security situation caused in part by South Africa's 1980 decision to take over patronage of RENAMO, threw their weight behind the reformers, insisting economic policies would have to be changed if the peasantry was to be won over for FRELIMO. The most important pragmatic initiatives were the 1983 Fourth Congress economic reforms, the 1984 Nkomati Accord, and the increasingly vigorous courting of Western aid and investment from 1980 on.

The pragmatism only partially paid off. South Africa did not comply with Nkomati, and RENAMO activities escalated. Western aid increased, but not to the extent FRELIMO needed. Mother nature continued to be harsh, and the economic reforms had little effect on the countryside because RENAMO activities prevented physical access to the peasants.

FRELIMO then turned another aspect of the colonial legacy to its advantage. It used the historical dependence upon its transport routes of nearby states to encourage neighbors to assist in the battle against the guerrillas sabotaging those routes.

Machel's death in 1986 did not seriously disrupt this policy evolution. President Chissano continued the same strategies, convincing black-ruled neighbors to help protect transport routes, partially defusing tensions with South Africa, and continuing to court Western aid, while not burning Mozambique's bridges with the socialist countries.

What will the future bring in Mozambique? The most likely prospect is continuing war. FRELIMO's return to its tradition of deriving policy from reality came soon enough to prevent its overthrow, but not soon enough to defeat RENAMO. Until the peasantry's needs are met, FRELIMO will find it hard to prevent RENAMO from intimidating the rural population into cooperation. And the peasants' needs cannot be met until the transport routes linking the rural and urban areas are secure, which in turn cannot be done until the war is brought under control.

United States Policy

What are the implications of this recent history for the United States, and most particularly for the policy options outlined at the beginning of this chapter?

Option 1: The Far Right's Argument

This argument claims that FRELIMO always intended, and still intends, to turn Mozambique into a classic Marxist-Leninist state serving Soviet interests, that RENAMO is the "freedom fighter organization nearest to victory," and that the United States therefore should both aid RENAMO, and cut all economic assistance to FRELIMO. Otherwise, this view holds, Washington would be assisting the expansion of Soviet influence in southern Africa.

Option 2: The Middle Right's Argument

A less extreme version of this argument, while not claiming slavish FRELIMO devotion to the Soviet cause, remains highly uneasy with FRELIMO's socialist outlook and perceived alliance with the Eastern bloc, but is also ambivalent about RENAMO's legitimacy. The proponents of the less extreme argument therefore advise that United States aid to FRELIMO should cease, and that no United States aid should go to RENAMO. However, those putting forward this argument also claim that the United States needs to get to know RENAMO better, and that its military successes qualify it for formal, official contacts with the United States government.

Option 3: The Argument for Continuation of Current Policy.

This argument holds that aid to FRELIMO should continue, and increase if possible, while both aid to and official contact with RENAMO should not be pursued. It points to the 1983-87 pragmatic initiatives in foreign and domestic policy as evidence of FRELIMO's willingness to cooperate with the West on a wide range of issues, and insists that public contact with RENAMO by Washington would severely damage FRELIMO's confidence, possibly jeopardizing United States influence with the government. In short, this view holds that United States interests can best be served by strengthening FRELIMO's ability to become independent of the Soviet bloc and less vulnerable to South African harassment and manipulation.

Which Policy?

The extreme right argument simply is not supported by the historical record. First, Mozambique is not a classic Marxist state serving Soviet interests. FRELIMO developed its socialist orientation gradually, and initially in response to specific conditions it encountered in the war against the Portuguese. Granted, an externally generated, highly ideological approach was adopted immediately after independence, but gradually FRELIMO has been returning to its pragmatic habits. That is not to say it intends to abandon socialism, but rather that it will pursue that goal more slowly, and is redefining the type of socialism it wants from one based on the Soviet model to one better suited to Mozambican conditions.

Second, the belief that continuation of FRELIMO in power means expansion of Soviet influence in the region is not supported by the recent factual record. FRELIMO has always had major policy differences with the Soviet Union, and while Soviet influence in Mozambique is unlikely to disappear, since the Nkomati Accord it certainly has not been dramatically increasing. Chissano has ruled out participation of non-African forces in the battle against RENAMO, and remains skeptical about the quality of Eastern bloc economic assistance.

Third, there is the question of the character of RENAMO. As outlined above, the movement's origins and its dependence on foreign patrons call into question its legitimacy as an indigenous party. It has historically been racked by internal problems. Thus the question arises: to whom does one give the check, to which representative, representing which faction? In addition, there is the problem of associating the United States with an organization that even its sympathizers admit has committed serious human rights abuses, and which has a history of support for white minority regimes. And finally, what would Mozambique's prospects be if RENAMO, after receiving United States support, were to oust FRELIMO? The organization's checkered history has left it with few professional administrators who could step in and run a government. Consequently a RENAMO-run Mozambique has little chance of being more stable than a FRELIMO-run Mozambique.

The less extreme version of the right's argument is flawed not so much by its version of the facts, although it too overstates the degree of alliance between FRELIMO and the Soviet bloc, but by the likely results of the policy it advocates. Without United States economic aid, Mozambique is more likely to remain chronically unstable, and therefore unable to control ANC guerrilla infiltration into South Africa. If the stated interest of the United States in a peaceful resolution of the South African conflict is genuine, then greater ANC infiltration is not a trend to be encouraged. Furthermore, if the United States disassociates itself from Mozambique by an aid suspension, South Africa will be even less constrained about manipulating Mozambique's rail routes to force regional dependence upon the Republic's transport system. South Africa will then be better able to hold the southern African region as a hostage against international anti-apartheid pressure, which will not only have humanitarian consequences, but will also hurt Western security and economic interests by hindering trade and reducing profitability of existing Western investments in the region. Public contact with RENAMO, the other element in the middle-right argument, also entails the risk of jeopardizing the position of those leaders in FRELIMO and the Front Line States who advocate trusting the West.

That leaves the third option, of continuing or even increasing aid to FRELIMO and avoiding public contact with RENAMO. This policy has the advantage of fitting into the historical record. Western aid to Mozambique had indeed contributed to an atmosphere within FRELIMO conducive to consideration of Western interests, as evidenced by the Nkomati Accord, the IMF membership decision, Mozambican cooperation with Western diplomats on southern Africa issues, and introduction of free market-style economic reforms. As its history shows, FRELIMO, more than many other nominally Marxist-Leninist parties, is open to changing its approach to suit new conditions. If the new conditions demonstrate that the West is a credible partner, FRELIMO's history suggests the party will adjust its actions accordingly.

Such a policy also has continent-wide benefits for the United States. Aid which helps Mozambican transport facilities operate is perceived by the rest of Africa to assist in the formation of an escape route for the Front Line states should South Africa seek to cut them off from world commerce. As Britain is discovering, African criticism of such a benefactor's perceived inaction on the South Africa question becomes less energetic.

Such a policy would also discourage U.S. contact with RENAMO, thereby avoiding undercutting and embarrassing those within FRELIMO and the Front Line States who advocate trusting United States pledges of good faith.

Avoidance of official contacts with RENAMO would not necessarily prohibit discreet, private contacts with the organization. These, indeed, could
be quite useful in identifying those individuals within the organization who
are not tainted by human rights violations and/or close South African contacts, and whose nationalist sentiments might make them acceptable can-
didates for an eventual reconciliation exercise.

The integrity of the Option 3 approach, however, rests on the extent of
its potential return not being exaggerated. United States assistance to Mozambique and avoidance of formal, public RENAMO contacts can enhance
Washington's influence, but it is unlikely ever to convince FRELIMO to break
relations with the Eastern bloc, or to abandon its long term goal of
establishing a socialist society. Just as in its heyday the Soviet Union could
not convince Machel to allow it a base facility, even under the most optimistic
assumptions Chissano is just as unlikely to give extraordinary consideration
to the United States. FRELIMO will continue to make decisions on the basis
of what it defines as Mozambique's interest. No amount of aid will change
that. But Option 3 can make accommodation of some United States concerns more attractive from the FRELIMO perspective.

In short, on several issues that really matter to the West—exclusion of
Soviet base facilities and Cuban combat troops from the southern Africa
region, participation in Western economic institutions, acknowledgement of
the role of free market mechanisms in development, and diplomatic cooperation on regional security matters—FRELIMO has already shown that its
definition of national interest can overlap with the definition by the United
States of Western interests. Option 3 appears to have the best chance of
facilitating continued and increased interest convergence. And the enhancement of such convergence is now particularly important, for as the situation
in South Africa develops over the next decade, the West will need contacts
and access in all countries able to influence the course of events, and Mozambique's geographical position makes it a key player.

Notes

1. Allen Isaacman and Barbara Isaacman, *Mozambique, From Colonialism to Revolution* (Harare: Zimbabwe Publishing House, 1985), 18; and Joseph Hanlon, *Mozambique: The Revolution Under Fire* (London: Zed Books Ltd., 1984), 16.
2. Isaacman and Isaacman, 17.
3. Ibid., 34.
4. Hanlon, *Mozambique: The Revolution Under Fire*, 17.
5. Isaacman and Isaacman, 33-36.
6. Ibid., 36.
7. Ibid.
8. Ibid.
9. Barry Munslow, *Mozambique: The Revolution and its Origins* (London: Longman, 1983), 28.
10. Ibid., 31-32.
11. Ibid., 34.
12. Isaacman and Isaacman, 40.
13. Hanlon, *Mozambique: The Revolution Under Fire*, 21.
14. Isaacman and Isaacman, 48.
15. Munslow, 28.
16. Isaacman and Isaacman, 102.
17. Hanlon, *Mozambique: The Revolution Under Fire*, 39.
18. Isaacman and Isaacman, 101.
19. FRELIMO, "Statutes and Program, First Congress, 1962" in *Documentos Base da FRELIMO,* (Maputo Tempographia, 1977), 33.
20. Ibid., 34-35.
21. FRELIMO, "General Declaration, First Congress 1962" in *Documentos Base da FRELIMO*, 15-17.
22. Ibid., 22.
23. FRELIMO, "Official Speech of the Central Committee, Second Congress" in *Documentos Base da FRELIMO*, 56.
24. Author's interview with FRELIMO official, Maputo, 1984.

25. FRELIMO, "Resolutions of the Second Congress" and "Official Speech of the Central Committee, Second Congress," in *Documentos Base da FRELIMO,* 101 and 86 respectively.

26. FRELIMO, "Resolutions of the Second Congress," in *Documentos Base da FRELIMO,* 103.

27. "Aliance Against Imperialism," *Mozambique Revolution,* 48, (July-September 1971).

28. Author's interview with FRELIMO official, Maputo, 1984.

29. "Alliance Against Imperialism," *Mozambique Revolution,* 48, (July-September 1971).

30. Phyllis Johnson and David Martin, *Destructive Engagement: Southern Africa at War* (Harare: Zimbabwe Publishing House, 1986), 2.

31. Johnson and Martin, *Destructive Engagement,* 3.

32. Ibid.

33. Ibid.

34. Isaacman and Isaacman, 106.

35. Hanlon, *Mozambique: The Revolution Under Fire,* 45.

36. Ibid.

37. Confidential interview with a South African diplomat, Pretoria, December 1985.

38. Confidential interview with a South African diplomat, Pretoria, December 1985.

39. Confidential interview with Mozambican source Maputo, 1985, and Joseph Hanlon, *Beggar Your Neighbors: Apartheid Power in Southern Africa* (Indiana: Indiana University Press, 1986), 136.

40. Confidential interview with a South African diplomat, Pretoria, December 1985.

41. Johnson and Martin, *Destructive Engagement,* 3-4.

42. Information provided by Donald Easum, September 1987.

43. Author's interview with Joaquim Chissano, Maputo, 1984.

44. "Stronger Links with Socialist Countries," *Mozambique Revolution: Special Independence Day Issue* (June 25, 1975) :3.

45. "A State Born of our People's Struggle," *Mozambique Revolution: Special Independence Day Issue,* (June 25, 1975) :23.

46. "The Independence Proclamation," *Mozambique Revolution: Special Independence Day Issue,* (June 25, 1975) :16.
47. Isaacman and Isaacman, 113.
48. Ibid., 146.
49. David Martin and Phyllis Johnson, *The Struggle for Zimbabwe: The Chimurenga War* (Harare: Zimbabwe Publishing House, 1981), 224.
50. Isaacman and Isaacman, 146.
51. Hanlon, *Mozambique: The Revolution Under Fire,* 220.
52. Johnson and Martin, *Destructive Engagement,* 6.
53. Ibid., 8.
54. Isaacman and Isaacman, 183.
55. Hanlon, quoting the Mozambique constitution, *Mozambique: The Revolution Under Fire,* 235.
56. Interview with Mozambican source, 1986.
57. Isaacman and Isaacman, 185.
58. Ibid.
59. Hanlon, *Mozambique: The Revolution Under Fire,* 77.
60. Isaacman and Isaacman, 161.
61. Ibid., 147.
62. Ibid., 150.
63. Ibid., 168.
64. Hanlon, *Beggar Your Neighbors,* 134.
65. Confidential interview with South African source, Cape Town, January 1986.
66. These were external factors in that a foreign state was causing the destruction. However, if FRELIMO had not supported ZANLA nor imposed sanctions, these costs would not have been incurred.
67. Johnson and Martin, *Destructive Engagement,* 10.
68. Ibid., 12-13.
69. Hanlon, *Mozambique: The Revolution Under Fire,* 102.
70. Isaacman and Isaacman, 156.
71. Ibid., 186.
72. Hanlon, *Mozambique: The Revolution Under Fire,* 84.
73. Ibid.
74. Ibid., 111.

75. Isaacman and Isaacman, 125.
76. Ibid., 142.
77. Hanlon, *Mozambique: The Revolution Under Fire,* 86-87.
78. Isaacman and Isaacman, 184.
79. Interview with Mozambican source, March 1987.
80. Isaacman and Isaacman, 187.
81. Johnson and Martin, *Destructive Engagement,* 15.
82. Hanlon, *Mozambique: The Revolution Under Fire,* 87.
83. Johnson and Martin, *Destructive Engagement,* 19.
84. 1986 interviews with former CIO officer, and a RENAMO official.
85. Isaacman and Isaacman, 182.
86. Hanlon, *Beggar Your Neighbors,* 138.
87. Ibid.
88. Hanlon, *Mozambique: The Revolution Under Fire,* 216-217.
89. Hanlon, *Beggar Your Neighbors,* 135.
90. Ibid., 135.
91. Ibid.
92. Isaacman and Isaacman, 174.
93. Ibid., 182, see footnote.
94. Hanlon, *Mozambique: The Revolution Under Fire,* 232-33.
95. Johnson and Martin, *Destructive Engagement,* 25.
96. Ibid.
97. Hanlon, *Mozambique: The Revolution Under Fire,* 39.
98. *Directivas Econômicas e Sociais,* Colecção 4, Congresso, Partido FRELIMO, 1983.
99. Hanlon, *Mozambique: The Revolution Under Fire,* 113.
100. Ibid., 254.
101. Hanlon, *Beggar Your Neighbors,* 139.
102. Hanlon, *Mozambique: The Revolution Under Fire,* 253.
103. Johnson and Martin, *Destructive Engagement,* 26-27.
104. Gillian Gunn, "Post-Nkomati Mozambique," *CSIS Africa Notes* 38 (January 8, 1985): 7.
105. Ibid., 2.
106. Ibid., 7.
107. Johnson and Martin, *Destructive Engagement,* 32.

108. Gunn, "Post-Nkomati Mozambique," 1.

109. Johnson and Martin, *Destructive Engagement,* 35-36.

110. Hanlon, *Beggar Your Neighbors,* 146.

111. Gillian Gunn, "Mozambique After Machel," *CSIS Africa Notes* 67, (December 29, 1986): 4.

112. *Documentos da Gorongosa,* (extractos).

113. Gunn, "Mozambique After Machel," 6.

114. Ibid., 4.

115. Ibid.

116. Ibid., 10.

117. Mozambique Information Agency, January 1987.

118. *The Observer* (London), March 22, 1987.

119. Confidential interview with Mozambican source, March 1987.

120. *Christian Science Monitor,* March 25, 1987.

121. *Mozambique Information Office News Review,* February 26, 1987.

122. *Christian Science Monitor,* March 25, 1987.

123. Ibid.; see also BBC's "Summary of World Broadcasts," reports of February and March 1987.

124. "Reasons for Fatal Plane Crash," *Mozambique Information Office News Review,* 104 (April 30, 1987), Mozambique Information Agency.

125. "Chissano Speaks," *Weekly Mail,* March 6, 1987.

126. "Pretoria Grants Reprieve to Mozambique Migrants," *Financial Times,* January 17, 1987.

127. "Chissano Speaks," *Weekly Mail,* March 6, 1987.

128. *Mozambique Information Office News Review,* February 13, 1987.

129. Ibid.

130. Gunn, "Mozambique After Machel," 3.

131. *Mozambique Information Office News Review,* January 16, 1987.

132. *Guardian* (London), January 20, 1987.

133. *Mozambique Information Office News Review,* February 13, 1987.

134. Mozambique Information Agency, January 1987, and Confidential interviews in Washington, 1987.

135. *Washington Post,* February 19, 1987.

136. BBC "Summary of World Broadcasts," January 23, 1987.

137. *The Times* (London), February 12, 1987.

138. *Tempo* (February 1, 1987).
139. BBC "Summary of World Broadcasts," March 31, 1987.
140. "Chissano on Eastern Ties, U.S. Envoy's Message," FBIS (January 5, 1987).
141. Gunn, "Mozambique After Machel," 3.
142. Confidential interview with Mozambican source, March 1987.
143. Gunn, "Mozambique after Machel," 9.
144. "New Mozambican President Turns Down Cuban Troop Offer," *Washington Report on Africa,* February 1, 1987.

7: Washington's Quest For Enemies in Angola

GERALD J. BENDER

Both Republican and Democratic administrations have demonstrated a peculiar ineptness in pursuing American interests in the Third World. The crux of the problem is frequently found in how they have identified "friends" and "enemies." All too often the determination of which parties or governments to support results from a knee-jerk reaction to the Soviet Union's position in a given country. The result is that the United States is prone to classify as "enemies" parties or countries that are not necessarily hostile to American interests.[1] No better example can be found than in Angola.

Under the Reagan Doctrine of supporting guerrilla movements that oppose Soviet-backed regimes in the Third World, Angola is considered an enemy and therefore the object of American covert intervention. Yet, while members of Congress or the American public advance reasoned cases for applying the Reagan Doctrine in other parts of the world (e.g. Afghanistan, Cambodia), rarely do they present a cogent case for considering the Angolan government as an enemy of the United States. On the contrary, most

American corporations, academia, and many in government, as well as all our NATO allies, emphatically reject the notion that the government in Luanda should be viewed as an enemy.

Pre-Independence Perceptions of the MPLA

American misperceptions in Angola are not new; they go back more than a quarter of a century. Days after his election as president of the MPLA (*Movimento Popular de Libertação de Angola,* or Popular Movement for the Liberation of Angola) in December 1962, Dr. Agostinho Neto travelled to the United States where he tried, according to the *Baltimore Sun,* "to remove pro-Communist coloring" from his "movement's image." [2] Neto appealed for American understanding and stressed that leftist "extremists" had been removed from the MPLA in conjunction with his election as president of the party.[3] His advocacy clearly made a strong impact in Washington. A CIA special report on Angola, issued shortly after his visit, favored a more even-handed approach toward the rival MPLA and FNLA (*Frente Nacional de Libertação de Angola,* or National Front for the Liberation of Angola) movements. The report noted that the MPLA, under Agostinho Neto's leadership, favored "genuine neutrality," and noted that both the MPLA and FNLA would "probably prefer Western assistance and neither desires a commitment to the Communist World."[4] The State Department adopted a similar position in a circular issued in July 1963, which directed that "United States policy is not, repeat not, to discourage MPLA (Neto-Andrade faction) move toward the West and not to choose" between the MPLA and FNLA.[5]

Washington's support for the MPLA, however, never materialized. Portuguese threats not to renew the Azores treaty, granting the United States military use of its strategically located island in the Atlantic, resulted in temporizing the Kennedy administration's support for any of the liberation movements in the Portuguese colonies.[6] Thus, Washington's intention to support Neto, as well as the positive attitudes toward the MPLA, apparently fell through the cracks. What remained was a residual hostility toward the MPLA—based on anachronistic phobias rather than on realistic political assessments.

A decade later these same anachronistic views determined the Ford administration's perception of the MPLA, even after the Soviet Union had cut off all aid to Agostinho Neto's party prior to the Portuguese coup in April 1974. Incredibly, the Soviet decision to give up on the MPLA did not alter Washington's perception of the party as "pro-Soviet." Washington's myopia was not shared, however, by American officials on the ground during the scramble that occurred between the Portuguese coup and the Angolan civil war. The American consul-general in Luanda, Thomas Killoran, "believed the MPLA was best qualified to run Angola and that its leaders sincerely wanted a peaceful relationship with the United States." [7] His views were echoed by the CIA Angola desk officer, who scoffed at the notion that MPLA leaders were hostile to the United States.[8]

Top CIA officials appeared to hold attitudes similar to those expressed by the agency's Angola desk officer right up to the end of the war. Senator John Tunney of California, prior to the Senate vote on his amendment in December 1975 that cut off American covert aid in Angola, asked James Potts, CIA director of African affairs, if it made a difference to the United States which party won the Angolan war. Potts responded that it made "no difference," and—when pressed by Tunney—conceded: "Well, perhaps five percent." [9] CIA Director William Colby also manifested this perspective in testimony before the House Select Committee on Intelligence in December 1975 in response to a question about the differences among the three contending factions: "They are all independents. They are all for black Africa. They are all for some fuzzy kind of social system, you know, without really much articulation, but some sort of let's not be exploited by the capitalist nations." [10] Colby told the committee that the simplest answer as to why the Chinese supported the FNLA and UNITA (*União Para a Independência Total de Angola,* or the Union for the Total Independence of Angola) was "because the Soviets are backing the MPLA." When Congressman Les Aspin responded that "it sounds like that is why we are doing it," Colby's retort was: "It is." [11]

The MPLA Before Marxism-Leninism

A major strength and weakness of the MPLA has been its broad, eclectic nature. During the first 21 years of its existence (1956-77) it was a wide front that accepted virtually all who opposed Portuguese colonialism. On those rare exceptions when individuals were excluded on ideological grounds, they tended to be on the left rather than the right. Although the party's non-political approach to membership helped to attract greater numbers of adherents, it also made the party difficult, if not impossible, for the leadership to control.

The subject of becoming a Marxist party arose several times before independence. During a party conference in February 1968 in Congo-

Brazzaville, the proposal to become a revolutionary vanguard party was deferred on the grounds that no nucleus of ideologically prepared cadres existed. Three months before independence, during the middle of the civil war, Agostinho Neto told a Nigerian editor:

> I must say that the MPLA is not a Marxist-Leninist organization. Also our leadership is not Marxist-Leninist. Some of us have read Marx and Lenin, but we don't consider ourselves Marxist-Leninists. We are a large organization with various shades of opinion and different types of groups united solely under the flag of liberation ... it is true that many people in the world consider the MPLA as a movement linked with Moscow, again, I say this is untrue. This image exists only in the imagination of outsiders. [12]

Neto told Senator Dick Clark that same month in Luanda that he personally had never read a book by Karl Marx.[13]

Neto's position on Marxism may help explain why he was never a favorite of Moscow. Colin Legum, a prolific writer on southern African affairs and one of the few experts on the region who supported the 1975 United States intervention in Angola, noted that "Moscow had a particularly troubled relationship with the Angolan [MPLA] leadership during the liberation struggle ... they had never found it easy to get along with the rather secretive and prickly Agostinho Neto."[14] Soviet negative attitudes toward Neto were vividly exposed by Arkady Shevchenko, a former Soviet diplomat who served as under secretary general of the United Nations before he defected to the United States in 1978. Shevchenko writes in his memoirs that "Moscow had never trusted Neto but had hailed him as a hero." He also related a conversation with a foreign ministry specialist on Africa who thought that the Soviets were behind "several assassination attempts on Neto before independence." [15]

An ultra-leftist faction within the MPLA, backed by the Soviet Union and two other Eastern European countries, attempted to eliminate Neto and his supporters in the party in an attempted coup on May 27, 1977. After initially hesitating, the Cubans intervened and helped Neto prevail. The Soviet and Cuban ambassadors were expelled from Angola and relations between Luanda and Moscow reached their nadir.[16] Many of those among the MPLA leader-

ship who could have been considered committed Marxists perished during
the attempted coup.

The question thus remains: "What propelled the MPLA to transform itself
into a Marxist-Leninist party in December 1977." The full answer to this
question is outside the scope of this study but a simple response is that the
decision to become a Marxist-Leninist party was not based solely on
ideological considerations. It would appear that it was more of a response
to perceived vulnerabilities than to ideological preference or conviction. Many
in the MPLA thought it would provide greater protection against South Africa
and, to a lesser degree, the United States. Although the MPLA's conversion
to a Marxist-Leninist party had not deterred Pretoria from constant attacks
and even occupation of parts of southern Angola, greater Soviet and Cuban
support had discouraged South Africa from repeating its 1975 attempt to
take over the country. Perhaps equally important is the fact that the change
greatly reduced Soviet meddling in the party. It is difficult to point to a single
change in party or government personnel that can be attributed to Soviet
pressure. On the contrary, most of those in the MPLA who were assumed
to have been favored by Moscow have been removed or demoted from power.

The formation of a Marxist-Leninist party also provided MPLA leaders
with a rationale for exclusively asserting their leadership. In most respects,
the party does not differ in structure or monopoly of power from most other
single party non-Marxist states in Africa. In fact, it is not possible to dif-
ferentiate systematically between Marxist-Leninist and other African states
in regard to their political structures or the role of the state in the economy.[17]
In some cases, as the *Wall Street Journal* reporter Jonathan Kwitney has
observed, "communist" Congo has a freer commercial system than
"capitalist" Zaire.[18]

It is clear that President dos Santos is more circumscribed politically by
his party in acting in an autonomous or dictatorial way than many of his
counterparts in one-party capitalist states, such as Gabon (Bongo), Zaire
(Mobutu), Togo (Eyadema), Malawi (Banda), the Ivory Coast (Houphouet-
Boigny), or even Kenya (Moi). Furthermore, it would appear that in Angola
under dos Santos there is greater freedom to criticize the party and government without suffering arbitrary arrest, torture, or death than is the case
in the six non-Marxist states cited above. Among other things, this suggests
that ideological labels do not always serve as a good guide for judging the

political or economic practices of one-party states in Africa.[19] The fact is that changes of personnel within the MPLA can be explained better by reference to race and ethnicity than to ideology.

The War

I have discussed the war in Angola in detail elsewhere and therefore prefer to touch only on a few highlights here.[20] Prior to 1981, UNITA's military operations were confined mainly to the sparsely populated southeastern part of Angola, which the Portuguese referred to as "the end of the world." Since 1981, however, UNITA has expanded its activities to all provinces in the country. Four factors help explain how UNITA has been able to spread its operations successfully to other parts of the country:

1. The failure of the MPLA to deliver minimal assistance to rural Angolans, who constitute over three-quarters of the population, alienated a sizable portion of the population who could be expected to be more open to appeals for an alternative government.

2. South Africa greatly augmented its military and financial support for UNITA during the 1980s. Not only did the South African air force fly combat missions during major offensives but, according to Magnus Malan, Pretoria's defense minister, soldiers from the SADF (South African Defense Forces) fought "side by side" with UNITA on the Angolan battlefield.

3. Zaire allowed UNITA to establish bases along its borders, reminiscent of those it provided for the FNLA for almost two decades. This greatly facilitated UNITA operations in the northern and eastern parts of the country. In addition, the American upgrading of the Kamina base in the Shaba province of Zaire aided UNITA's operations in northeastern Angola.

4. The United States provided UNITA with at least $30 million worth of military aid in 1986-87, including the infamous Stinger anti-aircraft missiles. Although it cannot be said that the American aid helped UNITA to expand its area of operations, it certainly assisted Savimbi's troops to resist major MPLA offensives, such as the battle for Mavinga in the fall of 1987.

While UNITA received increased help from South Africa and the United States, the MPLA was said to have obtained more than $1 billion worth of sophisticated Soviet military equipment between 1985-87. Perhaps more important was the fact that the government's military forces made great strides in learning how to use their new equipment effectively, including MIG-23 jets. Well-trained Angolan pilots not only replaced Cuban pilots but their success against Pretoria's aging Mirage jets in 1987 denied South Africa the near monopoly in air superiority it previously enjoyed. South African officers also reluctantly admitted that the MPLA ground troops acquitted themselves well in battles against the SADF.[21] One significant result of the government's improved fighting capacity was that from mid-1986 through 1987, UNITA was displaced from significant areas in the southern and eastern parts of the country, where they had previously operated more or less at will. Particularly disturbing to UNITA's external patrons was the loss of control over all major cities in the Cazombo salient, down to Cuito-Cuanavale, which UNITA had seized in 1984-85. Some officials in Washington expressed grave concern about this turn of events, especially since they coincided with the period of United States aid. One senior American official close to the American operation voiced his distress, saying that if UNITA did not regain its lost initiative, it would be difficult to sustain support for the covert assistance in Congress.

Thus, by the end of 1987, the military situation in Angola was confused at best. While the MPLA defeat at Mavinga was a humiliating debacle, it did not significantly alter the overall picture on the ground. Each side was put on the defensive in areas it had previously "controlled:" UNITA in the south and east and the MPLA in the north and parts of the central areas of Angola. While both armies managed to improve their fighting capacity considerably, the war remained hopelessly stalemated. Neither side was capable of inflicting a military defeat on the other. This view appeared to be shared not only by the contenders themselves, but by their outside supporters as well. In the United States the CIA, DIA, and State Department Bureau of Intelligence and Research all concluded that Savimbi is correct when he says that his troops cannot defeat the government militarily. Soviet experts also privately conceded that a military victory was beyond the capacity of the government. At the same time, neither party had any realistic prospect of victory off the battlefield by winning over the hearts and minds of the population.[22] Thus, only through a process of political reconciliation could the war be brought to a halt. Yet, this could not occur while there were significant numbers of foreign troops in the country supporting the two contending sides. The challenge therefore was to remove the foreign military presence so that Angolans could reach a stage that would allow them peacefully to resolve the issues that divided them. This required a diplomatic, not military, effort.

Prospects for Successful Negotiations

International attempts to negotiate a peaceful settlement of the conflict in this part of southern Africa have been based on a number of shared premises. Whether the principals in these negotiations have been the U.N., the Western Contact Group, (the United States, Great Britain, France, West Germany, and Canada), the Carter administration, the Reagan administration, or the Angolans, certain fundamental assumptions were a part of every attempt to solve the problems diplomatically rather than militarily.[23] These assumptions were:

1. Both South Africa and Angola have serious security concerns.

2. The Cubans in Angola helped protect Luanda's security against a major invasion from South Africa.

3. The government of Angola would not feel secure while South Africa had easy access from Namibia to carry out attacks and to occupy key areas of southern provinces.

4. Pretoria manifested grave concern over the presence of large numbers of Cuban combat troops in Angola and insisted it would not withdraw its troops and illegal administration from Namibia until those troops were removed from the region.

The Carter administration, working through the Western Contact Group, approached the problem by focusing on the cornerstone of a solution, namely by trying to convince South Africa to agree to withdraw from Namibia. This was achieved in April 1978 when Pretoria accepted United Nations Security Council Resolution 435, which called for South Africa to end its illegal occupation of Namibia. Pretoria added a number of conditions for implementation of Resolution 435, which none of the Contact Group was able to satisfy.

The Reagan administration, led by its chief strategist, Chester Crocker, the assistant secretary of state for Africa, attempted to negotiate a package deal that linked the premises outlined above. Although the *linkage* strategy went through several machinations, at the heart of the approach was the fundamental belief that the security concerns of the two principal parties (Angola and South Africa) had to be satisfied before any realistic hope of success could be envisioned. Despite the almost universal criticism of the linkage approach, it was interesting to note that it did not essentially differ from the plan advanced by Angola and Cuba. In a joint declaration signed February 4, 1982, the Angolan and Cuban foreign ministers asserted that Cuban combat troops would be withdrawn from Angola once South Africa ceased its military threats against the Luanda government and implemented U.N. Resolution 435, i.e. withdrew from Namibia.

Not unexpectedly, Pretoria initially insisted that the Cubans must exit prior to its withdrawal from Namibia, while Luanda demanded that South Africa fully implement 435 before Angola would initiate a withdrawal of the Cuban combat forces. American officials held dozens of negotiating sessions with South African and Angolan officials from 1982 onwards in an attempt to narrow this gap, i.e. to formulate a timetable, acceptable to both sides, that would allow for a parallel withdrawal of South Africans from Namibia and Cubans from Angola. Throughout most of this period, the Reagan administration's approach was based on the belief that Pretoria was acting in good faith when it claimed it was willing to get out of Namibia. Thus, most administration efforts focused on Angola in an attempt to obtain from the government in Luanda a timetable that would be acceptable to the South African government.

The Reagan strategy was seriously handicapped by domestic political constraints. The obvious key to success would have been for Washington to offer Luanda incentives or perks for narrowing the timetable—incentives that could range from diplomatic recognition to some assistance in the area of security. Fear of a right-wing backlash, however, discouraged the administration's chief strategists from offering the Angolan government little more than the promise that if they showed flexibility on the timetable Washington would make sure that South Africa would uphold its side of the bargain. This amounted to telling the Angolan government that it would have to risk its security on the belief that both South Africa and the United States were acting in good faith. Prior to 1987, the maximum that Luanda was willing to risk was contained in their *Plataforma*, spelled out in a letter from President dos Santos to the United Nations secretary-general in late 1984, which posited a timetable of three years for the withdrawal of some of the Cuban combat troops.

Little progress took place in the negotiations after the announcement of the *Plataforma*. The three-year withdrawal timetable satisfied neither Washington nor Pretoria, and the Reagan administration attempted to hammer out a compromise. The United States suggested that the timetable for the withdrawal of Cubans should correspond roughly to the timetable envisioned for the withdrawal of South African troops from Namibia under U.N. Security Council Resolution 435—i.e. that 80 percent of the Cuban troops south of the 13th parallel should be withdrawn within one year. Initially this was rejected by both Luanda and Pretoria, with Pretoria insisting that the Cuban withdrawal should take place in a matter of weeks, not years, nor even one year. By the end of 1985, however, South Africa showed signs that it was interested in the compromise as a basis for negotiating and wanted Washington to obtain Luanda's response. During the resultant talks in December 1985, the Angolan government asked the United States to get South Africa to demonstrate its good faith by, for example, setting a date for Namibian independence. Pretoria responded on March 4, 1986, with an announcement that set August 1986 as the target date for Namibian independence. By this time, however, the Angolan government showed no interest in pursuing the talks. The explanation for the silence could be attributed to some contention within the MPLA over how to proceed in the negotiations and to developments in the United States that undoubtedly contributed to the uncertainty in Luanda.

The Senate repeal of the Clark amendment in July 1985, which had prohibited United States covert military support in Angola, and Jonas Savimbi's highly visible and successful visit to Washington in early 1986, clearly heightened Luanda's anxieties over its security. Crocker and the State Department lost control of the policy to right-wing forces in the Congress who parlayed the momentum generated from Savimbi's visit into support for a covert program of military assistance to UNITA. The State Department recognized that such aid would be likely to scuttle the negotiations, which led them to work hard behind the scenes to prevent covert support for Savimbi's forces. They were unable, however, to stop the frenzy in Washington for support for the "Reagan Doctrine" of covert military assistance to "freedom fighters," especially since the American right wing considered UNITA to be the group of "freedom fighters" with the greatest prospects for success in overthrowing a Soviet-backed regime.[24]

American military support for UNITA in early 1986 was too much for the Angolan government to take. They cut off all negotiations with Washington and announced that they no longer accepted the legitimacy of the Reagan administration as a broker in the negotiations since the administration had become partisan in the Angolan war. Once having abandoned the diplomatic track, Luanda turned to the (futile) military option by investing over a billion dollars in purchasing weapons and training. This policy, however, was as poorly timed as it was hopeless. The dramatic drop in the price of oil (which provided the government with more than 80 percent of its foreign exchange) forced the government to adopt stringent economic austerity measures. Those measures only further alienated the Angolan population, which felt, with almost no exceptions, that they were already making economic sacrifices beyond the point of reasonable acceptance. By mid-1987 it was apparent to dos Santos that the economic situation in the country was deteriorating and that the government would either have to ask for a further belt-tightening or else would have to radically restructure the economy. It was also clear that the pace of military expenditures would have to be greatly curtailed. One possible alternative would be to resume the negotiations and once again attempt to achieve some major solutions to the government's problems diplomatically, rather than militarily. The challenge to dos Santos was how to accomplish this without losing face and/or losing support from his main backers.

Luanda Returns to the Table
President dos Santos made two bold moves in August-September 1987 that gave rise to hopes that dramatic changes would occur in the negotiations with the United States and in the structure of the Angolan economy. The Angolan government decided to resume negotiations with the United States in mid-July 1987 and invited Chester Crocker to visit Luanda. Foreign Minister Afonso Van Dunem (Mbinda) was Crocker's interlocutor, appearing for the

first time as the chief Angolan negotiator. Crocker had been led to believe that Luanda had developed a new, more flexible, position, but what he heard was little more than a rehash of the *Plataforma*. Disappointed at the lack of progress, Crocker announced that the trip had been a "waste of time." It was clear that the Luanda government did not have its act together.

Dos Santos apparently decided to take charge of the negotiations himself and made a quick trip to Havana (August 4, 1987) to discuss with Fidel Castro a new strategy for the talks, which he announced the following week in Lusaka at a meeting of the Front Line States. That approach called for an agreement that would have to be signed by representatives of Angola, Cuba, South Africa, and SWAPO (the South West Africa People's Organization)—the guerrilla group fighting to end Pretoria's rule of Namibia. It would be carried out under the auspices of the U.N. Security Council.

Although there was much speculation as to whether the inclusion of Cuba in the talks represented a clever maneuver on the part of Luanda to coopt Havana, or vice versa, the result clearly opened the way for a more flexible and open Angolan position at the negotiating table during Crocker's meeting with dos Santos in early September, 1987.[25] Angola shortened the timetable for the withdrawal of the first 20,000 Cuban troops from three to two years. The United States would have liked to reduce this further to one year. This was one of the subjects that Crocker discussed during his surprise visit to Brussels (late September) during President dos Santos' state visit to Belgium. The meeting resulted in Angola's further contracting the withdrawal timetable, moving it closer to 18 months.

The Reagan administration wanted Luanda to be even more flexible and to accept terms such as those presented in the compromise in late 1985, which called for a time frame of roughly one year, paralleling the time that South Africa would withdraw from Namibia under the provisions of U.N. Security Council Resolution 435. During that year approximately 80 percent of the Cuban troops south of the 13th parallel would be withdrawn, while a schedule for the withdrawal of the remaining 20 percent would have to be presented. This was more or less the bottom line for Washington. In other words, Washington would then have a package that it believed should be acceptable to Pretoria. If South Africa were to reject a deal that Washington found acceptable, the stage would be set for a collision course.[26]

There were a number of individuals in the administration who would have loved an excuse to come down hard on Pretoria, and they saw a rejection of an "acceptable compromise" on linkage as a perfect opportunity. If they were prevented from doing so by others in the administration who preferred not to offend Pretoria, the issue would likely move to the Congress. If the negotiations failed because of South African intransigence, the administration would not be in a position to ward off congressional calls for further punitive sanctions against South Africa and greatly increased economic support for the Front Line States. If Pretoria refused to cooperate with Washington, it could find itself considerably more isolated not only from the United States but from Western Europe as well.

None of this would transpire, however, unless Luanda manifested more flexibility and agreed to accept a package approximating the American compromise. Although some in the Angolan government argued that a one-year timetable was too risky, it would appear that this was not really true. On the one hand, if South Africa agreed, then Luanda could accomplish the goal it had sought for the last decade, namely to bring an end to South Africa's presence in Namibia. This would not end Pretoria's aid to UNITA but it would curtail it considerably, especially the ability of South Africa to employ its troops and planes in battles such as those at Cangamba and Mavinga. On the other hand, if South Africa rejected the compromise, Luanda risked nothing but could set in motion a process that would deeply strain relations between Washington and Pretoria.

Dos Santos' Volte Face

The combination of the war and economic mismanagement produced a situation in rural Angola that had reached catastrophic proportions that could not be ignored. During his August 1987 speech on the economy, dos Santos estimated that the war had produced $12 billion worth of damage between 1975 and 1987 and had cost over 60,000 Angolan lives. A report published by UNESCO in early 1987 estimated that the war had left almost one-tenth of the population homeless and had caused some 150,000 Angolans to seek refuge in neighboring countries. The UNICEF report also stated that in 1986 tens of thousands of Angolan children died from starvation and that even more were suffering from acute malnutrition.[27] The United States Committee on Refugees, a private organization based in Washington, issued a report that echoed the UNICEF conclusions and suggested that 200,000 tons of grain were needed by early 1988 to avoid catastrophic starvation and malnutrition in Angola's rural areas.[28]

President dos Santos laid out his radically new course for the economy at a meeting of party and government officials in mid-August 1987. Conceding that excessive socialist planning and bureaucratization of economic management were responsible for much of Angola's economic malaise, he announced plans to remove the state and party from economic (mis)management in many important sectors and to encourage private initiative and foreign investment, especially from the West. Private enterprise would be strongly encouraged, especially in the agricultural, trade, transport, and service sectors. Prices and wages would be determined by the market forces of supply and demand rather than by arbitrary government edicts.

Many observers were surprised by dos Santos' announcement that Angola intended to join the International Monetary Fund (IMF). Until recently, those Angolans who advocated IMF membership had found themselves in hot water. Dos Santos picked up important support for his country's IMF bid from each of the leaders of the four Western European governments (France, Belgium, Portugal, and Italy) he visited in September 1987, all of which pledged to help sponsor Angola's application for membership. The following month West Germany joined the ranks of the European countries supporting Angola's application to become a member of the IMF.[29]

While implementation of the new economic and financial stabilization program was deferred until January 1, 1988, its origins went back to 1984 when Angolan and Hungarian economic experts sketched out new directions for the Angolan economy. The resultant package, which was similar to the reforms announced by dos Santos in August 1987, was adopted at the MPLA party conference in January 1985 and ratified during the second party congress in December 1985. Yet, nothing was announced for almost two years, which can be explained, in part, by the high prices for oil that provided the government the option of papering over many of the country's deficiencies through expensive imports. The dramatic drop in oil prices changed all that by reducing foreign exchange earnings by almost half in 1986 compared with the previous year.

Implementation of the reforms was also delayed by some orthodox party members who feared that they were tantamount to selling out socialism. Their objections became moot, however, as dissatisfaction with economic deprivations became universal, even among members of the central committee. President dos Santos tried to demonstrate to the Angolan people that he was attentive to their complaints about the lack of food in the spring of 1987 by firing the ministers of foreign and internal commerce. But making scapegoats out of these two ministers convinced no one that there was reason to be hopeful for meaningful changes in their lives. Dos Santos, wisely noting in his August speech that no revolution could be consolidated without first satisfying the material needs of the people, decided that the only way to stem the widespread alienation in the country was to dramatically alter the economy from top to bottom.

Conclusion

If Angola were almost any other country in the world, the sweeping economic reforms and flexibility about negotiations with the United States would have received a positive response in Washington. Furthermore, in terms of our own economic interests, United States-Angolan trade exceeded $1 billion a year throughout most of the 1980s. Contrary to predictions by Henry Kissinger and others in the mid-1970s that an MPLA victory in the Angolan war would result in a loss of Angolan resources and markets, the United States became Angola's leading trading partner, taking over half the value of all Angolan exports. Moreover, Angola was among the top four importers of American goods in Africa.

It would be expected that Americans would want to encourage these trends, but the continued presence of Cubans blinded many, especially conservatives in Congress, to Angolan realities and to the United States' interests in the former Portuguese colony. Despite Savimbi's numerous assertions that he could not win a military victory, some conservatives in the United States were so hungry for a victory under the Reagan Doctrine that they refused to believe the evidence that victory was not possible in Angola. The failure of the Reagan Doctrine to produce a victory in the Third World clearly frustrated some of its supporters in Congress. This frustration would prove to be extremely dangerous; it would produce a *We've Got to Do Something* approach to East-West problems, which would lead to more harm than good.

Other members of Congress who were more sanguine about the prospects of a military stalemate in Angola were nevertheless prepared to use Angola to send symbolic messages to Moscow and Havana, regardless of the possible negative impact they might have on American efforts to bring about a

diplomatic solution to the problems of the region and regardless of the finan-
cially disastrous effects their efforts might have on American investments
in Angola. For example, Senate Minority Leader Robert Dole and Dennis
DeConcini (D-Ariz.) co-sponsored a bill in the Senate that would have prohibited American firms from operating in, or doing business with, Angola.
On the Senate floor, the senior senator from Kansas admitted that he har-
bored "no illusions" that his bill (S 1128) "will mean an end to Angolan
oil production or sales; or lead directly and quickly to the ousting of the
Cubans." [30] His stated purpose was to send a strong signal to Moscow,
Havana, and Luanda. In fact, what Dole, DeConcini, and others signaled
to both allies and adversaries was that the United States was floundering and
unable to recognize, let alone protect, its own best interests.[31] The Senate
wisely defeated the bill by a margin of almost two to one.

Another example of an American self-defeating policy toward Angola occurred when Congressman Jim Courter introduced an amendment to the
Defense Authorization Bill to prohibit the Department of Defense from contracting for petroleum products from Angola. The Defense Department
strongly opposed the amendment on the grounds that it would "drastically
curtail our military capability to maintain our operational readiness
worldwide." [32] The Joint Chiefs estimated that the effect would be to increase fuel costs by $72 million while carrier fleets would be unable to meet
their worldwide requirements, especially in the vicinity of Libya, where they
"would be reduced to an unacceptable level." Admiral William J. Crowe,
Jr., chairman of the Joint Chiefs of Staff, concluded in a letter to then Senator
Goldwater that "if the Angola sanction becomes law, we will concede far
more to the Soviets in reduced operational readiness than they could ever
gain through a Marxist regime in Angola ... While Congressman Courter's
motives are laudable, the consequences of his proposal will seriously hurt
our national security posture." [33] Despite the cogent case made against this
bill by the chairman of the Joint Chiefs of Staff, a watered-down version
of it was passed.[34]

What is clear from the above is that not only has there been a great
divergence of perceptions about whether the Angolan government represents
a danger to the United States but there have also been diametrically opposed
policies proposed to address the situation.[35] At time the White House,
State Department, Ex-Im Bank, Congress, NSC, and CIA have pursued their

policies toward Angola that reflect little, if any, consideration of the other branches. The result has been a series of confusing, contradictory, and futile policies that have displeased Americans from left to right and that have had almost no impact on engendering change in Angola. Clearly, this state of affairs is good neither for the United States nor for Angola.

After more than a quarter of a century of misperceiving Angolan realities, the time has come for Americans to transcend their phobias, myths, and paranoia over alleged "communist threats" and to deal directly with the Angolan government on the basis of mutually shared interests. While the negotiations pursued by the Reagan administration were slow and laborious, they nevertheless represented the only hope for the United States to realize its goals of reducing the number of Cuban troops and promoting national reconciliation in Angola. No one could be certain that the negotiations would succeed but the chances would be greatly enhanced if the administration were to pursue a coherent and coordinated policy. That policy must begin with the long overdue recognition that the MPLA is not an enemy of the United States and that with friends like South Africa as an ally in Angola, American policy is doomed to fail.

Notes

1. For an excellent study of this phenomenon, see Jonathan Kwitny, *Endless Enemies: The Making of an Unfriendly World* (New York: Congdon & Weed, 1984).
2. *The Sun* (Baltimore), 21 December 1962, found in John Marcum, *The Angolan Revolution,* vol. II (Cambridge: The MIT Press, 1978), 14.
3. Marcum, *The Angolan Revolution,* 14-15.
4. Special Report, Office of Current Intelligence, "The Angolan Rebellion and White Unrest," CIA, OCI No. 0274/63B, 5 April 1963; and Memorandum to the Secretary, From: INR-Thomas L. Hughes, Subject: Prospects for Angolan Nationalist Movement, RAF-51, 7 November 1963, found in Richard D. Mahoney, *JFK: Ordeal in Africa* (New York: Oxford University Press, 1983), 237.

5. Mahoney, *Ordeal in Africa.*
6. Mahoney, 201-22, 236-43. Also see: Gerald J. Bender, "American
    Policy toward Angola: A History of Linkage," in Bender et al,, eds.,
    African Crisis Areas and U.S. Foreign Policy (Berkeley: University of
    California Press, 1985), 111-12, and Witney Schneidman, "American
    Foreign Policy and the Fall of the Portuguese Empire" (Ph.D. diss.,
    University of Southern California, 1987), chapter 2.
7. John Stockwell, *In Search of Enemies: A CIA Story* (New York: Nor-
    ton & Company, 1978), 64. Stockwell was the chief of the CIA Task
    Force during the 1975 American intervention in Angola and his book,
    as the title suggests, is replete with information supporting my thesis
    about American misperceptions of the MPLA.
8. Ibid.
9. Personal communication from John Tunney.
10. House Select Intelligence Committee Report which became known as
    the "Pike Papers," after a version was leaked by former CBS newsman
    Daniel Schorr and published in the *Village Voice,* 20 February 1976,
    p. 40, n. 481.
11. Ibid.
12. See the penetrating interview of Neto by Uche Chukumerijie, Editor
    of *Afriscope* (Lagos), August, 1975, 10.
13. Personal communication with Dick Clark.
14. Colin Legum, "The Soviet Union, China and the West in Southern
    Africa," *Foreign Affairs* (July 1976) :749. Following a trip to Angola
    in February 1976, an aide to Senator John Tunney reported to the assis-
    tant secretary of state for Africa that a number of MPLA cabinet
    ministers and other top officials "all took great pains to point out the
    danger of forcing the MPLA into a cycle of ever-greater reliance on
    the Soviets by refusing to deal with them." See Gerald J. Bender, "Kiss-
    inger in Angola: Anatomy of Failure," in *American Policy in Southern
    Africa,* ed. René Lemarchand (Washington: University Press of
    America, 1978), 112.
15. Arkady N. Shevchenko, *Breaking with Moscow* (New York: Ballan-
    tine Books, 1985), 365. These negative Soviet attitudes toward Neto
    and possible Soviet involvement in assassination attempts may help
    explain why some members of the MPLA central committee prepared

a report (never released) following Neto's death in Moscow (September 1979) that accused the Soviets of murdering him.

16. For a detailed account of the coup, see Gerald J. Bender, "Angola, The Cubans, and American Anxieties," *Foreign Policy*, no. 31 (Summer 1978):23-26.

17. For a cogent analysis of these points see Richard L. Sklar, "Beyond Capitalism and Socialism," unpublished manuscript, October 1987.

18. Jonathan Kwitney, the *Wall Street Journal*, 2 July 1980.

19. For further elaboration on this point with respect to Angola, see Gerald J. Bender, "Angola: Friends and Enemies," *Africa Report* (January-February 1986):7-8.

20. See, for example, Gerald J. Bender, "The Eagle and the Bear in Angola," *The Annals of the American Academy of Political and Social Science*, no. 489 (January 1987):123-32; Gerald J. Bender, "American Policy toward Angola: A History of Linkage," in Bender et al., eds., *African Crisis Areas*, 110-28; and, Gerald J. Bender, "The Reagan Administration & Southern Africa," *Atlantic Quarterly*, vol. 2, no. 3 (Autumn 1984):235-47. Also see John Marcum's three perceptive articles in the Georgetown University Center for Strategic and International Studies; series *Africa Notes:* "The Politics of Survival: UNITA in Africa," no. 8 (18 February 1983); "Angola: A Quarter Century of War," no. 37 (21 December 1984); and "United States Options in Angola," no. 52 (20 December 1985).

21. Numerous stories appeared in newspapers in 1987 that referred to South Africa's growing respect for the fighting capabilities of Angola's armed forces. An excellent review can be found in "Angola: A Battle for Africa," *Africa Confidential*, vol. 28, no. 20 (7 October 1987):1-3.

22. An elaboration of this point can be found in Bender, "The Eagle and the Bear," 131.

23. For further background on the attempts to broker a diplomatic solution in Angola and Namibia, see the sources cited in note 20.

24. Secretary of State George Shultz deserves a portion of the blame for the State Department's failure to stop a move to provide military assistance to UNITA. Once President Reagan began to include UNITA in his speeches advocating military support for "freedom fighters," in early 1985, Secretary Shultz dutifully echoed the president in his own

speeches. This undermined his later opposition to covert support since, if it were true that UNITA was a group of freedom fighters deserving of support as he asserted in his speeches, then why should the Reagan administration deny them that very support.

25. The inclusion of the Cubans in the negotiations would make it easier for Havana to save face in any deal that would lead to a substantial troop withdrawal from Angola. On the other hand, including Cuba in the bargaining process would make any agreement more difficult to sell in Washington. For example, it could open the way for bureaus and agencies outside of the Africa Bureau in the State Department to demand a role in approving any final package. It could be expected that some who would demand such an input would not share the same goals as the Africa Bureau, i.e. they might prefer to see Cuba lose face and try to veto any agreement that fell short of this, even if it were to scuttle a deal that could produce the withdrawal of most of the Cuban combat troops.

26. South Africa had never spelled out its bottom line as to what constituted an acceptable timetable. Foreign Minister Pik Botha left no doubts that a two-year timetable was definitely out of the question when he stated that "if press reports are correct that the Angolan government proposed that 20,000 Cubans be withdrawn over a two-year period, the initiative is stillborn." Quoted in the *Windhoek Advertiser,* 21 September 1987.

27. UNICEF, *Children on the Front Line* (March 1987), see especially 6-27.

28. U.S. Committee for Refugees, *Uprooted Angolans: From Crisis to Catastrophe* (August 1987), 1-30.

29. This support was announced by West German Foreign Minister Hans-Dietrich Genscher during a two-day visit to Angola in late October 1987. Genscher, the highest-ranking West German to visit Angola since independence, called the economic reforms announced by dos Santos "a courageous step in the right direction." See *Reuter News Reports,* 30 October 1987.

30. *Congressional Record—Senate,* 19 May 1987, S6748.

31. Congressman Lee Hamilton (D-Ind.) asked Secretary of State George Shultz specifically if it is "U.S. policy to support the continued presence and involvement of American oil firms in Angola?" The State Department

responded (7 November 1986) that "it would be a mistake to consider trade with Angola as a form of economic aid to the [Angolan] regime. American companies are active in Angola because of the almost unanimous judgment by the private sector—American, West European and Japanese—that it is a good place to do business ... it is not our intention to make economic war on the Angolan people or prolong their suffering ... Their [American corporations] presence in Angola affords them a unique role in helping to educate the Luanda government to the possibilities of effective cooperation with the West and to the corresponding need to move toward political accommodation. We are satisfied that these firms understand this role and are playing their part." For copies of the exchange of letters between Representative Hamilton and the State Department on this subject see *Congressional Record, 7,* January 1987, E24-E25.

32. Contained in a letter from the chairman of the Joint Chiefs of Staff, William J. Crowe, Jr. to Senator Barry Goldwater who was then chairman of the Senate Committee on Armed Services, 2 September 1986.

33. Ibid.

34. The version that passed left implementation up to the secretary of defense, if he thought that it were in the best interests of the United States to invoke the provisions in the bill.

35. The full spectrum of American perceptions of Angola and the range of proposed solutions can be seen in the House debate over the Hamilton amendment. The amendment, which proposed that Congress must approve further covert aid to UNITA, was defeated 229 to 186. See the *Congressional Record—House,* 16 September 1986, 6966-6982 and 17 September 1986, 7009-7043.

8: U.S. Policy: Doctrine Versus Interests

RICHARD J. BLOOMFIELD

U.S. relations with Angola and Mozambique present a paradox. Both countries are self-styled Marxist regimes with ties to the Soviet bloc, from which both receive military assistance. In recent years, however, both regimes have become disenchanted with their official ideology: they have adopted more market-oriented policies, have welcomed foreign investment, and have been eager for close relations with capitalist countries. Both regimes have shown a willingness to cooperate with the United States in its efforts to bring about a resolution of their conflicts with South Africa, as part of a region-wide détente.

In spite of these parallels, the United States has warm relations with Mozambique, which include the provision of economic aid and diplomatic efforts on Mozambique's behalf, while relations with the People's Republic of Angola are poor. The United States has never had diplomatic relations with Angola and in 1986 began to provide military aid to UNITA, the guerrilla force fighting the government.

It is the thesis of this chapter that the contrast in U.S. policy toward Angola and Mozambique does not reflect differences in the interests of the United States in the two countries. Rather, it is the result of a confusion about what

U.S. interests in the region are. In Angola, in particular, the nature of U.S. interests has been obscured by national security doctrine. Since the adoption of containment of the Soviet Union as national policy in 1947, the dominant strain in U.S. national security doctrine has seen U.S. security interests as universal, a seamless garment. In such a world, the expansion of Soviet influence anywhere in the globe is per se a threat to the United States. Even in those areas that are not intrinsically important to the United States, what is at stake is U.S. credibility in the global struggle, which can only be demonstrated by confronting Soviet expansion wherever it occurs—and normally by the same means. Those who have taken a more particularistic view of U.S. security interests (including containment's intellectual father, George Kennan) and who have advocated judging local and regional U.S. interests on their own merits, have usually been on the defensive. In that respect, the history of U.S. policy toward Angola is a paradigm for a problem that has persistently bedeviled U.S. policy when the East-West rivalry has intersected with a regional conflict.[1]

The Globalization of a Regional Conflict

A shorthand way of explaining the different U.S. policies toward Angola and Mozambique is to point out that there are no Cuban troops in Mozambique. It is the Soviet bloc military presence in Angola, and especially the Cuban expeditionary force, that has been the bone in the throats of U.S. leaders. The State Department admits as much:

"The United States ... has made clear that normalization of U.S.-Angolan relations can be considered only within the context of a comprehensive settlement involving implementation of the UN plan for Namibia and the withdrawal of Cuban combat forces from Angola."[2]

Why should normal relations with Angola depend on a Namibia settlement? South Africa is the outlaw in Namibia, not Angola. Why should normal relations with Angola depend on the withdrawal of Cuban combat forces from Angola? These forces play a defensive role, as attested by the fact that, until the great battles of 1988, they have remained as a rearguard, some distance from the southern combat zone. It has been South Africa that time and again has invaded Angolan territory.

U.S. leaders have answered these questions in terms of the superpower competition: Thus, Henry Kissinger:

"The issue in Angola... was not a direct threat to our security, but the long-term danger of allowing Soviet surrogate forces to intervene globally to tip the scales in local conflicts."[3]

This theme—the strategic significance of the Soviet bloc military intervention—has had a decisive influence on policy toward Angola through both Democratic and Republican administrations since 1975.[4]

In Mozambique, on the other hand, regional interests have succeeded in driving U.S. policy. The reasons for this are simple. In that country, the Soviet bloc military presence has been modest as compared to Angola. There was only one independence movement—FRELIMO—and independence was achieved without outside intervention. While Cold War ideology has affected U.S. policy toward Mozambique from time to time, those in the U.S. government who believe that U.S. interests in Mozambique are largely regional, rather than global, by and large have managed to prevail. This has been possible even during the ideological Reagan administration because those in charge of regional policy have convinced the White House that their approach is weaning Mozambique away from the Soviet Union. In effect, the regionalists have managed to make their preferred policy consistent with the Reagan Doctrine.

The Impact of National Security Doctrine: 1975-1980

It must be asked whether those who, in the name of U.S. strategic interests, have had the decisive influence on policy toward Angola during three administrations have been correct. Does U.S. national security justify the refusal to establish cordial, or at least official, relations with the Angolan government, the emphasis on withdrawal of the Cubans, and the shift to intervention on behalf of the Angolan government's opponents in the civil war?

Answers to those questions begin in 1975, when the collapse of Portuguese authority in the colony led to the outbreak of civil war among the three independence movements. At that point, the United States had a choice. It could have tried to enlist its allies and the African states to support the establishment of an international peacekeeping force provided by the OAU or the UN to assist the Portuguese in enforcing the Alvor accord, which provided for a coalition government of transition. Instead, it chose to throw its support to one of the warring factions. This move—and the South African invasion of Angola—provided the Soviet Union and Cuba with a pretext for coming to the rescue of their ally, the MPLA (*Movimento Popular de Libertação de Angola*). This is not to say that the Soviet/Cuban intervention might not have occurred anyway, but only that the United States did not attempt a strategy that might have succeeded in forestalling or nullifying it. In the ensuing civil war the U.S. side was badly beaten; the MPLA established itself as the government in Luanda, and, with the exception of the United States, most of the international community soon extended it diplomatic recognition.

In the immediate aftermath of the debacle in Angola, it is not surprising that the Ford administration refused to recognize the new government in Luanda. Ford and Kissinger were bitter at the U.S. Congress for having refused to go along with their plans to increase military aid to the U.S.-backed Angolan faction fighting the MPLA. Accepting the MPLA's victory as a *fait accompli* would have seemed to belie their previous impassioned rhetoric about its dire consequences. But looked at dispassionately, the policy made little sense. There is no doubt that Soviet interests in a continuation of détente suffered from a backlash in the United States as result of its intervention in Angola. However, the U.S. refusal to establish relations with the new government in Luanda in itself was meaningless except as a symbol of U.S. pique. It certainly did not deter the Soviets and Cubans from doing the same thing in 1978 in Ethiopia. If U.S. hostility toward the Angolan government was designed to teach the Soviet Union a strategic lesson, the pupil was a poor learner.

The powerful grip of strategic doctrine on American attitudes towards regional conflict was forcefully illustrated by the policy split over Angola that occurred in the Carter administration. This was an administration that began in office determined to reject the "inordinate fear of Communism"[5] of its predecessors and with a view of southern Africa that promised to see U.S. interests there in regional, rather than global terms. In his 1976 campaign for the presidency, candidate Jimmy Carter had declared:

"I think that the United States position in Angola should be one which admits that we missed the opportunity to be a positive and creative force for good in Angola... We should also realize that the Russian and Cuban presence in Angola, while regrettable and counter-productive of peace, need not constitute a threat to United States interests, nor does that presence mean the existence of a satellite on the continent."[6]

This was certainly the view of Secretary of State Cyrus Vance, who believed that removing the threat from South Africa was the way to get the Soviet Union and Cuba out of Angola. To Vance, Namibia was the key: if the Namibia problem were allowed to fester it could lead to a wider war in southern Africa which would draw the Soviet Union and Cuba even deeper into the region.[7] On several occasions, he recommended that relations with Angola be established as a first step in the process of enlisting Angolan support for U.S. efforts to arrange an area-wide settlement, which would include independence for Namibia. Although Carter was sympathetic to such an approach, events elsewhere soon made him hesitate. In 1977, a Somalian invasion of the disputed Ogaden triggered a Soviet-sponsored Cuban expeditionary force to help Ethiopia. This event revived the debate over how to deal with Soviet intervention in Africa that had raged during the Angolan civil war. Similarly invasions of the Shaba region of Zaire by Katangan refugees in Angola in March and December 1977, led some in the U.S. to charge that the Cubans were conspiring to destabilize a U.S. client, although, as it turned out, U.S. intelligence was probably faulty on this score.[8]

While Vance and others in the administration tended to view events in the Horn of Africa and Shaba as being rooted in local problems and tried to avoid having them linked to overall U.S.-Soviet relations, they were opposed by a powerful voice within the administration, National Security Adviser Zbigniew Brzezinski, who saw the Soviet/Cuban presence in Africa as threatening U.S. strategic interests.[9] Brzezinski opposed establishing relations with the Angolan government without first extracting concessions on the Cuban presence, and there are indications that he may have advocated that the U.S. provide aid to UNITA.[10] Carter was fearful of being seen as "soft" on the Cubans, and leery of making moves that would arouse the conservatives in Congress and further complicate high priority objectives such as the Panama Canal treaties.[11] This made him more susceptible to the strategic arguments of Brzezinski. As time went on, and his administration became beleaguered politically, the possibility of establishing relations with Angola became increasingly remote.[12]

A decade later, the strategic interpretation of the Soviet/Cuban actions in Africa in the 1970s strikes one as fanciful. In one fell swoop, Soviet and Cuban interventions in a few backward and fractious nations widely separated on the African continent were painted as bold moves in a master plan for world domination, instead of the costly dead-ends for the Soviet Union that they now plainly have become. At the time, however, they fed the vision of the Soviet Union as an implacable empire on the march, a foe that had to be contained. In these circumstances, it was argued, it would appear to be sheer appeasement to be cozying up to a Soviet ally, such as Angola.

In contrast, there were Vance's views on how to deal with the Soviet and Cuban presence in Africa. Vance felt that Soviet actions in Africa "were not part of a grand Soviet strategy, but rather attempts to exploit targets of opportunity. It was not that Soviet actions were unimportant, but I felt realism required us to deal with those problems in the local context in which they had their roots.''[13] Accordingly, in southern Africa, Vance and his advisers proposed to outflank the Soviets and Cubans by becoming as influential as possible with the Angolan government and using that influence to draw Angola into a U.S. effort to stop the conflicts in the southern African region, stabilize the new states in the area, preempt further opportunities for Soviet and Cuban meddling, and isolate South Africa.

The Impact of National Security Doctrine:
The Reagan Administration and U.S. Interests

Let us imagine that the regime in Pretoria were one that accorded full political rights to the black majority. If that were the case, it is likely that the guerrilla movements in Angola and Mozambique would be weak, if they existed at all. There would be no Cuban troops in Angola and the Soviet bloc presence in both countries would in all likelihood be minimal and largely civilian. While the infrastructure of the two countries might not be as devastated as it is now, Marxist economic policies would still have proven a failure and the two regimes would still be eager for Western investment, trade, and aid. Consequently, U.S. economic interests would be as large and probably larger than they now are. That being said, however, U.S. political interests in the two countries would be modest. Neither Angola nor Mozambique would be salient issues in the African policy of the United States.

In fact, both countries are important to the United States because their neighbor is powerful, racist, and hegemonic South Africa. For the Reagan administration, it has been difficult to accept that fact because it arrived in office armed with a set of views that predisposed it to a sympathetic view of South Africa and a hostile one of Angola and Mozambique. As it did the rest of the world, the Reagan administration saw South Africa through the ideological prism of the Soviet-American confrontation. The regime in South Africa was, after all, Western-oriented and fiercely anti-communist.

In contrast, in Angola, and to a lesser extent in Mozambique, the administration saw two clients of the Soviet Union. Angola, in particular, represented everything Ronald Reagan and his supporters had said was wrong with policies during previous administrations, policies that in their view had allowed the Soviet Union and its Cuban ally to get away with intervention in the trouble spots of the Third World. Thus, almost from the outset, the new administration insisted that the departure of the Cuban troops from Angola was a *sine qua non* of normal relations with Angola and a settlement of the conflicts in southwest Africa. As it happened, this posture coincided with that of South Africa and was, therefore, consistent with the administration's new strategy toward that country, which was to build a position of influence with Pretoria through what came to be called "constructive engagement."

In Mozambique, the Reagan administration reacted positively to overtures from Maputo for better relations, as it saw an opportunity to distance the Mozambicans from the Soviet Union and, at the same time, broker a deal between Maputo and Pretoria that would enhance its influence with both. The result was the Nkomati accord. South Africa would stop aiding RENAMO and Mozambique was to suppress activities of the African National Congress (ANC) on its territory. On balance, this accord has probably served Mozambique's long run interests, even though it was for a long time flouted by South Africa. However, it also confirmed Mozambique's vassalage to South Africa.

Thus, in both Angola and Mozambique, the United States seemed to be legitimizing South Africa's policies toward its neighbors. This strengthened the hand of the hardliners in South Africa and helped to make the regime in Pretoria even more impervious to change.

Defining U.S. Interests

How can the United States resolve the contradictions in its policies in southern Africa? Evidently, it must be clear about what its interests in the region are, and, more important, about which interests are paramount. The process must start with South Africa, as the most dynamic power in the region.

The principal and overriding U.S. interest in South Africa is the existence of a state in which non-whites have full civil and political rights. This interest is the product of the U.S.'s own racial history and the repugnance that experience has bred in most Americans for a white-ruled regime that practices racial injustice and denies political rights to the non-white population.[14]

To argue, as many do, that political change is only one U.S. interest and that it must be balanced by U.S. strategic interests in South Africa is to pose a false dilemma. The United States does have a strategic interest in South Africa, which is continued access to several rare minerals produced in that country. It is in fact unlikely that any South African regime, regardless of its political coloration, would find it in its interests to forego foreign exchange income by denying these minerals to the United States. That being said, access would be most secure under a democratic regime based on the will of the majority. Such a regime and the United States would be likely to have close ties based on shared ideals and common interests, making it unlikely that there would be an interruption of trade due to political conflict. In contrast, the outcome of a prolonged and violent struggle between whites and blacks could be a radical xenophobic regime of either the Left or the Right, which is hardly likely to serve U.S. strategic interests.

The question of how the United States can best advance its interests in political change in South Africa is outside the scope of this book. It seems clear, however, that a new U.S. strategy toward South Africa is needed.[15] Part of such a new approach must be that U.S. policies in neighboring states reinforce its policy in South Africa, rather than work at cross purposes. Although South Africa is much the stronger neighbor, developments in Angola and Mozambique nevertheless have an influence on the political evolution within South Africa. South Africa's military attacks on Angola and Mozambique, its support for anti-government guerrillas in both countries, and its portrayal of the regime in Angola as a Soviet beachhead have all been designed as much to strengthen the Pretoria regime's ability to carry out its repression of internal dissent as to ward off external foes. These actions help it to convince its own white population of the need for repression and to persuade South African blacks of its invincibility. In addition, of course, weak and battered regimes in Maputo and Luanda will be unable to be of much help to the African National Congress and the Southwest African People's Organization (SWAPO). Nor will besieged governments in the two countries be strong partners in the Front Line States' efforts to support change in South Africa.

In contrast, the primary interest of the United States in Angola and Mozambique is the existence in both countries of regimes that will cooperate with U.S. diplomacy vis-á-vis South Africa. Such regimes, by definition, will be sufficiently strong and stable to pursue foreign policies independent of the wishes of South Africa. They should likewise be able to act independently of the Soviet Union. While the Soviet Union has adopted of late a more moderate line regarding the struggle in southern Africa, its long-term interests in the region are not the same as those of the United States.

Once we are clear about this paramount U.S. interest in Angola and Mozambique, it becomes easier to define what objectives the U.S. should pursue in both countries.

U.S. Objectives in Angola and Mozambique

(1) An end to the civil wars in both countries.

The insurgencies in Angola and Mozambique have weakened both regimes to such an extent that they are vulnerable to South Africa and, in varying degrees, to the Soviet Union. In Angola, the MPLA regime depends on Soviet bloc military assistance and Cuban troops to protect it from the South African-backed UNITA insurgents and from direct attacks by the South African Defense Force. In Mozambique, there are no Soviet or Cuban troops and Soviet assistance is less important to the beleaguered FRELIMO government than military aid from neighboring Zimbabwe and Tanzania, but outside help has been unable to prevent the RENAMO rebels from ravaging large parts of the country.

If it is in the U.S. interest that the regimes in both countries be able to act independently of either Soviet or South African manipulation, a primary U.S. objective should be the cessation of the guerrilla wars in the two countries, or at least their reduction to a level that frees the central governments from either Soviet or South African hegemony. At that point, they could become positive forces for the achievement of U.S. goals in South Africa and the region as a whole.

(2) The reopening of the rail and port facilities in both countries that provide an alternative outlet to the sea for the foreign trade of neighboring black states, most of which now must pass through South Africa.

It is not in the U.S. interest that South Africa enjoy leverage on the policies of the Front Line states, whose objectives, insofar as South Africa is concerned, coincide with those of the U.S.

(3) The expansion of U.S. economic relations in both countries via the American private sector as well as through foreign aid.

Both the MPLA and the FRELIMO have long since recognized that the economic development of their countries—on which the survival of their regimes may ultimately depend—will not be achieved through Soviet bloc aid nor by policies inspired by Marxism. Both have welcomed foreign private investment and have eagerly sought economic assistance from the West. The greatest advantage the United States has in dealing with both regimes is its ability to orchestrate private investment and public economic assistance.

(4) The elimination of the Soviet bloc military presence in both countries or its reduction to at the most a training and maintenance function.

Dependence of either Angola and Mozambique on Soviet bloc military aid or troops is inimical to U.S. objectives in a variety of ways. The most obvious is that it provides the Soviets and the Cubans with leverage on their clients' policies, who may consequently be less able to cooperate with the U.S. in achieving common objectives. This is more of a problem in Angola than in Mozambique, where the government has chosen to seek military assistance from outside the Soviet bloc and, in spite of the inroads of the insurgents, has resisted asking for Cuban troops.

There is another reason why the U.S. should seek to eliminate (or in the case of Mozambique avoid) dependency on Soviet bloc military protection, and that is that it gives South Africa a pretext for its policies of internal repression and destabilization of neighboring countries. Both Angola and Mozambique at times have served as havens for guerrillas operating in South Africa or Namibia. This fact, coupled with their ties to the Soviet bloc, has allowed white South African hardliners to portray internal unrest as foreign-inspired and ultimately masterminded by the Soviet Union. The U.S. decision early in the Reagan administration to make the Cuban presence in Angola a major issue lent credibility to South Africa's claim that it was beleaguered by a Soviet conspiracy. That is not to deny that it is in the U.S. interest that the South African regime be deprived of the Soviet bugaboo. That will not be accomplished, however, by giving the issue of Soviet bloc military presence top priority.

Courses of Action: Getting the Means Right

Without a clear definition and ordering of interests and objectives, it is impossible to establish effective courses of action. But the appropriate courses of action do not automatically follow from having succeeded in getting the objectives right. It is argued by the American Right, for example, that the best way to assure that the two countries help the U.S. work for an end to apartheid in South Africa would be by replacing the regimes now in power in Luanda and Maputo with ones dominated by the forces seeking their overthrow. Yet a victory of the insurgents would not achieve the U.S. objective of freeing the two countries from the hegemony of South Africa. On the contrary, rebel victories would enhance South Africa's position in the region.

A RENAMO regime in Maputo would be heavily dependent on its South African patrons and unreceptive to U.S. overtures that might run counter to the interests of Pretoria. It would also be faced with a monumental task of reconstruction and very likely with guerrilla warfare from the remnants of FRELIMO. There would be great pressure on the U.S. for humanitarian reasons to continue to provide large amounts of assistance, which, if it materialized, would put the U.S. government in the unhappy position of paying the bills for an ally of South Africa.

The case of UNITA is somewhat different. UNITA is heavily dependent on South African support, but Savimbi also receives aid from other sources, including lately the United States. He has more claim to being the leader of a legitimate nationalist movement than his counterparts in RENAMO. A Savimbi government might thus prove to be more independent of Pretoria than a RENAMO government. That is a moot point, however. The Soviet Union and Cuba have a large political stake in Angola. They have made it clear that they are not going to allow the MPLA regime to be overthrown without a major escalation of their military effort, an upping of the ante the United States is unlikely to be willing to match. A clear-cut defeat of the MPLA regime is not a credible objective for U.S. policy.

In short, attempts to replace the current rulers in these two countries with their enemies would put the United States in a far worse position than it is now. In Mozambique, the U.S. could find itself dealing with (and perhaps subsidizing) a puppet of South Africa; in Angola the result would be to provoke massive military intervention by the Soviet bloc.

To its credit, the Reagan administration has resisted pressure from its right wing and has pursued a policy of doing what it can to bolster the Mozambican government. It has provided substantial food aid and some development assistance and it has encouraged an international effort to improve the seaport of Beira and to secure the rail corridor linking that port with the Front Line states in the interior of the continent. Its early attempt to provide military assistance was blocked by congressmen opposed to arming a self-styled Marxist regime. It has withstood the pressures of the pro-RENAMO lobby in Washington, which counts on a number of influential sympathizers in Congress. The administration's policy toward Mozambique has obviously been an aberration, however, given that its ideology, the "Reagan Doctrine," would seem to coincide with that of the pro-RENAMO lobby. However, the president had been persuaded—correctly—that the supportive policies being followed by the United States have been successful in helping the Maputo government loosen its dependence on Moscow and move toward the West.

On the critical issue of South Africa's use of RENAMO to weaken the FRELIMO regime, however, the mutual non-aggression pact that the administration brokered between Mozambique and South Africa (the Nkomati accord) has up to now failed to weaken RENAMO. At least until recently, the South Africans ignored the agreement and continued to aid the rebels. While direct aid may now have ceased, the South African government is believed to have turned a blind eye to the use of its territory by revanchist Portuguese citizens and others who are supplying RENAMO. One is entitled to be skeptical regarding Pretoria's motives in moving in mid-1988 to revive the Nkomati accord; South Africa's conciliatory gestures often turn out to be tactical maneuvers, facilely discarded when they no longer serve their purpose of feint and delay.

In Angola, it is not surprising that a Reagan administration would not move to establish official relations. As we have seen, the Soviet and Cuban role in the MPLA's accession to power, the presence of Cuban troops in the country, and the regime's links to Moscow, which are closer than those of Mozambique, have all given the issue of Angola a heavy ideological cast. Even the Carter administration, which adopted a clearly antagonistic policy toward South Africa and wished for better relations with Angola, could not bring itself to establish diplomatic relations. How then could an administration to the right of Carter's be expected to be bolder?

However, the Reagan administration, by making the withdrawal of the Cuban expeditionary force in Angola a prior condition for the consummation of Namibian independence, dramatically changed the politics of the Angola-South Africa equation. Although the Carter administration had recognized that the Cuban military presence in Angola made a Namibia settlement more difficult and would ultimately have to be addressed in some fashion, its strategy was to make the major issue of the Namibia negotiation South Africa's compliance with United Nations resolutions mandating an independence process for Namibia. It had organized its European allies in a Contact Group to keep the pressure on South Africa and, in effect, negotiate the terms of South Africa's compliance with UN Resolution 435.

The Reagan administration, in contrast, made Cuban troop withdrawal the *sine qua non* of a Namibia settlement. This let South Africa off the hook. It shifted the focus away from South Africa's illegal occupation of Namibia and its attacks on Angola. Moreover, it set for the U.S. negotiators an unenviable task—that of convincing an Angolan government (that felt itself vulnerable to both the UNITA rebels and the South African Defense Forces) to give up the shield of the Cubans. While Angola has been eager for diplomatic relations with the United States—which presumably would pave the way for U.S. economic assistance and would enhance its political legitimacy—it will not send the Cubans home as long as it feels threatened by South Africa. And—Catch 22—until recently, South Africa has refused to stop its aggressive behavior, which it has justified in large part by the Cuban presence in Angola.

The U.S. role as the honest broker of a grand settlement in southwest Africa was further complicated in 1986 by the success of the proponents of the Reagan Doctrine in getting congressional approval of military aid to UNITA, apparently over the objections of the State Department, which correctly saw that this would impede the negotiating track the U.S. was pursuing.[16]

The 1988 Breakthrough

In the summer of 1988, the negotiating situation changed dramatically. The United States, with the support of the Soviet Union, was successful in bringing about an agreement among South Africa, Angola, and Cuba. This agreement would provide a framework for a settlement of the conflict between Angola and South Africa, and would also lead to independence for Namibia. If a timetable for withdrawal of the Cuban force can be agreed upon, South Africa is to abide by UN Resolution 435 and elections in Namibia, withdrawal of South African forces from Namibia, and Namibian independence are to follow. The question of UNITA was not discussed in the negotiations, but that is obviously the next item on the agenda for U.S. diplomacy.

Would such an outcome be a vindication of the Reagan policy toward Angola? Does it mean that making the Cuban troop issue the fulcrum of the U.S. diplomatic strategy was correct, after all?

Given the many obstacles in the path of the U.S. negotiators—some of them self-imposed—the breakthrough in the summer of 1988 was a considerable achievement. However, it must be pointed out that the tripartite agreement was possible only because of two fortuitous changes in the environment, for neither of which can U.S. policy take the slightest bit of credit. First, and foremost, South Africa seems to have decided that the cost of continuing the conflict in Angola now outweighs the benefits. In the 1988 battles in southern Angola, the South African/UNITA forces were met by a Cuban army that has been reinforced and armed with more sophisticated weapons. The result was that the South Africans were driven back and suffered, for them, a substantial number of casualties. White South Africans, whose sons have been killed and maimed, have questioned the need for the war in Angola, and important white institutions, like the Dutch Reformed Church, have called for a reexamination of the government's policy. In addition, the South African military are thought to fear that future engagements with the Cubans could turn into a military debacle, which would tarnish the image of invincibility that the South African Defense Force has enjoyed in southern Africa. The Botha administration apparently decided that it needed to end the war in Angola for these domestic political reasons. It also may have concluded that for a peace to be permanent, it would be necessary to go beyond a mere cease-fire and withdrawal from Angolan territory and to give up control of Namibia, that is to disengage from the Angolan border entirely. This was plainly an extremely difficult draught for the Pretoria regime to swallow and, as of this writing, it is still uncertain whether the South Africans are in fact sincere, or by making demands as to the timing and manner of the departure of Cuban troops from Angola that are unacceptable to the other side, are trying to set up Cuba and Angola to take the blame for a failure of the Namibia independence plan. Be that as it may, there is no doubt that there has been a significant change in the domestic South African political situation as it relates to the war.

The second changed circumstance that has made a settlement in southwest Africa a possibility is that the Soviet Union has decided that it wants to get out of Angola badly enough to risk an increase in U.S. prestige and influence in Angola and the rest of the region. This decision is the result, like the one in South Africa, of a change in domestic politics. Gorbachev has decided that *perestroika* requires a retrenchment of Soviet military commitments in the Third World and a redeployment of resources to internal development. Although the Cubans are not the slavish puppets of the Soviet Union that they are often made out to be, and do have an important political investment in their fraternal revolutionary role in Angola, they also have incentives to find an honorable way to end their intervention in that country. They have suffered many casualties during their long presence, which doubtless is the cause of some anguish and disaffection at home, and their economic dependence on the Soviet Union cannot help but make them sensitive to Soviet desires.

It is ironic that if the U.S.-brokered settlement comes into effect, it will be in large measure due to the fighting ability of the very Cuban forces that the United States has insisted for so long were the chief obstacle to such an agreement and to a decision by the Soviet Union that Angola was not such a strategic prize after all.

A Fallback Position

It is useful to consider a fallback position in the event that the tripartite agreement of 1988 fails to materialize. Even if it does, the sketching-out of an alternative strategy serves another purpose: it will indicate what kind of approach might succeed in similar situations elsewhere in which fortuitous circumstances like those that changed the Angolan situation do not occur.

Should the tripartite agreement fall apart, a new U.S. negotiating strategy should take into account the following realities:

(1) It is most likely that a failure of the 1988 agreement will be due to demands from South Africa regarding the timing of the Cuban troop withdrawal from Angola—demands that Angola and Cuba consider would create unacceptable risks. Whether or not this would be the result of a deliberate ploy of the South Africans to put the blame for the collapse of the accords on the Angolans or would be an honest difference in the two sides' assessment of their security needs is beside the point. A failure to reach agreement under the favorable conditions that now prevail should confirm once and for all that South Africa is unlikely to withdraw from Namibia in the foreseeable future.

(2) With South Africa still on its southern border, Angola would continue to need a substantial Cuban force. The impasse of linkage would continue.

(3) The re-thinking of Soviet policy toward the Third World that has been one of the products of *perestroika* makes the Soviets amenable to a settlement in which the Soviet/Cuban military presence in Angola is ended, even if that means a sharp reduction of Soviet influence. However, the Soviets will not abandon the MPLA regime to its fate, nor will the Cubans, who have an even greater stake in a "victorious" end to their long intervention in Angola than do the Russians. Any U.S. strategy that makes military power a central issue plays to Soviet strength.

(4) In addition to the threat from South Africa, the Angolan government faces a formidable foe in UNITA. As long as UNITA continues to receive sufficient foreign assistance, either from South Africa, the U.S., or elsewhere, the Angolans will continue to depend on Soviet arms and advisers and be reluctant to give up the protection afforded by the Cubans.

In these circumstances, there would be little hope that the United States could soon find the key to the grand regional settlement for southern Africa that it has sought for two administrations. Instead, a step-by-step approach should be adopted. The first step should be an end to the civil war in Angola. It is, after all, that conflict that has provided South Africa with an entrée to intervene in Angola and keeps Angola a weak pawn in South Africa's game of regional hegemony. A unified—and reconstructed—Angola could make a significant contribution to strengthening the Front Line states vis-á-vis South Africa. Angola's great economic potential and maritime location could make it an important partner in the development of the other black African states in the region.

To play a decisive role in ending the civil war, the United States should end its ostracism of the Angolan government and move to put itself in a position of greater influence with that regime. The point of departure for the United States would be to accept the realities on the ground and to discontinue setting impossible tasks for itself—such as brokering a grand bargain that would achieve Namibian independence and a Cuban withdrawal at one stroke. The U.S. failure, after many tries, to deliver on such a deal has weakened its credibility. U.S. progress in obtaining commitments from the Angolans on reducing the Cuban contingent has been repeatedly sabotaged by the South Africans, who inevitably have found the Angolan proposal inadequate. Each time that has happened, it has made the United States look either foolish or duplicitous to the Angolans.

The first step in the process of building a new relationship with Luanda would be to establish diplomatic relations. This should not be a unilateral act. Instead, a package deal should be negotiated with the MPLA government that responds to the political needs of both sides. The United States would wish to make it clear that its agreement to accord diplomatic recognition to the MPLA regime did not mean that it had ceased to regard UNITA as a legitimate political movement with a valid claim to a role in the future of Angola. However, the United States would not assist UNITA in attempts to overthrow the MPLA government; rather it would work for a peaceful settlement between the two sides.

In the economic area, the United States would point out that Angola had recently taken steps to free its economy from the dead hand of the state apparatus and to introduce free market principles. It would also point to the excellent record Angola had in its relations with U.S. companies that had invested in the country and its punctilious performance of its international financial obligations. The United States would state that it looked forward to cooperating with the People's Republic of Angola in various economic development efforts.

Finally, the U.S. would have to take a clear position condemning South African incursions into Angolan territory. Indeed, the new approach to Angola implies a more forthright posture by the United States toward South Africa's destabilization of its neighbors than has heretofore been the case, including voting for sanctions in the United Nations when such incidents occur.

For its part, the Angolan government could reasonably be expected to provide a quid pro quo on several issues of importance to the U.S. Foremost would be the issue of UNITA. It would not be necessary that the Angolan government publicly approve the U.S. position on UNITA. Indeed, it would probably insist on reiterating its view that the best way for UNITA to play a role in the future of the country would be to lay down its arms and join the MPLA in reconstruction. It would be important, however, that the two sides work out a private understanding relating to UNITA. The U.S. would commit itself to using whatever influence it had with Jonas Savimbi to accept an unspoken truce with the MPLA—keeping the territory he has traditionally controlled but not seeking to harass the MPLA where it has normally held sway. U.S. leverage on Savimbi would seem to be considerable. The Cubans regard the U.S.-supplied Stinger missiles as a very important qualitative strengthening of the UNITA forces, more important in many respects than the quantitatively larger South African contribution.[16] Also, even if the framework agreement fails to lead to Namibian independence, the cease-fire between South Africa and Angola might remain in effect with a pullback of forces from both sides of the border. In that case, South Africa might decide it was prudent to curtail its support for UNITA, leaving Savimbi even more dependent on U.S. goodwill. As a quid pro quo, the Angolan government would commit itself to cease its annual offensives against UNITA. The cooperation of the Soviet Union, which has supplied the arms for these offensives and some of the tactical leadership, would be essential, but both the Soviets and the Cubans are now pushing for an internal reconciliation. It would probably not be possible at the outset to accomplish more than a cease-fire, but that itself would be a major element in establishing a new dynamic in the situation.

Such a bargain between the U.S. and Angola would provide a basis for the U.S. over time to allay the MPLA's insecurity and thus set the stage for further movement toward an end to the civil war. If a rapprochement between the MPLA and UNITA were to be worked out, an important instrument for destabilization would be denied to South Africa. Of course, the threat of South African cross-border attacks would remain. However, the battles of 1988 on the southern front seemed to have permanently changed the military situation. The willingness of the Cuban forces to give up their rearguard role and engage the South Africans and the Cubans' superior equipment should make the South Africans wary of future forays into Angola. Also, some scaling down of the Cuban force should be possible if there were an MPLA-UNITA settlement. Under the scenario described, Angola would be in a position to tackle the enormous task of reconstruction and development, which should make it better able to cope with an aggressive South Africa. At the same time, the pretext for South African aggression would be even more flimsy than it is now, and the responsibility for further conflict would be clearly laid at South Africa's door. It should be possible under these circumstances to revive the interest of the international community in a settlement of the Namibia question and to focus that attention squarely on South Africa. This could not be effectively done, it should be repeated, if the United States were to continue to insist that an agreement on Cuban troop withdrawal is a pre-condition for South African compliance with Resolution 435.

Mozambique

In the near term, Mozambique presents fewer obstacles to United States policy than does Angola. It achieved independence without Soviet bloc military intervention and did not become as dependent on Soviet military assistance in the struggle with its guerrilla opponents as did Angola. Consequently, President Samora Machel was able to move toward the West decisively when his regime decided that Western help was necessary for it to survive. After his death, his successor, Joaquim Chissano, has continued the policy of seeking closer relations with Western Europe and the United States.

Yet, in many ways, Mozambique's situation is more desperate than that of Angola. Its economy, intrinsically weaker than Angola's, has been devastated by drought and famine, and at various times RENAMO has seemed able to operate at will in the entire countryside, rather than being confined to one region. Unlike Angola, Mozambique is economically dependent on South Africa.

While the country's problems are daunting, the obstacles to effective U.S. action are not nearly so great as they are in Angola. So far, the Reagan administration has succeeded in keeping Mozambique out of the East-West straightjacket. Nevertheless, right-wing lobbyists and their congressional allies have made it difficult for the administration to extend the amounts and kinds of assistance that its policy of helping Mozambique escape from the clutches of South Africa requires. The Mozambican government needs assistance in building the military capability necessary to defeat RENAMO and to pacify the countryside, as well as large amounts of economic aid for reconstruction. The United States should put itself at the head of the major international effort that the situation requires, but to do so it needs to be free to provide a broad range of assistance to the Mozambican government without the restrictions of the past. The new U.S. president should speak out forthrightly to the American people to explain why it is in the U.S. interest to strengthen a "Marxist" regime in Maputo. Otherwise, U.S. assistance to Mozambique is likely to continue to have a bumpy time in the Congress and the task of turning the desperate situation in Mozambique around will continue to falter.

Conclusion

The specific courses of action required to advance American interests in Angola and Mozambique are different in the two countries, but the general principles that should inspire U.S. policies in both are the same. The first is to be clear about what U.S. interests are. In both, the paramount U.S. interest is in the existence of regimes that will cooperate with the U.S. in the pursuit of its goals in South Africa. Other presumed interests—e.g. making the Soviet bloc "pay the price" for intervention or demonstrating that Marxist regimes are failures—must not be allowed to interfere with the advancement of the primary interest. The second principle is that U.S. objectives in each country must be consistent with U.S. interests. This seems obvious, but in the policy debate it is as often as not disregarded. Thus, the objective of replacing governments that are "Marxist" and friendly to the Soviet Union with their enemies in these two instances would only lead to governments that would be even less likely to cooperate with U.S. policy vis-á-vis South Africa.

Focusing on the right objective at the wrong time is also a common problem. Getting the Cubans out of Angola is a worthwhile objective but if the 1988 negotiations fail once again, to continue to pursue this goal is folly. There are other important objectives in Angola that can be achieved without it.

At the time of writing, it would appear that for the first time the underpinnings of the doctrinaire approach that has dominated U.S. thinking about Third World conflicts for four decades are now being seriously under-mined. Gorbachev evidently is turning away from the expansionary policies of his predecessors, as intervention in the Third World is seen as conflicting with the top national priority of internal reform. These new Soviet attitudes could affect broad areas of the superpower competition, including the possibility of cooperation through the United Nations to tamp down or resolve regional and local conflicts.

Whether these hopeful changes will endure remains to be seen. Even if they do, the Soviet Union may on occasion find it difficult to seem to aban-don clients or to restrain them. In any event, retrenchment by the Soviet Union is an unsatisfactory basis for U.S. policy. In fact, it can be downright misleading, if it is interpreted as a vindication of doctrinaire hardline U.S. policies rather than internal changes in the Soviet Union itself. What is needed is a reexaminaton of premises; that has been the lesson of Angola.

Notes

1. For the origins and evolution of U.S. national security doctrine, John Lewis Gaddis, *Strategies of Containment: A Critical Appraisal of Postwar American National Security Policy,* Oxford University Press, 1982; and Leslie H. Gelb with Richard K. Butts, *The Irony of Viet-nam: The System Worked,* The Brookings Institution, 1979, especially Chapters 1, 6, and 13.

2. *Background Notes: Angola,* United States Department of State, Bureau of Public Affairs, June 1987.

3. "Continuity and Change in American Foreign Policy," Arthur K. Salomon lecture, September 19, 1977, in Henry Kissinger, *For the Record, Selected Statements, 1977-80,* Little Brown, Boston, 1980.

4. For a careful and thoughtful analysis of the motives for U.S. policy in Angola from Ford to Reagan, see Jonathan Michael Crystal, *Ex-plaining United States Policy,* honors thesis, Department of Govern-ment, Harvard University, March 1987. Crystal distinguishes between "ideological" and "strategic" explanations of U.S. policy toward radical regimes in his case study of Angola, Mozambique and Zim-babwe. For him, an "ideological" explanation of U.S. policy is one

in which the primary motive for the policy is the ideology of the radical regime. His "strategic" (or "realist") explanation is one in which the primary motivation is U.S. perception that the radical regime's "connection with a powerful hostile power—that is, the Soviet Union, China, or one of its allies, such as Cuba"—constitutes a security threat to the United States. Crystal concludes that, in the case of the three southern African states he has studied, the "strategic" explanation best explains U.S. policy.

5. Carter's speech at Notre Dame, May 22, 1977, cited in Gaddis, *Strategies of Containment,* p. 345.

6. "Jimmy Carter on Africa," *Africa Report,* vol. 21, No. 3, May-June, 1976, as quoted in *Explaining United States Policy Toward Radical Regimes: The Case of Southern Africa.*

7. Cyrus Vance, *Hard Choices: Critical Years in America's Foreign Policy,* New York, Simon and Schuster, 1983. p. 274.

8. Vance, *Hard Choices,* p. 90.

9. Zbigniew Brzezinski, *Power and Principle: Memoirs of the National Security Adviser 1977-81.* New York: Farrar, Straus, & Giroux, revised edition, 1985, pp. 178-90. In particular, Brzezinski believed that the Soviet/Cuban presence was a threat to the Suez Canal and the Persian Gulf.

10. I could find no flat statement in Brzezinski's memoirs as to what position he took on the issue of establishing relations with Angola, although there are certainly plenty of hints as to what it was (e.g. p. 143); however, senior officials in the Carter administration have confirmed to me that he was opposed. On the question of aid to UNITA, the evidence is circumstantial, see Crystal, *Explaining U.S. Policy,* p. 69; Vance, *Hard Choices,* p. 71 and p. 89.

11. Vance, *Hard Choices,* p. 275. and conversations of the author with a senior official in the Carter administration.

12. The Carter administration did go far towards establishing good working relations with the Angolan government. The point here is that those who, like Vance, wanted to give priority to resolving the local and regional aspects of the Angolan/South African problem rather than to its symbolism in the East-West rivalry were unable to do so.

13. Vance, *Hard Choices,* pp. 84-85.

14. It will be argued that values like freedom and racial justice are

ideological and therefore doctrinaire. Values are not ideology, however; ideology is a theory about how the world works.
15. For a persuasive description of such an alternative policy, see Michael Clough, "Southern Africa: Challenges and Choices" in *Foreign Affairs,* Vol. 66, No. 5, Summer 1988.
16. See Chapter 7, pp. 195-96.
17. Conversation between the author and a senior Cuban official, April 1988.

The Authors

Gerald J. Bender is Director of International Relations at the University of Southern California. He taught in the departments of Political Science at UCLA and UCSD from 1970-79, and since 1979 has been a member of the faculty of the School of International Relations at USC. He is a past president of the African Studies Association. Professor Bender conducts research in Africa, making an average of two trips a year to central and southern Africa. After spending time in Portugal and Angola in the late 1960s, he wrote *Angola Under the Portuguese* (University of California Press, Berkeley, 1978). He is also the co-editor of *African Crisis Areas and U.S. Foreign Policy* (University of California Press, Berkeley, 1985), and edited a special volume of the Annals entitled *International Affairs in Africa* (January 1987).

Richard J. Bloomfield is Executive Director of the World Peace Foundation, a private non-profit foundation based in Boston that conducts studies of international issues. He is a former career diplomat of the United States; among his assignments in the Foreign Service were those of Ambassador to Portugal (1978-82) and Ambassador to Ecuador (1976-78). He is the editor of *Puerto Rico: The Search for a National Policy* (Westview Press, 1985) and has contributed articles on foreign affairs to the *New York Times*, the *Boston Globe*, the *Miami Herald*, and the *Los Angeles Times*.

Kurt M. Campbell is a lecturer in public policy and international relations at the Kennedy School of Government and Assistant Director of Harvard's Center for Science and International Affairs. In 1987, Dr. Campbell was appointed a Council on Foreign Relations International Affairs Fellow. He previously was a Fellow at the International Institute for Strategic Studies in London and worked in Moscow for the Rockefeller Foundation. He is the author of *Soviet Policy Towards South Africa* (Macmillan, 1987).

Carlos Gaspar is diplomatic adviser of the Civil Household of the President of the Republic of Portugal. He studied law and history at the Faculties of Law and of Letters at the Universidade Clássica de Lisboa, and pursued postgraduate studies in political science at the Institut d'Études Politiques de Paris. He has served as a consultant on the planning staff of the Portuguese Ministry of Foreign Affairs and as political adviser of the Civil Household of the President of the Republic of Portugal.

Gillian Gunn has been a Fellow in the African Studies Program of the Center for Strategic and International Studies, Washington, D.C., since 1986. She contributed four chapters to the book *Angola, Mozambique and the West*, ed. Helen Kitchen (Praeger, CSIS, 1987), and is a frequent contributor to *CSIS Africa Notes*. From 1981 to 1984, she was Africa editor of *Business International*, a London-based research, publishing and consulting firm. In 1984, she was named a Rockefeller Foundation International Relations Career Development fellow and spent the next two years doing in-country research on Mozambique's and Angola's relations with the West.

Kenneth Maxwell is currently the Director of the Camões Center for the Portuguese Speaking World at Columbia University. He was previously Program Director of the Tinker Foundation of New York and Herodotus Fellow at the Institute for Advanced Study at Princeton. He holds degrees from Princeton and Cambridge Universities, and has lectured and written extensively on Portugal, Brazil, and Lusophone Africa.

Robert I. Rotberg is Academic Vice-President for Arts, Sciences, and Technology at Tufts University. From 1968-87 he was Professor of history and political science at the Massachusetts Institute of Technology, and was also a Research Associate at the Center for International Affairs, Harvard University Press. Graduate of Oberlin College, Princeton University, and the University of Oxford, he previously taught at Harvard University. He is the author and editor of 30 books, including *Suffer the Future: Policy Choices in Southern Africa* (Howard University Press, 1980), and *South Africa and Its Neighbors: Regional Security and Self-Interest* (Lexington Books, 1985). He is a contributor to the *Christian Science Monitor*, the *New York Times*, and the *Boston Globe*.

Wayne S. Smith is an Adjunct Professor of Latin American Studies at the Johns Hopkins University's School of International Studies in Washington, D.C. He is the Founding Director of the Program of Argentine Studies at the School and the Coordinator of its Exchange Program with the University of Havana. From 1982-85, he was a Senior Associate at the Carnegie Endowment for International Peace in Washington, D.C. Dr. Smith was a career Foreign Service Officer from 1958-82. Among his diplomatic assignments were those of Chief of the U.S. Interests Section in Havana from 1979-82 and Director of Cuban Affairs in the State Department from 1977-79. Earlier he served in Havana, Brazil, Moscow, and Argentina. He is the author of a book on U.S.-Cuban Relations, *The Closest of Enemies* (W.W. Norton, 1987).

Bibliography

Abshire, David M., and Michael A. Samuels, eds. *Portuguese Africa: A Handbook*. London: Pall Mall Press, 1969.

Albright, David E. "The Communist States and Southern Africa." In *International Politics in Southern Africa*. Gwendolyn Carter and Patrick O'Meara, 3-44. Bloomington: Indiana University Press, 1982.

Axelson, Eric Victor. *Portugal and the Scramble for Africa, 1875-91*. Johannesburg: Wittwatersrand University Press, 1967.

Bell, Coral. *The Diplomacy of Détente*. London: Martin Robertson, 1976.

Bender, Gerald J. *Angola Under the Portuguese: The Myth and the Reality*. Berkeley: University of California Press, 1978.

_____. "Political Socialization and Political Change." *Western Political Quarterly* 20 (July 1967):390-407.

_____. "The Limits of Counterinsurgency: An African Case." *Comparative Politics* 4 (April 1972):331-60.

_____. "Angola: History, Insurgency and Social Change." *Africa Today* 19 (Winter 1972):30-36.

_____. "Portugal and Her Colonies Join the Twentieth Century: Causes and Initial Implications of the Military Coup." *Ufahamu* 4 (Winter 1974):121-62.

_____. "Kissinger in Angola: Anatomy of Failure." In *American Policy in Southern Africa: The Stakes and the Stance,* edited by René Lamarchand, 63-144. Washington, DC: University Press of America, 1978.

_____. "Angola: Left, Right & Wrong." *Foreign Policy* 43 (Summer 1981) :53-69.

_____. "American Policy Toward Angola: A History of Linkage." In *African Crisis Areas and U.S. Foreign Policy,* edited by Gerald J. Bender, James S. Coleman, and Richard L. Sklar. Berkeley: University of California Press, 1985.

Bender, Gerald J. and Allen Isaacman. "The Changing Historiography of Angola and Mozambique." In *Africa Studies Since 1945: A Tribute to Basil Davidson,* edited by Christopher Fyfe, 220-48. London: Longman, 1976.

Bender, Gerald J. and P. Stanley Yoder. "Whites on the Eve of Independence: The Politics of Numbers." *Africa Today* 21 (Fall 1974):23-37.

Birmingham, David. *The Portuguese Conquest of Angola.* London: Oxford University Press, 1969.

Bissel, Richard and Chester A. Crocker, eds. *South Africa in the 80s.* Boulder, Colorado: Westview Press, 1979.

Brandenburg, Frank. "Transport Systems and Their External Ramifications." In *Portuguese Africa: A Handbook,* edited by David M. Abshire and Michael A. Samuels, 320-44. London: Pall Mall Press, 1969.

Bragança, Aquino de and Immanuel Wallerstein, eds. *The African Liberation Reader.* London: Zed Press, 1982.

Brzezinski, Zbigniew. *Power and Principle.* New York: Farar, Strauss and Giroux, 1984.

Caetano, Marcello. *Relações das colónias de Angola e Moçambique com os territórios estrangeiros vizinhos.* Lisbon: Imprensa nacional, 1946.

_____. *Colonizing Traditions, Principles and Methods of the Portuguese.* Lisbon: Agéncia Geral do Ultramar, 1951.

_____. *Os nativos na economia africana.* Coimbra: Coimbra Editora, 1954.

_____. *Razões da presença de Portugal no Ultramar.* Lisbon: n.p., 1973.

_____. "Os antecendentes legislativos do Acto Colonial." *Estudos Ultramarinos* 1 (October-December 1951):1-9.

_____. "É na linha das reformas profundas que temos de prosseguir." *Notícias de Portugal* 23 (October 1970).

_____. Interview with German newspaper *Die Welt* and reprinted in *Notícias de Portugal* 27 (8 September 1973).

_____. "Linha de rumo para o Ultramar." Speech presented to the National Assembly, Lisbon, 5 March 1974. Reprinted in *Notícias de Portugal* no. 1401 (9 March 1974).

_____. "Conversa em familia." Speech over Portuguese radio and television, 28 March 1974. Reprinted in *Notícias de Portugal* no. 1405 (6 April 1974).

Campbell, Kurt. *Soviet Policy Towards South Africa.* London: The Macmillan Press, 1986.

Challiand, Gerard. *L'enjeu africain.* Paris: Editions de Seuil, 1980.

_____. *Où va l'Afrique du Sud?* Paris: Calmann-Levy, 1986.

Chilcote, Ronald. *Portuguese Africa.* Englewood Cliffs: Prentice-Hall, 1967.

_____. *Emerging Nationalism in Portuguese Africa: Documents.* Stanford: Hoover Institution Press, 1972.

_____, ed. *Protest and Resistance in Angola and Brazil.* Berkeley: University of California Press, 1972.

Clement, Peter. "Moscow and Southern Africa." *Problems of Communism* 34 (Summer 1986).

Clough, Michael, ed. *Reassessing the Soviet Challenge in Africa.* Policy Papers in International Affairs, No. 25. Berkeley: Institute for International Studies, University of California, 1986.

Coker, Christopher. *NATO, the Warsaw Pact and Africa.* London: The Macmillan Press, 1985.

_____. *The United States and South Africa: Constructive Engagement and its Critics.* Durham: Duke University Press, 1986.

_____. "L'Afrique du Sud, l'Afrique australe et la sécurité régionale." *Politique Etrangère* 49 (Summer 1984):287-300.

Coutau-Bégarie, Hervé. *Géostratégie de l'Atlantique Sud.* Paris: PUF, 1985.

Davidson, Basil. *The African Awakening.* London: Macmillan, 1955.

_____. *The African Slave Trade: Precolonial History, 1450-1850.* Boston: Little, Brown, 1961.

_____. *The Liberation of Guinea: Aspects of an African Revolution.* Baltimore: Penguin Books, 1969.

_____. *In the Eye of the Storm: Angola's People.* Garden City: Doubleday, 1972.

_____. "An Inside Look at Angola's Fight for Freedom." *Africa*

Report 15 (December 1970):16-18.

Directivas Economicas e Sociais. Colaccão 4 Congresso. Partido FRELIMO, 1983.

Documentos Base da FRELIMO. Maputo: Tempographica, 1977.

Duffy, James. *Portuguese Africa.* Cambridge: Harvard University Press, 1961.

_____. *Portugal in Africa.* Cambridge: Harvard University Press, 1962.

_____. *Portugal's African Territories: Present Realities.* Occasional Paper No. 1. New York: Carnegie Endowment for International Peace, 1962.

Ebinger, Charles K. "External Intervention in Internal War: The Politics and Diplomacy of the Angolan Civil War." *Orbis* 20 (Fall 1976):669-99.

Figueiredo, António de. *Portugal and Its Empire: The Truth.* London: Gollancz, 1961.

_____. "Portugal and Africa." In *Portugal: Ten Years After the Revolution,* edited by Kenneth Maxwell. New York: Columbia University, School of International and Public Affairs, Research Institute on International Change, 1984.

_____. "Portugal and Africa." In *Portugal in the 1980s: Dilemmas of Democratic Consolidation,* edited by Kenneth Maxwell, 89-108. London: Greenwood Press, 1986.

Fontoura, Luis. "A cooperação, destino inevitável. *Democracia e Liberdade* (Oct.-Dec. 1985).

Franco Nogueira, Alberto. *Diálogos interditos: A política de defesa.* Braga: Intervenção, 1979.

Freitas do Amaral, Diogo. *Política externa e política de fedesa.* Lisbon: Cognitio, 1985.

Fukuyama, Francis. *Moscow's Post-Brezhnev Reassessment of the Third World.* Rand Report R-3337-USDP, February 1986.

Gama, Jaime. *Política externa 1983-85.* Série Diplomática. Lisbon: Ministério dos Negóios Estangeiros, 1985.

_____. "Portuguese Foreign Policy." Paper presented at The Wilson Center conference, Portugal: Ancient Country, Young Democracy, Washington, D.C., 1987.

Gann, Lewis. H. and Peter Duignan. *White Settlers in Tropical Africa.* Baltimore: Penguin Books, 1962.

_____. "Reflections on Imperialism and the Scramble for Africa." In *Colonialism in Africa.* Vol. 1, *The History and Politics of Colonialism 1870-1914,* 100-132. Cambridge: Cambridge University Press, 1969.

Gelman, Harry. *The Brezhnev Politburo and the Decline of Détente.* Ithaca, NY: Cornell University Press, 1984.

Gonçalves Pereira, André. *Uma experiencia política.* Lisbon: Atica, 1982.

Grundy, Kenneth. *Confrontation and Accommodation in Southern Africa.* Berkeley: University of California Press, 1973.

Gunn, Gillian. "Post-Nkomati Mozambique." *CSIS Africa Notes* 38 (January 8, 1985).

_____. "Mozambique After Machel." *CSIS Africa Notes* 67 (December 29, 1986).

Hammond, R.J. *Portugal and Africa, 1815-1910: A Study in Economic Imperialism.* Stanford: Stanford University Press, 1966.

_____. "Race Attitudes and Policies in Portuguese Africa in the Nineteenth and Twentieth Centuries." *Race* 9 (1967):205-16.

Hanlon, Joseph. *Mozambique: The Revolution Under Fire.* London: Zed Books Ltd., 1984.

_____. *Beggar Your Neighbors: Apartheid Power in Southern Africa.* Bloomington: Indiana University Press, 1986.

Heimer, Franz-Wilhelm. *Social Change in Angola.* Munich: Weltforum Verlag, 1973.

_____. *Decolonization Conflict in Angola: An Essay in Political Sociology.* Geneva: IUHEI, 1979.

Henriksen, Thomas H. *Mozambique: A History.* London: Rex Collings, 1978.

Hosmer, Stephen and Thomas Wolfe. *Soviet Policy and Practice Towards the Third World.* Lexington, Mass.: Lexington Books, 1982.

Hurrell, Andrew. "The Politics of South Atlantic Security." *International Affairs* 59 (Spring 1983):179-93.

Isaacman, Allen F. *Mozambique: The Africanization of a European Institution.* Madison: University of Wisconsin Press, 1972.

Isaacman, Allen and Barbara Isaacman. *Mozambique: From Colonialism to Revolution.* Harare: Zimbabwe Publishing House, 1985.

Jowitt, Kenneth. "Scientific Socialist Regimes in Africa: Political Differentiation, Avoidance and Awareness." In *Socialism in Sub-Saharan Africa: A New Assessment,* edited by Carl Roseberg and Thomas Callaghy. Berkeley: University of California Press, Institute of International Studies, 1979.

Kitchen, Helen and Michael Clough. *The United States and South Africa: Realities and Red Herrings.* Significant Issues Series, vol. 6, no. 6. Washington: Georgetown University, CSIS, 1984.

Klinghoffer, Arthur Jay. *The Angolan War: A Study of Soviet Policy in the Third World.* Boulder, Colorado: Praeger, 1986.

Laidi, Zaki. "L'URSS et l'Afrique: vers une extension du système socialiste mondial?" *Politique Étrangère* 48 (Fall 1983):679-99.

Legum, Colin. *Southern Africa, The Secret Diplomacy of Détente: South Africa at the Crossroads.* London: Rex Collings, 1975.

_____. "The Role of the Big Powers." In *After Angola: The War Over Southern Africa,* edited by Colin Legum and Tony Hodges, 3-44. New York: Africana Publishing Co., 1976.

_____. "The Soviet Union, China and the West in Southern Africa." *Foreign Affairs* 54 (July 1976):745-62.

_____. "Angola and the Horn of Africa." In *Diplomacy and Power,* edited by Stephen Kaplan, 570-640. Washington: The Brookings Institution, 1981.

Legum, Colin and Tony Hodges. *After Angola: The War Over Southern Africa.* New York: Africana Publishing Co., 1976.

Lemarchand, René, ed. *American Policy in Southern Africa: The Stakes and the Stance.* Washington, D.C.: University Press of America, 1978.

LeoGrande, William M. "Cuban-Soviet Relations in Africa." *Cuban Studies* (January 1980) :??-??.

Litvak, Robert. *Ideology and the Conduct of Soviet Policy in the Third World.* Washington: The Wilson Center, 1984.

MacFarlane, S. Neil. *Superpower Rivalry and Third World Radicalism.* London: Croom Helm, 1985.

_____. "Intervention and Security in Africa." *International Affairs* 60 (Winter 1983-84) :53-73.

Mondlane, Eduardo. *The Struggle for Mozambique.* London: Penguin Books, 1969.

Marcum, John. *The Angolan Revolution.* Vol. 1, *The Anatomy of an Explosion.* Studies in Communism, Revisionism and Revolution. Cambridge: MIT Press, 1969.

_____. *The Angolan Revolution.* Vol. 2, *Exile Politics and Guerrilla Warfare (1962-1976).* Studies in Communism, Revisionism and Revolution. Cambridge: MIT Press, 1978.

_____. "Angola." In *Southern Africa: The Continuing Crisis,* edited by Gwendolyn Carter and Patrick O'Meara. Bloomington: Indiana University Press, 1979.

_____. "Angola: A Quarter Century of War." *CSIS Africa Notes* 37 (1984).

Matias, Leonardo. "A diplomacia portuguesa em Africa." *Democracia e Liberdade* (Oct.-Dec. 1985).

Maxwell, Kenneth. "A New Scramble for Africa?" In *The Conduct of Soviet Foreign Policy,* edited by Eric Hoffmann and Frederic Fleron, 515-34. New York: Aldine Publishing Co., 1980.

_____. "Portugal and Africa: The Last Empire." In *The Transfer of Power in Africa: Decolonization 1940-1960,* edited by Prosser Gifford and W.W. Roger Louis, 337-85. New Haven: Yale University Press, 1984.

_____. "As colónias portuguesas e descolonização." *Revista de Ciências Sociais* (Portugal 1974-1984: Des anos de transformação social), no. 15-17 (May 1985).

Medeiros Ferreira, José. *Elementos de política externa.* Lisbon: Ministério dos Negocios Estrangeiros, 1977.

_____. Estudos de estratégia e relações internacionais. Lisbon: INCM, 1981.

_____. *Portugal en transe: Notas de política internacional e de política de defesa.* Aveiro: Pandora, 1986.

Melo Antunes, Ernesto. "Vector africano da política externa portuguesa." Paper presented at the World Peace Foundation-Calouste Gulbenkian Foundation conference, Portugal, os estados africanos de língua oficial portuguesa e os Estados Unidos da América, Lisbon, May 1985.

Martin, David and Phyllis Johnson. *The Struggle for Zimbabwe: The Chimurenga War.* Harare: Zimbabwe Publishing House, 1981.

_____. *Destructive Engagement: Southern Africa at War.* Harare: Zimbabwe Publishing House, 1986.

Minter, William. *Imperial Network and External Dependency: The Case of Angola.* Beverly Hills: Sage Publications, 1972.

_____. *Portuguese Africa and the West.* New York: Monthly Review Press, 1972.

Moita, Luis. "Elementos para um balanço da descolonização portuguesa." *Revista de Ciências Sociais* (Portugal 1974-85: Dez anos de transformação social), no. 15-17 (May 1985).

Moreira, Adriano. *A nação abandonada.* Lisbon: Intervenção, 1977.

_____. "Factores de coesão e dissociação portuguesa." *Estudos Políticos e Sociais* 11 (1983):7-25.

Munslow, Barry. *Mozambique: The Revolution and Its Origins.* London: Longman, 1983.

Newitt, M.D.D. *Portuguese Settlement on the Zambesi.* New York: Africana Publishing Co., 1973.

————. *Portugal in Africa: The Last Hundred Years.* London: Longman, 1981.

Niddrie, David L. "The Role of Ground Transport in the Economic Development of Angola." *Journal of the American Portuguese Cultural Society* 3 (Winter-Spring 1969):1-13.

————. "The Cunene River: Angola's River of Life." *Journal of the American Portuguese Cultural Society* 6 (Winter-Spring 1970) :1-17.

Nogueira, Franco. *The United Nations and Portugal: A Study in Anti-Colonialism.* London: Sidgwick and Jackson, 1963.

————. *The Third World.* London: Johnson, 1967.

Oliveira, Mário Fernandes de, et al. *A descolonização portuguesa.* Lisbon: Instituto Democracia e Liberdade, 1979.

Ottaway, David and Marina Ottaway. *Afrocommunism.* New York: Africana Publishing Co., 1980.

Porter, Bruce. *The USSR in Third World Conflicts, 1945-1980.* Cambridge, Mass.: Cambridge University Press, 1984.

Rotberg, Robert I. *Suffer the Future: Policy Choices in Southern Africa.* Cambridge: Harvard University Press, 1980.

————, ed. *Namibia: Political and Economic Prospects.* Lexington, Mass.: Lexington Books, 1983.

Rotberg, Robert I., Henry Bienen, Robert Legvold, and Gavin Maasdorp. *South Africa and its Neighbors: Regional Security and Self-Interest.* Lexington, Mass.: Lexington Books, 1985.

Sa Machado, Victor. "O conflicto na Africa Austral." *Nação e Defesa* 9 (Jan.-Mar.), 1984.

Samuels, Michael A., Chester A. Crocker, Roger W. Fontaine, Dimitri K. Simes, and Robert E. Henderson. *Implications of Soviet and Cuban activities in Africa for US Policy.* Significant Issues Series, vol. 1, no. 5. Washington: Georgetown University, CSIS, 1979.

Schneidman, Whitney. *American Foreign Policy and the Fall of the Portuguese Empire.* Ph.D. Dissertation, University of Southern California, 1987.

Seiler, John, ed. *Southern Africa Since the Portuguese Revolution.* Boulder, Colorado: Westview Press, 1980.

Shevchenko, Arkady N. *Breaking With Moscow.* New York: Ballantine Books, 1985.

Silva, António, et al. *A cooperação portuguesa: Balanço e perspectivas â luz de adesão â CEE e do alargamento da Covenção de Lomé III.* Lisbon: IED, 1986.

Singleton, Seth. "The Shared Tactical Goals of South Africa and the Soviet Union." *Africa Notes* 12 (April 6, 1983).

Smith, Wayne S. *The Closest of Enemies: A Personal and Diplomatic History of the Castro Years.* New York: W.W. Norton, 1987.

Smith, Wayne S. *Castro's Cuba: Soviet Partner or Non-Aligned?* Washington, D.C.: The Woodrow Wilson Center for Scholars, 1984.

Soares, Mario. *Democratização e descolonização: Dez meses no governo provisório.* Lisbon: Publicações Dom Quixote, 1975.

Sommerville, Keith. *Angola: Politics, Economy and Society.* London: Frances Pinter, 1986.

Soremkun, Fola. "Portugal, Angola and Mozambique: The Trends of Future Relationships." In *Africa and Europe,* edited by A. Sesay, 86-103. London: Croom Helm, 1986.

Spinola, António. *Portugal e o futuro.* Lisbon: Arcádia, 1974.

_____. *Ao serviço de Portugal.* Lisbon: Atica-Bertrand, 1976.

_____. *País sem rumo.* Lisbon: Scire, 1978.

Stockwell, John. *In Search of Enemies: A CIA Story.* New York: W.W. Norton, 1978.

Szulc, Tad. "Lisbon and Washington: Behind the Portuguese Revolution." *Foreign Policy* 21 (Winter 1975):3-62.

Vanneman, Peter and Martin W. James III. "The Soviet Intervention in Angola: Intentions and Implications." *Strategic Review* 4 (Summer 1976):92-103.

_____. "Soviet Strategy in Southern Africa in the Eighties: The Rise of Coercive Diplomacy." *South Africa International* 12 (July 1981):261-82.

Wheeler, Douglas L. "The Portuguese in Angola, 1836-91: A Study in Expansion and Administration." Ph.D. dissertation, Boston University, 1963.

_____. "A Note on Smallpox in Angola, 1870-1875." *Studia* (Lisbon) 13-14 (January-July 1964):351-62.

_____. "Reflections on Angola." *Africa Report* 12 (November 1967):58-62.

_____. "Nineteenth Century African Protest in Angola: Prince Nicolas of Kongo (1837-60)." *African Historical Studies* 1 (1968):40-59.

_____. "The Portuguese Army in Angola." *Journal of Modern African Studies* 7 (October 1969):425-39.

_____. "An Early Angolan Protest: The Radical Journalism of José de Fontes Pereira (1823-1891)." In *Protest and Power in Black Africa,* edited by Robert I. Rotberg and Ali Mazuri, 854-74. New York: Oxford University Press, 1970.

_____. "Origins of African Nationalism in Angola: Assimilado Protest Writings, 1859-1929." In *Protest and Resistance in Angola and Brazil,* edited by Ronald H. Chilcote, 67-87. Berkeley: University of California Press, 1972.

_____. "Portugal in Angola: A Living Colonialism." In *Southern Africa in Perspective,* edited by Christian P. Potholm and Richard Dale. New York: The Free Press, 1972.

_____. "The Portuguese Revolution of 1910." *Journal of Modern History* 44 (June 1972):172-94.

Wheeler, Douglas L. and René Pelissier. *Angola.* New York: Praeger, 1971.

Wiles, Peter, ed. *The New Communist Third World.* London: Croom Helm, 1982.

Young, Crawford. *Ideology and Development in Africa.* New Haven: Yale University Press, 1982.

Index